BEYOND REVOLUTION

BEYOND REVOLUTION

A New Theory of Social Movements

Daniel A. Foss
Ralph Larkin

Introduction by Stanley Aronowitz

Critical Perspectives in Social Theory Series

Bergin & Garvey Publishers, Inc.
MASSACHUSETTS

First published in 1986 by
Bergin & Garvey Publishers, Inc.
670 Amherst Road
South Hadley, Massachusetts 01075

6789   987654321

Printed in the United States of America

LIBRARY OF CONGRESS CATALOGING-IN-PUBLICATION DATA

Foss, Daniel A., 1940–
   Beyond revolution.

   (Critical perspectives in social theory)
   1. Social movements. 2. Radicalism—United States.
I. Larkin, Ralph W., 1940–   . II. Title.
III. Series.
HM281.F57 1986   303.4′84   85-20157
ISBN 0-89789-077-9
ISBN 0-89789-087-6 (pbk.)

This book is dedicated to
the memory of
William F. O'Donnell,
1939–1973,
sociologist, artist, social activist,
visionary, friend:
Casualty of a failed revolution.

Contents

ABOUT THE AUTHORS

DANIEL A. FOSS was born in The Bronx, N.Y., on July 26, 1940. He received his B.A. in Sociology at Cornell in 1961; his M.A. and Ph.D. were granted by Brandeis University in 1962 and 1969, respectively. Foss' dissertation was published, in abridged form, as *Freak Culture*. He taught at the School for Critical Studies at the California Institute for the Arts, and at Livingston College and the Newark College of Arts and Sciences, Rutgers University. Upon finding himself unemployable as a sociologist, Foss took courses in data processing at Syracuse University and New York University. He has been employed as a computer programmer and data base manager for academic and government researchers. He continues to have an abiding interest in the historical study of social movements, medieval Europe, and China.

RALPH LARKIN was born in Los Angeles on May 27, 1940. He was graduated from the University of California, Santa Barbara, in 1961, and taught elementary school in California. He received a Master's degree in education at California State University at Northridge in 1966 and a Ph.D. in Sociology of Education at UCLA. Larkin moved to New York in 1970, where he worked as a Research Associate at the Center for Urban Education. In 1973, he became an Assistant Professor of Sociology at Rutgers University, Newark, where he and Daniel Foss met. They collaborated on the study of social privilege, social movements, and post-movement phenomena, which resulted in several articles and this book. The publication of Larkin's controversial *Suburban Youth in Cultural Crisis* by Oxford University Press resulted in the denial of tenure at Rutgers. Larkin presently operates his own research consultancy in New York City. His scholarly interests remain focused on the reproduction of social domination and the various struggles against it.

Preface

This book occurred due to the circumstance that sociologists no longer read history. In a discipline which canonizes those who read history as classical theorists, we succumbed to the delusion that reverence for them had relevance to practice. What is more, history was our pornography in that it dealt with the dirty parts of human life unmentioned and unthought about in polite social discourse. We observed that social conflict is both as old as social privilege as well as ever-recurrent, and that the form in which social movements have become stereotyped within sociology is representative of only a thin time slice in the historical record. To correct the irrational stereotypes, we wrote this book, fully aware that the prevalence of irrational stereotypes and distorted images are no accident and are valid objects in the investigation of sociology itself. Where we find eternalizing or other ahistorical distortions, we so indicate and try to account for their existence, from whatever part of the political spectrum they derive.

The practice of the sociology of social movements and the construction by psychologists of personality profiles of social-movement participants dictate that the object of investigation in the respective disciplines remain both stable and quantifiable (e.g., size of membership rolls, frequency of meeting attendance, conservatism-liberalism). Additionally, on the behavioral level, the procuring of external grant support requiring up to a year for approval, the hiring of the soft-money staff, design of the data set, blocking out of data records, sampling and/or subject recruitment, methodological choices regarding data not collected, and so forth—these concerns are familiar to the reader and constitute a lead time element of up to two years. During which time the object of investigation has transmuted itself beyond anything envisaged in the research design or has completely disappeared, or has, worse, been superceded by phenomena of an avowed, albeit spurious, "social movement" character. The confluence of intellectual dispositions with contracted promises to the funding agency, and personal interest in research outcomes, can create a situation in which funds are returned unspent, papers go unpresented, articles unwritten, and promotions unsought. This can render the object of investigation to the realm of low probability exogenous event and nothing may eventually be studied. *Something* must be studied and the appropriateness of studying it proceeds therefrom.

We are suggesting, nay, committing, an unseemly disruption from the back halls of social science, that the hallmark of the object of investigation as it confronts the would-be investigator is its evasion of, resistance to, or, in the most extreme case, destruction of, the processes whereby it is conventionally objectified. We deny, however, that investigation is impossible: it must proceed from observed patterns of qualitative change in the object of investigation, one of whose defining processes is the emergence of the human subject in history such that in a social movement a huge psychic leap occurs. *Anyone who was there will never be the same and, correspondingly, and dialectically, anyone who was not there is constituted as no longer the same in relation to those who were, however much they deny it*. The investigation of social movements which proceeds from an open-minded alertness to qualitative changes in participants, as well as in their observed behavior, is *decisive—beyond the study of social movements—to the creative formulation of macrosocial theory*. We herein will suggest that the critique of capitalism in its most recent phase requires that one cease fixation on the exploitation of productive labor to focus instead upon wasting time for its own sake and social discipline for its own sake.

Symptomatic of the discontinuity of our thinking with the rest of the profession and the disarray of social-movement theory was our placement at association meetings in paper sessions that included, among other topics, earthquake disasters and pedestrian behavior at intersections. Most of our published work on postmovement phenomena ended up in journals focusing on sociology of religion. With a few exceptions, our work seemed incomprehensible to other sociologists, even when it was appreciated. In 1978 we decided that the remedy to the problem was to write a comprehensive explication of our theory of social movements. This volume is the result of that effort.

While writing this book, we received help from friends and associates who read the manuscript and commented on it, provided resources, and encouragement. We would like to thank and express our appreciation to Maurice Stein, Henry Eskowitz, Mike Brown, Andy and Harriet Lyons, Ray Calluori, Murray Karstadt, and Miriam Fischer for their comments on the manuscript in its various stages. We would especially like to thank Stanley Aronowitz for his support and help in publishing this work. We would also like to thank him and the staff at *Social Text* for publishing what was once an appendix to this work called, "A Lexicon of Folketymology of the 1960s," in their book, *The 60s Without Apology*.

Ralph Larkin would like to single out Peter Freund for his support, encouragement, and careful reading and critique of the manuscript. In addition, I would like to thank my wife Debra, for her support and unfailing confidence in me; my parents Ralph and Edna Larkin; my in-laws Herman (now deceased) and Jennie Douglass; and my children Stephen, Thomas, Andrew, and David for their love and emotional support.

Introduction

Until the 1960s, the study of social movements, particularly in the United States, was safely subsumed within social science as just another field of empirical study. The tendency in American sociology and political science to renounce "grand theory" in favor of theories of the middle range, or no theory at all, effectively limited social movement study to things that could be counted. Although some very good work was done, social movement study became an ethnographic enterprise, a branch of the "participation" subfield of political science. Rarely, if ever, did researchers consider the question of the relation of social movements to the processes of historical change. This relation, like many other issues, was generally considered better dealt with by silence.

Of course, the one exception was marxist social theory. But even here, the subject was confined to the study of working class organizations, trade unions and left-wing parties. Views of other social movements were limited to those in precapitalist societies, in which peasant revolts, middle-class rebellions, and even proletarian movements were discussed, say, in terms of the transition from feudalism to capitalism, or in any event were subsumed under broadly conceived class theories.

Since 1968, investigators and social theorists have elevated the status of social movement research to the level of grand theory. The reason seems quite clear: the May '68 events in France, part of a world-wide student revolt, and the Cuban, Chinese, and other "third-world" revolutions signified the appearance of new social actors on the historical stage. For many writers—Andre Gorz and Alain Touraine in France, Alvin Gouldner in the U.S., Jürgen Habermas in Germany, to name a few of the most important—the marxist problematic of working-class revolution had come to an end; either new classes, such as the intellectuals, or movements whose relationship to class was ambiguous or nonexistent, had entered History without the old parties and their constituents. Peasants, feminists, intellectuals, ecologists, and youth—these social movements prefigured an entirely new historical paradigm. Social movements became the euphemism for the "new" subject.

Today the study of social movements has taken on an intellectual urgency unparalleled since the rise of working-class movements in the nineteenth century. Although the old empiricism has by no means disappeared from the discourse, the entrance of social theory into the consideration of issues surrounding the appearance of new social movements has already replaced the old questions: it is no longer sufficient to study how social movements arise and what the character of their activities is. Now the questions are: What are social movements? What is their relationship to class categories? What is their place in the general and specific processes of social transformation?

Prior to the pivotal decade of the sixties, social research, implicitly or explicitly, understood social transformation almost exclusively in terms of class, i.e. economic, terms. "Collective" action was said to occur at those moments in history when workers, middle classes, and peasants were no longer able to consent to the policies of the state, the "hegemonic" ideologies of ruling classes, or prevailing economic conditions. Although social theory has hotly contested the causal agents of collective action (some attributed its appearance to crisis in the economic sphere, others to the "revolution of rising expectations" identified with better times), the key idea in almost all cases was that strikes, demonstrations, and other disruptive manifestations of mass discontent were the function of class deprivations that were somehow ignored by the forces of social order. Even when this notion was disputed, the underlying agreement among most students of mass movements was that their impetus could be ascribed, generally, to a rational calculation among their subjects that disruptive forms of action were more efficient for achieving certain goals than normal methods of peaceful petition or electoral participation.

Beyond Revolution is perhaps the most sweeping challenge to these theories that has appeared since social movements became an appropriate subject for theory. Foss and Larkin have examined effectively and comprehensively the major variants of theories that explain the appearance of new social movements on the basis of some form of rational calculation, whether "resource deprivation"-driven or motivated by the capacity of social categories to engage in a contest over resource mobilization. Moreover, Foss and Larkin have refused the narrowly construed concept that social movements are invariably class-determined, although they do not deny that class forces remain an important underlying structure in accounting for various types of social struggle. For them, class movements are one important type of social movement, but in analyzing the most recent decades of mass struggle, they find that these movements have involved many other sections of the population. For Foss and Larkin, the youth, race, feminist, and religious movements of the sixties and seventies are not to be understood as the displacements of class struggle but should be engaged on their own terms as valid responses to the historical conjunctures, *including* economic forces, that produced them.

But *Beyond Revolution* is more than critique. It advances its own theory of social movements, one that defines *what they are* (in contrast to much of the recent literature on the subject), and *what they do* in terms of the social reproduction of prevailing social relations. Social movements are not the same as purely cultural movements, such as intellectual tendencies, religious movements, and art trends; they involve a specific form of political intervention. Foss and Larkin argue that social movements disrupt the form of social reproduction, even if temporarily; that they entail, for their adherents, a reinter-pretation of social reality; and that they almost always propose a transformation of social relations and of "human nature." So, not every strike, demonstration, or riot is identical with the appearance of a social movement—striking workers belong to bureaucratic unions that have long ceased to possess the character-istics of social movements; counterdissidents may only engage in demonstra-tions; and riots can take place within the context of a football rally. What the authors have achieved is to place social movement in a specific framework, showing that its appearance, throughout history, is largely unanticipated by ruling groups or social observers because its leading characteristic is the re-bellion against the prevailing social structure which is thought by those in control to be a fact of nature.

Second, *Beyond Revolution* is concrete. Throughout the text, four key world-historical events are drawn upon to illustrate their theory: the English revolution of the seventeenth century; the French revolution a century later; the Bolshevik revolution; and the revolts of the 1960s and '70s, which includes much more than the so-called western new left, embracing the Iranian Revolution and other third-world movements. The historical and global character of the examples strengthens the claims of the text. Foss and Larkin boldly have adduced "laws" of social development corresponding to the emergence of new social movements.

Third, *Beyond Revolution* offers not only a theory of entailment but of stages in the rise and decline of these movements. According to the authors, social movements are short-lived and arise only under determinate conditions. In both victory and defeat the tendency to routinization (in winning cases) destroys the institution-shaking quality of the movement, and decadence (in losing cases) produces demoralization among even its most fervent actors, and, consequently, the old order reestablishes itself.

Although Jean-Paul Sartre's monumental *Critique of Dialectical Reason* is not invoked in the text, there are striking parallels with this work. Sartre's philosophy of history can be considered a "marxism of spontaneity." He posits the dialectic between the "practico-inert" (the givens of the social world: the past) and the emergent transformation of seriality (isolated individuals) into groups-in-fusion that are constrained by the practices of the past but can transform social relations. Sartre's is not a theory of history in which parties and elites play the crucial role in changing society; rather, change is seen as the result of the unanticipated formation of rebellious movements in which the mind/body split, the contradiction between the individual and the collective realms, and differences between ideology and conscious intervention are tem-porarily overcome. Sartre's book (1960) had the immediate impetus of the Algerian revolution, which for him constituted the main case in point for the argument. Needless to say, this work is only now beginning to receive the attention it deserves, for even the French "left" has dissociated itself from Sartre's insistence that movements cannot be "built" according to party edict or bureaucratic plan. Together with Henri Lefebvre, whose work on everyday urban life anticipated the famous student and worker rebellion of May '68, Sartre insists on the primacy of the social to explain the political in the face of the marxist tendency (since Kautsky and Lenin) to privilege the state (the political institutions) and most importantly, the party, as the real arena/agents of social change. So, Foss and Larkin place themselves in a different tradition, a tradition now represented in France most notably by sociologist Alain Touraine, one that insists on the self-production of society. *Beyond Revolution* is not only the best work on social movements since Touraine's important work of 1968–77, deriving from the significance of the May events, but the authors have gone beyond that work by reading back into history the general conditions for the formation of social movements. That is, they have not explained the unanticipated appearance of new social movements as the product of specific late capitalist conditions of, say, post-scarcity; they have shown that the attempt to disrupt social structure is the key to understanding the revolutionary process in any society marked by classes and economic and political hierarchy. For, in concert with Sartre and Lefebvre, Foss and Larkin have insisted that the reproduction of social relations—ideologically, economically, and politically—must be disrupted by movements that constitute themselves as an alternate community in the wide meaning of the term, in order to really make change, and that these changes are not limited and instrumental in character but propose to revolutionize the human condition.

In essence, a social movement is simultaneously utopian and practical: it engages in collective action to make changes, but will not be satisfied by concessions from the ruling group. Feminists demand an end to male domination and patriarchy even as they wrest jobs and social equality within the existing order; the most radical sections of the Black freedom movements in the U.S., U.K., and South Africa demand human rights, including voting rights, at the same time as they propose to transform race and other social relations. These movements are like Halley's comet: they shoot up and light the sky and fall. But it is the stuff of which social transformation is made. Foss and Larkin take their place in the tradition that regards trade unions, socialist parties, organizations of social reform as the *sediment* of failed social movements, the forms in which the future becomes the past.

This perspective locates *Beyond Revolution*. It is clearly influenced by the social movements of the 1960s, most of which regarded their immediate predecessors such as trade unions, left-wing organizations, and single-issue pressure groups as obstacles rather than allies. These institutions, in many cases, were once social movements that felt obliged, in the long periods between upsurges, to function within and not against the state and its bureaus. As many observers have noted, they tend to become bureaucracies themselves and therefore part of the existing order. Their revolutionary and radical phrases are part of their legitimating baggage but have little to do with their practice. When the new social movement period arrives, even against their will, the established liberal and left organizations find themselves defending the arrangements they have made with the existing order, discover they have become agents of social reproduction and condemn the new social movements as irresponsible. In turn, the hostility of the establishment left helps radicalize the new social movements.

For an illustration of the dynamics at play here, consider the birth and fate of Students for a Democratic Society (SDS). It began as a student movement seeking to democratize liberal representative institutions that had evolved into hierarchies excluding ordinary people from processes of decision making. In 1962, SDS felt it was by no means a new social movement in the sense discussed here. It had begun to reinterpret reality in political terms, but was not seeking a "new human individual" or a new definition of social relations. The antagonism of labor and liberal leaders towards these fairly limited goals produced the beginning of radicalization among a generation of students that believed in civil rights and later opposed military intervention in the third world. SDS became part of a social movement when it no longer defined itself in terms of "issues" but demanded nothing less than social transformation. Even as a fairly substantial majority of liberals and a growing minority of labor officials supported the antiwar program of student radicals, the "movement" had already surpassed its own program, which had presupposed working within and not against the prevailing structure. By the late sixties, SDS was proposing a new mode of life in which social, cultural, political, and economic relations would be radically changed and the whole ethos of self-interest and competitive advantage overthrown. The profound radicalization of the youth and student generation was not matched, of course, by a general radicalization among workers, professionals, and others. With the possible exception of the most radical wing of the Black freedom movement, the youth movement found itself politically and ideologically isolated. Foss and Larkin do not discuss the particulars of the ebbing of the world-wide counter politics of the youth movement, but discuss in some detail the results. The seventies are marked by a massive reinstitution of the social order. The disruption is over: radicals carry their fervor in their heart but return to school, most typically, to law school; others enter mainstream reproductive institutions like electoral politics and trade unions; still others raise families in that peculiarly private way that seems unique to America. In short, "life" goes on.

Sociologists and psychologists tend to interpret "normality" as a life-cycle phenomenon. Youth rebel, but the 30s and 40s of a person's life are times for careers and families. So, radicalism turns out to be a generational phenomenon, something that passes with age. Others take a purely conjunctural position: the movement dies when repression breaks its ranks, or factionalism causes damaging splits or economic and political conditions change as reforms are enacted to thwart the radical motion. Foss and Larkin take these historical conjunctures seriously, but by making a transhistorical analysis, they show that as social movements become power groups, as the revolution settles into reform, in *all* social movement periods the dynamic is lost and bureaucracy settles in.

Since *Beyond Revolution* posits the persistence of ineluctable contradictions, the period of calm and order is more or less temporary. New social movements arise as reforms wear thin or promises go unkept. If a new social contract is often able to produce decay in the upsurge, its abrogation by those in power is a built-in feature of the structure. Reforms are a way of preserving hierarchy and exploitation. They contain the "seeds" of their own dismantling: either the power group renounces them in the name of efficiency, law and order, and so on, or they fall of their own weight. Times change, and with them, the demands.

Beyond Revolution constitutes a new standard against which all other books on social movements should be measured. However, since its authors have refused a simple linear causality, many will find its insights more satisfying than its "theory." Those social scientists whose research is still locked into methodologies of the eighteenth century will have a difficult time with the book's multilayered causality. And history will continue to play its tricks on them.

STANLEY ARONOWITZ

Chapter 1

The Guises of Social Movements

The theory in this volume is discontinuous with all prior work concerning social movements. It is not only discontinuous with the analyses of mainstream sociology and political science, it is also at variance with Marxist perspectives, which tend to disavow the social movement perspective for such concepts as "political action," "vanguard party," and "revolution." Because of the broad scope of our project, we have not only developed a theory of social movements, we have also posited metatheories of society and human nature. Societies are historical phenomena every bit as much as they are structural entities. The human subject is also an artifact of historical development and is determined within broad limits by the level of material surplus. Thus, our metatheory is necessarily dialectical and humanistic, in that the human subject is presumed to be part of the material conditions of a given historical period.

To the best of our knowledge, no society exists that does not have some mechanism for the suspension of social structure. It is in this sense that rituals in so-called primitive societies are viewed by anthropologists as universal phenomena. In class societies, the suspension of social structure and normal everyday functioning (in addition to vacations, holidays, and ritual occasions) occurs during periods of social movement in which there is widespread popular insurgency. Members of social categories usually excluded from history begin asserting themselves as historical actors. This forceful assertion of "antistructure" determines the parameters of a social-movement period, which is necessarily shorter than the intervening periods of social quiescence. During the interim between movements, elites reappropriate their positions as controllers of historical development and pursue their own self-interests relatively unfettered by the unwashed masses. This is also true following social revolutions, when new elites have emerged and have taken control of the instruments of domination.

It is the hope of the authors that this work can, in some small way, help enhance the understanding of social movements by analyzing them in historical and comparative perspectives. Only then can we appreciate them in their

1

complexity. Social movements are the collective expression of the highest sensibilities of the species—the desire for freedom, liberation, and self-determination. The ultimate value of our work must be judged on its contributions to understanding the historical development of society, especially during social-movement periods.

What is a Social Movement?

To this end we offer the following definition of a social movement: *A social movement is the developing collective action of a significant portion of the members of a major social category, involving at some point the use of physical force or violence against members of other social categories, their possessions, or their institutionalized instrumentalities, and interfering at least temporarily— whether by design or by unintended consequence—with the political and cultural reproduction of society.*

The preceding is deliberately worded to exclude as irrelevant the issue of whether a given social movement "succeeds" or "fails" to permanently transform the prevailing relations of exploitation and domination. This therewith excludes from further consideration the idealist and economist errors of those who apply this standard of evaluation even to the extent of denying the legitimacy of the appellation "social movement" to episodes in social history marked by dissidence on the part of the "wrong" social categories or by dissidence articulated in terms of the "wrong" ideology. For example, from a 1975 statement of a group affiliated with the Weather Underground: "The New Left of the 1960s failed because it lacked a class analysis and a working-class base." Likewise, the wording is contrived to exclude cultural changes. That is, religion, ideas, art, shamanism (including psychotherapy), and so forth—where these are not accompanied by overt collective forcible conflict (including nonviolence and civil disobedience) with the representatives of established relations of exploitation and domination. The same device is also intended to distinguish between social change and social movements proper. By social change, we mean the quantitative and qualitative changes in the appearances of social relations, which continue throughout periods of dissidence and quiescence alike.

By social category is meant a human aggregate defined by one or more of the lines of cleavage within the social order. In their ensemble, such cleavages give rise to the "normal appearances" (to borrow Goffman's phrase) of society; that is, of society in its routine condition or as encountered by the isolated individual in its everyday-life nomenclature. Social categories that have served as the basis of social movements at one time or another in history have been enormously diverse. They have included status groups (that is, groups ranked hierarchically by prestige deriving from privilege recognized in law or custom, e.g., the medieval titled nobility, knights or gentry, bourgeoisie, free peasants and laborers, villeins, slaves); orders, guilds, and confraternities; castes (that is, occupational categories ranked hierarchically in order of ritual purity); social fractions defined by reference to visible styles or levels of consumption (poor versus rich or sansculottes versus culottes); categories defined by religious or secular ideological belief (believers versus heretics and infidels or socialists versus liberals, conservatives, monarchists, fascists, and so forth, with all of these in times of social quiescence organized into political parties accepting votes and volunteers from all strata); genders; age grade (e.g., youth or students); sexual-orientation categories (homosexual versus heterosexual); "the people" represented as a category antithetical to the state or regime (especially if the state or governing clique is of alien provenance or, as in the Iranian Revolution, because the governing clique has persecuted all rival or potentially rival sources of political initiative impartially and thus lacked a base of support in any major social category); military versus civilians; and ethnic groups. As to the latter, it should be recognized that the operative lines of ethnic cleavage are a good deal more fluid than is asserted by the ideological representations of ethnic "traditions." For example, the Greeks in the sixteenth century supported their "historic" enemy, the Turks, against Italians and Spaniards as the East against the West. Southern Slavs separately rose against common enemies (Turks, later Hungarians) only to give vent to the most ferocious conflict when united in their own state, Yugoslavia. Also, ethnic groups may be either geographically compact or dispersed (e.g., Jews and Zoroastrians), with U.S. Blacks[1] displaying some of the characteristics of the first in the rural South and of the second in the urban North. Ethnic groups may likewise divide (or combine) along lines of language, religion, culture (in the sense of "way of life" other than language or religion), political history (including those instances where ethnic divisions were themselves the outcome of social movements, e.g. the Dutch, the Swiss, or the WASPs of the United States; the latter were themselves divided in the course of social movements and countermovements into Yankee and Dixie versions, which subsequently recombined), appearance (the "prejudice of mark"), and race (the "prejudice of origin"). In short, there are hardly any appearances of society entailing invidious distinctions among humans that have not at one point or another in history constituted the basis or the point of departure for social-movement behavior.

It will be noted that this list omits the word *class*. There is no doubt that class relations, that is, relations of exploitation, underlie or heavily influence the course of all social movements and countermovements. However, it is quite rare that the "appearances" of society, as embedded in the everyday interpretation of social reality, correspond with any precision to class relations. The exceptions occur in those periods in which new axes of exploitation emerge rapidly from older social relations.[2] It is precisely the developing interference with the reproduction of this everyday interpretation of social reality that represents a defining characteristic of any social movement. A dissident social category necessarily begins with the "appearances" of society, including its own; whether or not the reinterpretations of social reality that emerge in the course of the movement embody class analyses is immaterial. The expression "class struggle" will be avoided here because it lends itself so readily to confusion and does not help us understand, historically speaking, the interference with the reproduction of social reality.[3]

Problems of Interpreting Social Movements

A classic example of the problem of the reinterpretation of social reality arises with regard to the English Revolution of 1640. From 1637, England was perturbed by mounting dissidence, to which legitimacy if not leadership was lent by Puritan clergy and professional jurists associated with, protected by, or recruited from the gentry, a leisured, landowning, subaristocratic status group whose distinctive badge of status was the right to display family coats of arms. By 1640, nearly the whole of the gentry—as evidenced by the outcome of the election of the House of Commons in that year—was in opposition to the government of Charles I, in which it was joined by a section of the titled aristocracy, and was at first united in its determination to curb the monarch's pretensions to the continental-style absolutism. Christopher Hill, Lawrence Stone, and Perez Zagorin have emphasized the fact that the whole of the ideological struggle, that is, the reinterpretation of social reality, conducted within and by gentry was couched in the language of religious sectarianism and constitutional legal theory.[4] From Hill, in particular, one may draw the following explanation of why this was necessarily true: The gentry was a status group that displayed considerable homogeneity in its appearances, that is, in its consumption styles and mental life; but it did not constitute a *class* in that the character of the exploitative relationships were subject to considerable variation. Some landlords, especially in the commercially developed south and east, had long since become profit-maximizing capitalists who increased their revenues through rack renting, enclosures, and sensitivity to market conditions. Others, concentrated in the backward and traditionally turbulent north and west, thought in more feudal terms of maximizing military power on the spot and regarded their peasants as potential infantry in time of war; these accordingly adopted a patriarchal policy of restraint in raising rents beyond the traditional level. Between these extremes there were gradations and local peculiarities. (Meanwhile, a minority, resented by the remainder, augmented their landed revenues by access to redistributed surplus in the form of the proceeds of state office and monopolistic privileges "in the king's gift," after the fashion of the continental nobility.)

Secular economic change differentially disturbed the gentry, unsettling some in their rise as others were unsettled in their decline; but the impact of the aggregate of these disturbances upon the gentry as a whole could only have been to focus their attention collectively upon their shared appearances as privileged status group. Specifically, it penetrated their shared differences in political philosophy—founded upon their entrenched position in Parliament and as unpaid local magistrates—with a regime that aimed at despotism yet lacked the revenue and coercive machinery to impose it; and upon their differences in religious faith—Catholic, Puritan, or sectarian—with the same regime that was visibly manipulating the tenets, structure, and ritual of the established church to mold it into an instrumentality of that despotism ("thorough"). The increasingly radical measures adopted by the Long Parliament to secure itself against a resurgence of the royal power, especially the abolition of the church hierarchy, then repolarized the gentry. By the outbreak of war in 1642, the gentry stood against the crown along lines partly ideological (in terms of religious faith, political allegiance, and willingness or reluctance to contemplate mobilizing the multitude for the defense of the revolutionary regime) and partly territorial (in terms of the military situation at the outbreak of war). Hill (1958), in a brilliant article, "The Agrarian Legislation of the Long Parliament," demonstrates most convincingly that the immanent logic of the revolution, expressed in emergency wartime expedients, was the generalization and systematization of bourgeois social relations: (1) Confiscated lands of the crown, the church, and absentee royalists were sold off in large parcels to new owners who moved quickly to recoup their outlays in the shortest possible time by subjecting these properties to profit-maximizing procedures (rack renting, enclosures, etc.), either out of principle or because they feared that the fortunes of war or politics might bring retrocession to the original proprietors. Other royalists were fined and consequently went into debt to preclude confiscation; however patriarchally minded they may have been, they were obliged to become profit maximizers to pay off the principal plus interest. (2) The underbrush of medieval survivals in land law was cleared away for the landlords but not for the peasantry; thus large property was protected by the abolition of the status of tenant-in-chief of the crown. Meanwhile, the "customary tenants" received no parallel proprietorship in their small holdings. (3) The process of redistributing land, as well as the receipt of fines levied upon royalists and the rents from impounded or confiscated but unsold lands—not to mention the whole of the state finance of the revolutionary regime—was concentrated in the hands of the London moneylenders, who were thereby enabled to make a quantum leap toward the development of a centralized, sophisticated, and resourceful money market that could within decades surpass that of Amsterdam. In still other essays, such as those of the conservative parliamentarian James Harrington and the reactionary royalist Earl of Clarendon (both cited in *Puritanism and Revolution*), Hill indicates that by the time the democratic thrust of the Levellers had been smashed in 1649, the awareness of the importance of property interests during and after revolution had come to pervade the propertied class as a whole whether royalist or republican to the point that they depicted such interests if anything more simplistically than the facts of the revolution warranted.[5]

The period in which social movements, especially those of the working class, were permeated by explicitly formulated secular-rationalist doctrines, exhibited acute class consciousness, and lent themselves readily to formal-organizational cohesion was, in the developed (or "core") countries of bourgeois society, peculiar to a period beginning in the early nineteenth century and ending about 1960. At least in the United States, formal organization was accompanied by the emergence of occupational specialties such as those of the organizer, the professional revolutionary, the radical journalist, and the theoretician. (Those who regarded the trends in these directions as inexorable laws of history consequently were called the Old Left during the 1960s.) In retrospect, these trends now appear as logical consequences of the increasingly despotic authority relations embedded within the capitalist labor process. By this is meant not only the arbitrary command exercised through foremen and straw bosses, but increasingly also the fruits of the capitalists' seizing of control of every aspect of the labor process and embodying it via production engineering, first in the assembly line and more recently in the "continuous flow" process.

Consequently, the mythology surrounding bureaucratized dissidence took on the appearance of self-evident validity, culminating in the first four decades of the twentieth century: Workers manifested their dissidence in part by spontaneously joining in the thousands of mass organizations, such as trade unions and political parties, within which bourgeois social relations were systematically reproduced. So, just as in times of social quiescence the "captains of industry" commanded the "labor forces" unhindered, the leaders of working-class organizations in social movements of the first four decades of the twentieth century ordered about "the great army of labor" or the "rank and file" in strategies, tactics, offensives, lines of defense; even individuals and small groups were alluded to as "elements" and "echelons."[6]

In bourgeois society, the subsiding of working-class movements was commonly disguised by the deposit of an imposing mass of bureacratic sediment which continued to call itself "the labor movement" or "the socialist movement" long after overt social conflict had ceased (except for periodic and highly routinized strikes). One curious result has been the institutionalization of the position of the shop steward or "union rep," who notoriously collaborates with management in the supresion of threats to factory discipline in intervals between contract negotiations. Closer to the concern here, another result has been a thorough obfuscation of sociological analysis of social movements, perhaps worst of all among avowed Marxists who are still characterized by the use of the mixed metaphor "building a movement." We find, therefore, to this very day a strange identity of perspective between the bourgeoisie and avowed subversives of the Marxist persuasion, which denies the capacity of the working class to accomplish anything collectively unless so ordered by trained experts.

The "traditional" working-class movement of the nineteenth and early twentieth centuries is therefore a thing of the past in the developed "core" of bourgeois society and may well be obsolete in parts of the periphery as well, Poland notwithstanding. In those parts of Europe in which "class consciousness" is most rigorously institutionalized, the end was heralded first in France in 1968, when the authority of the Communist party over the working class collapsed at the height of the movement in May 1968 under the impact of the slogan of "autogestion," in effect a demand for the liquidation of the despotic authority relations embedded in the capitalist labor process. This was to some extent replicated in northern Italy in 1969–70. In Britain, first in 1974 and then in 1979, it became apparent that the Labour party and the Trades Union Congress (TUC) hierarchy quite lost the ability to dictate to the working class and consequently became permanently estranged from each other, as the Labour party must appeal to the electorate whereas the TUC must follow their followers since they are their leaders.

In the socialist world, the expropriation of the bourgeoisie, whether by revolution or by military conquest, has everywhere been followed by the emergence of a new exploiting class that has in each instance reinstituted a variant or plain copy of the capitalist labor process. Charles Bettelheim, in his stimulating book, *Class Struggles in the USSR: 1917–1923*, discerns the original sin, so to speak, in errors of policy made by the Bolsheviks in that period. But he is himself guilty of an idealist error, since the institutionalization of collegial relations beyond the social-movement period proper (from the outbreak of political strikes in 1916 to the suppression of the Kronstadt Rising of 1921, or perhaps until the suppression of strikes and peasant revolts against the Bolsheviks lasting up to 1923), would have presupposed a degree of development of the human subject beyond what was historically possible.[7]

Excepting only the socially sanctioned display of the splendor and luxury of the rich and the circumstance that the exploiting class bureaucratically possesses—without formally owning—the means of production, contemporary socialist society is comparable in its stratification of classes and status groups to bourgeois society, though it forswears certain powerful instrumentalities of bourgeois social control: (1) organized religion; (2) parliamentary processes, that is, "working within the system to secure meaningful change through the electoral process"; and (3) escapist fantasies of "striking it rich" coupled with alienated identification—promoted by the media—with big-spending celebrities such as Jackie Onassis and her ilk, mink-clad Rolls-driving athletes, film and video superstars, and fashion models. As a result, it is interesting that collective action by the working class has brought down—temporarily—the regimes of Hungary (1956) and Czechoslovakia (1968) and thrice induced major changes in that of Poland (1956, 1970, 1980–81).

The social movements of the 1960s in the United States witnessed the entire disappearance of "class" as the basis of visible dissident social categories, though certainly not as an underlying reality. The dissidents were drawn from two principal sources: (1) the lower strata of the working class, whose core consists of the racial minorities, together with adjoining strata of the racial-minority population; whence the Black movement and its parallels among Chicanos, Puerto Ricans, and Amerindians; and (2) persons who in times of the social quiesence would have been candidate members of the bourgeoisie, whence the "youth," "students," "counterculture," etc. The women's movement spun off from that, and the gay movement spun off from the latter in its turn. In each case, the principal factor in dissident social cohesion was subculture rather than formal organization. Dissident ideological formulations were of the "subjectivist" type, that is, they emphasized the intensification of inner mental life and the importance of the subculture as the outward shared manifestation of this; reinterpretation of reality was conducted in each case from this standpoint. The dissident categories were each in some sense biologically defined, that is, in terms of race, age grade, gender, and sexual preference.

The entertainment industries in the 1970s reacted to their experience of the previous decade by deliberately overpackaging stylistic fads with the least modicum of rebellious overtones; in the instance of punk rock this postponed the possibilities of commerical success. On the other hand, there has been an unqualified success in transmuting the "ex-counterculture" into elitist and expensive "alternative life-styles," which serve not only as emblems of social privilege but as stimulators of the volatility of household consumption and thus the real possibility of being publicly branded as a "life-style failure" on top of the older penalties attendant to occupational failure.

It would, consequently, be futile to expect that the next round of social movements will resemble those of the 1960s any more than the latter replicated the working-class movement of the 1930s: New contradictions have been piled on top of the older ones and will doubtless be attacked from new directions by new methods; these are as certain to be as incomprehensible to Bobby Seale, Abbie Hoffman, and Robin Morgan as the 1960s were to George Meany. The subcultural cohesion of the movements of the 1960s had, as their precondition, the existence of bourgeois culture which was restrictive and conformist. With the incorporation of "alternative life-styles" into contemporary culture, the presumption that the next social movement will be based on dissident subcultures is highly questionable.

A Brief Restatement

This chapter is titled "The Guises of Social Movements" because they take such varied form. Although they may or may not permanently alter social relations, they are one of the prime mechanisms for doing so. Certainly as

important, within a social movement there is *always* an alteration in the development of the human subject, which influences social change beyond the
social-movement period.

Although social movements have been engaged in by numerous collectivities,
taken on religious, formal-organizational, and subcultural forms, and involved
great varieties of strategies and tactics, all social movements are characterized
by three mutually reinforcing characteristics: (1) intensifying overt conflict, (2)
the reinterpretation of social reality by members of dissident collectivities, and
(3) the reappropriation or "disalienation" of human capacities alienated from
dissidents as part of their socialization to subordinate positions in the social
structure.

It is the manifestation and mutual reinforcement of these three characteristics
within a social formation that delimit a social-movement period, during which
dissident collectivities engage in conflict with the regime and its instrumentalities, calling their right to dominion into question. By overtly challenging
and interfering with the reproduction of the relations of social privilege and
participating in forms of mass collegialization themselves, dissident collectivities become agents of antistructure. Statuses are temporarily suspended, role
structures are interfered with, and people who once knew their places refuse
to accept them. As long as the three characteristics are mutually reinforcing,
the social movement is ongoing. When relationships between them attenuate
and become fragmented, society has entered into what we have referred to as
a postmovement period (Foss and Larkin, 1976), in which social structure is
reimposed by dominant elites and movement participants are forced by necessity
to accommodate themselves to the return of quiescence.

By concentrating our attention on the internal laws of motion and development
of social movements (i.e., the natural history), issues of motivation and success
are put into the perspectives of historical and comparative analysis. Conceptualizations in social-movement theory have been so overly concerned with
motivation in the search for social-psychological "causes," and success in the
analysis of organizational "mobilization," that social-movement theory has been
doubly distorted. First has been the psychologization of social movements by
those who have operated in the tradition of Gustave LeBon ([1899]1960),
currently represented in the work of the relative deprivation school. Second is
the work of neo-Weberian resource mobilization theorists, most recently joined
by Marxists and New Left theorists, who have taken seriously the Old Left
criticism of the 1960s that they "failed" because they had an insufficient
organizational base and lacked doctrine. Before proceeding to our own theoretical statement, we will first examine relative deprivation and resource mobilization theories.

Notes

1. The capitalization of "Black": It is technically proper to use the capital "B" to
denote USA-born persons of sub-Sahara African descent, since "Black" is the term by
which they themselves denote their ethnic group and by which they identify ethnically.
The lower-case "b" is technically correct for generic allusions to recent Anglophone
and Francophone immigrants (Jamaicans, Trinidadians, Guyanans, Haitians, etc.) from
the Caribbean region and to Hispanophone immigrants of sub-Saharan African appear-

ance (such as Dominicans), since these draw ethnic lines among themselves and Blacks, who reciprocate in kind. Sub-Saharan African immigrants should likewise be lower-cased to distinguish them from Blacks. Thus one may for example write, "The Blacks are by far the largest of all black ethnic groups in the United States."

Analogously, the whole of the U.S. population socially defined as of European descent (that is, e.g., Portuguese immigrants regardless of color), should be called "white," with a lower-case "w," since these comprise numerous groups of distinct ethnic identification whose names for their particular ethnic groups should be capitalized (e.g., Poles, Italians, Jews, Irish, Hungarians, Ukrainians, etc.). An exception must be made for the largest white ethnic group, the WASPs, whose members have an unfortunate tendency to call themselves "Americans."

Certain immigrants who, though perhaps of darker color than some Blacks, are not of sub-Saharan African descent, e.g., Dravidians of south India, Melanesians, Australian aboriginals, Yemeni Arabs, etc., should be denoted by their place of origin.

2. See E. P. Thompson (1966) for his remarkable elaboration of the mechanism of capitalist exploitation developed by English factory operatives during the early nineteenth century.

3. Properly speaking, the concept of "class struggle" includes (1) the fact that exploitative class relations posit as their precondition the possession of the effective means of violence by the exploiting class either as the guarantee of the conditions of exploitation or as part of the mechanism of exploitation or both; (2) everyday pushing and shoving activity within the confines of the exploitative relation between exploiters and exploited; and (3) the actual overt collective resort to force and counterforce, explicable in terms of class relations, observable during social movements.

4. Cf. Christopher Hill, *Puritanism and Revolution*. London: Secker & Warburg, 1958; *The Century of Revolution: 1603–1714*, New York: Norton, 1961; *The World Turned Upside Down*, Harmondsworth, England: Penguin, 1973; Lawrence Stone, *The Crisis of the Aristocracy*, New York: Oxford, 1965; *The Causes of the English Revolution: 1529–1642*. New York: Harper, 1972; and Perez Zagorin, *The Court and the Country*, London, Atheneum, 1970.

5. It was Harrington, by the way, who coined the term "superstructure" in 1651, 200 years before the revelation unto Marx.

6. All this gave an unanticipated advantage to the Fascists, who could supplement the military metaphor with authentic militarism (the socialism of the trenches), and who not only copied their opponents' organizational methods down to the last detail, including the red flag, but vastly surpassed them in fields of street theater and pageantry. What is more, though the fascists were under no obligation to engage in class conflict, they did make free use of the combativeness of all sorts of hooligans whom their opponents spurned as too disreputable and whose antics offended their bourgeois feeling for tidiness and order.

7. If further proof is needed, consider the fate of the Maoist experiment dear to Bettelheim's heart of replacing the "capitalist road" management of industrial production with "revolutionary committees": This has apparently contributed mightily to the immense popularity enjoyed in the working class by Teng Hsia-p'ing (Deng Xiaoping), whose program is akin to that of Stalin, that is, a rising standard of living based on rapid industrialization coupled with the development of a military capability comparable to the USSR. (The Chinese regime has an advantage that Stalin lacked: As an ally of the United States against the USSR, it can draw upon foreign capital and need not resort to the "primitive socialist accumulation" associated with Stalin's five-year plans.)

Chapter 2

Relative Deprivation and Resource Mobilization

Relative deprivation (RD) and resource mobilization (RM) theories view movement participants as rational calculators seeking to maximize psychic, social, or material profits and minimize losses. Wheras RD theory centers on motivation, RM theory presupposes it, while examining internal organization, recruitment, and mobilization of forces, including sentiment.

Relative Deprivation Theory

Relative deprivation theory received its impetus from James Davies in his classic article "Toward a Theory of Revolution" (1962), in which he generated a synthesis between Marx and Toqueville on the causes of a social movement. Although he noted that Marx mentioned both "absolute" (i.e., immiseration) and "relative" deprivation in his work, he dismissed the former and accepted the latter, since it conformed more closely to Toqueville's observation that the French Revolution of 1789 occurred following a sharp economic decline preceded by a long period of progress. Davies saw revolutions occurring as a consequence of rising expectations, which, because of an economic downturn, outstripped society's ability to satisfy them. For Davies, psychology was the critical factor: "Political stability and instability are ultimately dependent on a state of mind, a mood, in a society" (1962:6). In Davies's simplistic causal scheme, he was guilty of both economism and psychologism. The reason he saw Marx stating antithetical positions on the causality of revolution is because Marx always focused on social relations; in his "Economic and Philosophical Manuscripts of 1844" (1963), he stated that in periods of economic decline, the working class experiences immiseration as they are called upon to suffer the brunt of the crisis, sometimes being forced to exist below the level of subsistence. In periods of economic expansion, he noted, the bourgeoisie was able to extract increasing amounts of surplus value from the labor of the workers, elevating their relative position vis-à-vis labor. The important fact, ignored by Davies, was that both immiseration and relative deprivation are a consequence of the relations of exploitation between the bourgeoisie and the proletariat. Davies's attempt to focus on the psychological well-being ("mood") of the people and tie it to a specific economic trend eliminated other probable causes of revolutions. Consequently, Davies's conception was recast by Ted Gurr (1970:52-58) as "progressive deprivation" and subsumed under a more comprehensive theory of relative deprivation.

Because of the comprehensiveness, sophistication, and scholarly acclaim he has received, we will center our attention on Gurr's most important theoretical work, *Why Men Rebel*.[1] Gurr's book was presented in the form of a logico-deductive axiomatic theory. The core of the theory is a set of probabilistic hypotheses that relate dependent to independent variables. The major dependent variable is "political violence," which may or may not take the form of a social movement. The issue of political violence and social movements is addressed in Chapter 7, "Social Movements Versus Political Violence and Mobilization."

As evinced by the title of Gurr's work, the major focus is motivation:

> This study proposes some general answers to three basic questions about our occasional disposition to disrupt violently the order we otherwise work so hard to maintain: What are the psychological and social sources of the potential for collective violence? What determines the extent to which that potential is focused on the political system? And what societal conditions affect the magnitude and form, and hence the consequences, of violence? [1970:7-8]

Thus, Gurr set out to establish the conditions under which the propensity to commit violent acts are maximized and those conditions under which such violent acts are politicized, that is, directed at the state. The relative deprivation model posits social conditions as preconditions for violence—they influence the probabilities of the occurrence of violent acts of a collective nature. Though such variables as socialization, tradition, and legitimacy of the system will influence the probability and shape of violence, the critical factor exists in the minds of individuals. Collective violence has as a necessary condition the existence of a gap between the "value expectations," that is, what people feel they are entitled to by virtue of their membership in a collectivity, and their "value capabilities," or what they expect the future to bring to them given past experience. Gurr saw this gap as a continuous variable defined as relative deprivation. It exists in all societies at all times. However, its rapid acceleration signals problems for the maintenance of social order.

RD theory is based on the frustration-aggression hypothesis, which states that when goal-directed behavior is interfered with, subjects who are frustrated in successful achievement will increase their propensity to resort to violence. Gurr saw the frustration-aggression hypothesis as reflecting a basic truth about human nature:

> The frustration-aggression mechanism is . . . analogous to the law of gravity: men who are frustrated have an innate disposition to do violence to its source in proportion to the intensity of their frustration, just as objects are attracted to one another in direct proportion to their relative masses and inverse proportion to their distance. [1970:37]

However, as Gurr noted from the evidence, frustration is not sufficient to produce violence to its source. Anthropological and clinical evidence indicated that frustration could induce many behaviors, only one of which is direct violence against the object of frustration: submission, dependence, avoidance, scapegoating, and self-destruction are equally viable alternatives. The inconclusiveness of the frustration-aggression hypothesis renders it questionable as the basis for a theory of collective political violence, as McPhail (1971) has noted in his review of studies of correlations between frustration-aggression indices and riot participation. The problem becomes magnified when attempts are made to measure and assess indices of frustration at the level of macrostructure. The virtue of such concepts as "value expectations" and "value capabilities" is that they are subject to public opinion survey measurement. If a regime were to assess the variety of collectivities under its control, it is likely to be able to spot centers of ferment. It must, however, be pointed out that these two variables are heuristic and the regime might do just as well, if not better, by employing spies and informants or reading police blotters or newspapers. Gurr's theory is probabilistic, not causal; the reason being that it is a quantitative theory and eliminates those factors (e.g., the collective reinterpretation of social reality on the part of dissident collectivities) that may be more important but are not subject to quantification.[2]

The circulating medium for relative deprivation theory is "values." For Gurr, there are three types of values: Welfare values are concerned with economic and psychological well-being. Power values constellate around the desire to participate in decisions affecting one's life and security. Although Gurr uses the terms "participation" and "security," they seem to be confused with "influence" and "autonomy," which are implied in his definition: *"Power values are those that determine the extent to which men can influence the actions of others and avoid unwanted interference by others in their own actions"* (1970:25). Finally, there are interpersonal values. They include status, community, and ideational coherence. Briefly, although slightly redefined from Gurr, these values are, respectively: the desire to attain a respectable station in life; support, companionship, and affection; and meaning in life.

Each collectivity in the social order can be defined by its value position, value potential, and value opportunities. Its value position is the amount of value it has attained. The value potential of a collectivity is what its members see it as capable of achieving. The value opportunities can be separated into three categories: personal, societal, and political. Personal opportunities are the possibilities for individuals within a collectivity to enhance their value. Societal opportunities are those avenues for a collectivity to become socially mobile. Political opportunities are those that allow a collectivity to "induce" others to provide them with value satisfactions. Each social category, then, can be located in the social order according to its position, potential, and opportunities, given the value structure, values being all those things that "men" want.

Gurr identifies three types of relative deprivation: decrimental, aspirational, and progressive. Decrimental deprivation occurs when the value capabilities of a social order decline and value expectations remain constant. Such can occur when a social category experiences downward mobility. Aspirational deprivation occurs when the value expectations increase without a simultaneous increase in value capabilities. Such a case occurs when people are exposed to societies that have higher standards of living that are not open to them. Progressive deprivation is, as mentioned above, Davies's J-curve form of deprivation, or the revolution of rising expectations as, say, in evidence during the French Revolution of 1789.

Gurr's theory of relative deprivation predicts that revolution can occur when things get better, stay the same, or get worse. By doing so, he is saying that *any* or *no* fluctuation in the economy can generate political violence, since relative deprivation can occur at any time in the economic cycle. Thus, Gurr's simplistic economism is reduced to absurdity. Add to this the political violence in the Western world by the social category of "youth," that is, the candidate members of the bourgeoisie, in the 1960s throughout a period of increasing economic well-being, declining in concomitance with the recession of 1969–70, induced in the United States by the Nixon administration at least partially for the purposes of social control. One begins to question (1) what it is in the macrostructure that leads to relative deprivation, and (2) whether relative deprivation can be assessed prior to violent outbreaks. (We are in no way claiming that the the youth movement of the 1960s declined because of recession.) This leads us to the difficulty that relative deprivation may only be able to be assessed *ex post facto* since it cannot be tied to any quantitative social change, nor can it apparently be inferred prior to social disruption. Additionally, actual participation within a social movement generates an alteration in the locus of motivations of participants, which neither social scientists nor activists could possibly have anticipated.

It seems a truism that people rebel because they are discontented and they are discontented because they feel they are not getting that to which they believe they are entitled. The obvious is being labored over in a social-scientific, logico-deductive, hypothesis-verifying way. The mystique of language, charts, boxes, and arrows covers the overriding simplistic conceptions of Gurr. First, the dependent variables, collective and political violence, are overblown and vague (see Chapter 7 of this book for a complete analysis of the term "political violence"). Second, it is an attempt to prove the obvious, which is obvious because it is resurrected in hindsight. Third, Gurr is attempting to turn what is an explanation after the fact into a predictive theory. In this he fails because of the lack of relationship between relative deprivation and violence directed at the system of exploitation and stratification; it does not concur with fluctuations in the economy; and he stumbles at precisely the same place every theory that attempts to explain social behavior on the basis of espoused or inferred attitudes stumbles—there is very little correlation between the two, be they acts of racial discrimination or of political violence. In Gurr, we have the triumph of form over content.

Resource Mobilization Theory

One of the most recent developments in social movement theory has been the increasing concern of sociologists about the ability of groups in movement to marshal resources to their cause. Useem (1975) saw the problem of mobilization of resources from the perspective of the protest organization. He was concerned with the ability of an organization to exploit issues, generate constituencies, develop programs, build infrastructures, and maintain commitment and solidarity. He saw these as problems that protest organizations must solve if they are to be effective. He was writing for an audience that is interested in forming groups directed at social change. Although Oberschall (1973) took a more "value-free" approach, he shared with Useem the belief that a social movement could not develop unless it was able to exploit a resource base.

Oberschall viewed mobilization from a macrostructural position by analyzing the various features of a society that accelerate or retard and give shape to social conflict. Using a more or less neo-Weberian approach, he classified social systems on a *gemeinschaft-gesellschaft* dimension. Midway between the two ideal types, Oberschall included the category of "weakly or unorganized" collectivity. He cross-tabulated *gemeinschaft-gesellschaft* with a hierarchical dimension. Societies were identified as segmented if they had castelike boundaries between higher and lower social categories. They were termed integrated if such boundaries were somewhat permeable. Thus, in an integrated communal (*gemeinschaft*) society, the probability of collective protest was minimized, since the community had access to the problem-solving centers. However, in a segmented associational (*gesellschaft*) society, collective dissidence would be much more probable. Dissidence would more likely be sustained and intense than in other social formations. Without going into detail, we can view Oberschall as refining Smelser (1964) by differentiating the types of social strain generated by social structures. In addition, he proffered a rough idea of the forms and intensity social movements would take within certain social structures.

Oberschall's resource mobilization (RM) theory posited the same motivational axiom found in relative deprivation theory: that the individual rationally/calculatedly maximizes scarce goods. His point of departure was Mancur Olson, Jr.'s, *The Logic of Collective Action*. Olson presented a model of the formation of interest groups for the purpose of obtaining "collective goods" whose existence for the membership (higher wages for workers, higher prices for farmers) presupposes the existence of a formal organization empowered to discipline individual members. As individuals, they maximize returns not by joining or contributing, but as members maximize returns still more by precluding the isolated action of any of them in the former capacity. For Olson and Oberschall, then, we have a sociological Keynesianism: the assumption of the rational-accumulating egoistic individual is retained, whereas the assumption of the capitalist "free market" is explicitly rejected.

They fixed upon a model of bureaucratic mass organization and pressure-group formation to start with. However, such organizations normally abstain from social conflict except as episodic dissidence. Oberschall, nevertheless, approached the problem of social movements by way of "conflict group formation in large collectivities," for which Olson's theory admittedly is inappropriate:

> Olson's theory would predict that large collectivities deprived of civil liberties and political rights would not develop from within an opposition organization for obtaining these goals if the members of the collectivity pursued their own selfish interests in a calculated, rational way and if they have complete freedom to join or not to join an opposition movement. In effect, each member of a large negatively privileged collectivity might as well wait until others take the risks and pay the price of mobilization and of opposition. But if each member follows this rule, then no opposition

movement is ever likely to be formed. Nevertheless, we know from history and from our own experience that opposition movements and conflict groups are formed quite frequently. Since Olson's theory is basically sound, one is led to question some of his assumptions with a view to modifying and extending his theory for the case of political opposition and conflict groups. [Oberschall, 1973:114]

Oberschall tried to get around this by questioning Olson's "assumption that the members of a large collectivity are unorganized individual decision makers similar to the numerous, small, independent producers in the market of the classical economist" (1973:117). Oberschall consequently pointed to the pre-movement prevalence of established collectivities. Where society is still on the *gemeinschaft* side, dissidents supposedly follow the lead of their traditional leaders. One would ordinarily suppose this to be more appropriate to counter-dissidence, except perhaps for colonial countries where the European powers handed over the state under fairly amicable conditions. Not surprisingly, Oberschall relied on cases such as these, especially in Africa, to the detriment of instances such as Vietnam, Angola, Mozambique, Guinea-Bissau, Algeria, and the like.

Where society has become *gesellschaft*, Oberschall suggested that "[the collectivity's] members might already be partly organized along associational lines for purposes other than opposition" (1973:117). Under such conditions, he posited that the "collectivity" behaves "rationally" in maximizing power. He said:

The very real theoretical gain achieved is that a theory of mobilization of opposition and conflict groups, social and mass movements, of protest behavior and collective political action, is essentially the same as the theory of mobilization for economic interest groups, and that the simple assumption of rationality in economic theory is sufficient in this theoretical effort. Thus, one need not make assumptions about individual motivation based on alienation or psychopathology, and a single theory spans the entire range of political and social movements, regardless of whether they are designated as extremist, leftist, rightist, centrist, or mass movements by their opponents and detractors. [1973:118]

It is apparent that collectivity is a most central term here; but what is it? Oberschall equates collectivity (1973:118) with "quasi group," a term attributed to Dahrendorf; but this is incorrect. We propose our own definition as follows: Humans may be said to constitute a collectivity to the extent and for whatever reason they act collectively. Multinational corporations and peasant villages of the sort that practice agriculture involving collective technique (e.g., wet rice culture or medieval open fields) constitute *ongoing* collectivities. Trade unions, religious bodies in secular society (excepting the clergy), and friendship groups meeting informally constitute *occasional* collectivities. The military and other total institutions are *enforced* collectivities. Subdivision of these categories and devising of cross-cutting categories is obviously possible ad infinitum. "Women" are not normally a collectivity except of the informal friendship-group type. We prefer on these grounds to use the term "social category" after Poulantzes (1975), to designate commonplace pigeonholes ordinarily employed by everyone in everyday life to depict the appearances of society. Ongoing social-movement collectivities are emergent in the course of social movements themselves. Thus we may have and in several periods have had ongoing women's movement collectivities; and "the working class" or "the industrial proletariat" has constituted itself as an ongoing collectivity on such occasions as Russia from 1917 to 1923; the United States in the 1930s; and France in May and June of 1968. Our objection is not so much to the word itself as to the degree of solidarity—voluntary or compulsory—denoted by it, which renders the usage appropriate in certain contexts and out of place in others.

Even within social-movement collectivities, the generalized prevalence of cost-benefit accounting procedures remains to be proven: Obviously, where dissidence is highly bureaucratized, as under the leadership of Marxist-Leninist vanguard parties with their accountantlike computations of the "correlation of forces," strenuous efforts in this direction may be inferred, but the substantive rationality of the same—evaluating their policies post facto—may not. For earlier periods when movements were permeated by religious ideology, the idea makes no sense: What "sensible" person, that is, of the rationally calculating bourgeois persuasion, would have joined in Albigensianism at the time of Innocent III, knowing perfectly well that this entailed at best a fight to the death (and otherwise not even the chance to defend oneself)? Would the Jews similarly have taken on the whole Roman Empire in A.D. 66-73? It was much more likely that dissidents in these epochs would appeal to the alienated supernatural, as the Boxers in the China of 1898 depended on spells and incantations for protection from bullets. (The same was done by Native Americans and Africans.)

More recently, where social movement cohesion has depended on culture rather than formal organization, the same assumption has led Oberschall to equal and opposite errors: Where riots and insurrections occur without visible guidance by a rationally calculating entity, he refuses to impute to them any substantive rationality: "The lower-class urban riots of the 1960s by black slum dwellers in the U.S. are an example . . . of collective outbursts devoid of leadership, organization, and explicitly articulated goals that arise in a collectivity that is both segmented from the rest of society and weakly organized within itself" (1973:122-23). To imply that these riots were without achievements—and substantial ones at that—is obviously conterfactual. One dimension of these achievements, in the form of federal programs, was in its content dictated by the selfsame "leaderless" character of the riots, as the preexisting leaders had evidently lost their moral authority over the masses they were supposed to keep in hand. Recall, for example, Governor Spiro Agnew's anger at the Black elite of Baltimore following the eruption of that city's ghetto in April 1968. Moreover, given the control, surveillance, and infiltration capabilities of the state in the present epoch, the very existence of a leadership cadre wielding effective powers of guidance over a Black population regimented in mass organizations would have precluded any possiblility of riots or insurrections taking place. What actually happened was substantively rational. Vide the near extermination of the Black Panther party, whose intentions in this direction were mostly notional and who were substantively more effective as a media myth than as a Marxist-Leninist vanguard party.

The state apparatus tended to persecute most ferociously those entities organized as a mirror image of itself, this having been facilitated by the *eo ipso* susceptibility to infiltration. Consider the thirty-one-year FBI harassment and surveillance of the Socialist Workers party, whose devotion to the forms of legality certainly far exceeded that of J. Edgar Hoover. Consequently, the "mobilization" idealized by Oberschall was not only (1) impossible and (2) contrary to the trend of the times toward cultural rather than formal-organizational solidarity in social movements, but also (3) self-defeating, as it would have rendered a laboriously built organization hostage for the good behavior of its members while rendering potential bribees conspicuous.

Contrarily, where "organizations" appear to have existed, this was accepted at face value:

> [T]he overnight rise of the Free Speech Movement (FSM) at Berkeley in the fall of 1964 was possible only because of the existence of a prior network of political, civil rights, and special interest groups in an already highly politically mobilized and ideologically sophisticated student population. All groups, right and left, felt their interests threatened by the sudden ban on campaigning at the Telegraph-Bancroft entry to the campus during the 1964 national election campaign. The FSM grew out of an overnight merger of these various campus groups. On a campus where most students are social isolates and organizational networks weak, the rapid rise of a student protest movement would have been impossible. [1973:127]

The preceding used as evidence what must rather be proven, specifically (1) that most Berkeley students were not "social isolates" as much as students anywhere; (2) that the various campus "organizations" primarily had in common the ban on political activity; (3) that Right and Left were meaningful designations and the students consequently "ideologically sophisticated," yet somehow the Right, in the midst of the Goldwater campaign, did not fly at the throat of the Left in support of the Board of Regents, of its own political coloration, but concluded an "overnight merger" with the Left to form the FSM; and (4) that the number of "members" of these "organizations" was sufficiently large to warrant the usage of "highly politically mobilized." This is reasoning *ex hypothesi*.

What in our opinion distinguished the Berkeley campus in 1964 from other schools of the same size was the intensity of the development in the South Campus area of a dissident subculture wherein bohemian cultural radicals and political radicals mingled promiscuously (in every sense of that word), for which the corner of Bancroft and Telegraph (and the plaza beyond) constituted a species of agora much like the corner of Lenox Avenue and 125th Street in Harlem at that time. This subculture was already quite visible by 1960. By 1964 its emergence was three to four years in advance of anything comparable with the possible exception of Cambridge, Massachusetts. As we analyzed the situation, if the South Campus subculture was to be taken as the "pond," then the "organizations" were to be understood as "ripples."

In consonance with his emphasis on formal organizations, Oberschall viewed ideologies as concrete givens. He noted:

> It is best to think of protest ideas and opposition ideologies as producing a collective response in conjunction with the presence of real or felt grievances, discontents, and suffering. The ideas serve to explain private

wrongs and sufferings experienced by individuals in terms not of private shortcomings of accidental events, or of eternal, unalterable states, but in terms of shortcomings of the society that can be remedied and of particular groups for the collective welfare. [1973:179]

Here we find that the RM approach tends to conceive of ideology as rationally calculated and in the form of doctrine. Within the natural history framework, a social movement is characterized by a continual reinterpretation of reality. It is only in the advanced stages or in the wake of the movement that such reinterpretations assume the characteristics of an ideology. (See Chapter 5, "The Reinterpretation of Social Reality," for an elaboration of this point.)

With the decline of social movement activity in the United States in the 1970s, social movement theorists of the Left, Center, and Right have concerned themselves with the "causes" of social movement success and failure. This has led to increased emphasis on the formally organized aspects of social movements. For such New Left theorists as Michael Useem and William Gamson, it has meant examining "protest organizations" with history only providing context. The more moderate or centrist theorists have focused more on "resource mobilization," which presupposes the existence of a formal-organizational structure at the core of the movement that must carry on exchange relationships with potential clientele, suppliers of material resources, and other organizations. Whereas the Left, is more given to analyzing the goals and structures of the protest organization (Useem, 1975) and its sociohistorical context (Gamson, 1975), RM theory emphasizes rational calculation on the part of social-movement organizations in interaction with their environments. In all these cases, collective action and even dissident behavior is subordinated to the analysis of behavior within organizations that are identified with social movements. Surprisingly, this sort of analysis has been applied to the movements of the 1960s, when formal-organizational activities were at a minimum, spontaneous collective dissidence was at a maximum, and, the basis of cohesion was the maintenance of a dissident subculture (Foss and Larkin, 1976, 1979). The assumption of bureaucratized dissidence is tied into desires on the part of the Left that the 1970s would be a time of consolidation of the political gains of the 1960s in liberal-reformist directions. In addition, it is a repudiation of cultural dissidence and overt conflict that was characteristic of the period in much the same way Jesus freaks, Hari Krishnas, and Marxist sectarians rejected the validity of their former behaviors within the movement. For the more moderate theorizers, this means focusing on the more "legitimate" or, perhaps, "serious" aspects of agitation for social change.

The work of McCarthy and Zald (1977) is a classic example of this trend. First, they define a social movement (SM) as "a set of opinions and beliefs in a population which represents preferences for changing some elements of the social structure and/or reward distribution of that society" (1977:1217-18). Therefore, social movements need not take on any behavioral attributes at all, since they are defined wholly in terms of public sentiment. Second, within this structure of sentiment exists organizations that are dedicated to promoting changes in line with sentiments. These organizations are called "social movement organizations" (SMOs) by McCarthy and Zald. They are the building blocks of social movements. We emphasize the term "building blocks" because

McCarthy and Zald see social movements as edifices in the body politic. Third, "social movement industries" (SMIs) are the collectivities or organizations that cater to the social movement, the movement being, of course, the sentiment structure. Finally, there is that section of the social order that is organized around social movements.

McCarthy and Zald view social movements as having a continuing existence within the social order. During periods of quiescence, they occupy an extremely minor and narrow sector. The activity that can be attributed to them is relatively small. (We would suspect that McCarthy and Zald would see such organizations as CORE, NOW, Naders Raiders—subsequently known as Public Citizen—and Common Cause as SMOs in the latter half of the 1970s.) The social movement sector competes with other sectors of society for resources in a sort of capitalist-free enterprise market. In this sense, resource mobilization theory maintains the myth of the free enterprise of ideas. Social movement organizations (SMOs) must compete as part of the social movement sector with non-movement organizations for the allegiance and resources of the population. Within the social movement sector (SMS), there is competition between SMIs and SMOs. An example of the former would be the recruitment of Black women by NOW—the women's movement industry would be competing with the Black movement industry. Competition between SMOs would be exemplified by intramovement rivalries, such as the rivalry between Orientalist sects, Jesus freaks, and Marxist sects for the hearts and minds of youth in the early 1970s.

Once the elements of their theory have been explicated, McCarthy and Zald turn their attention to the development of hypotheses concerning the relationships of SMSs, SMIs, and SMOs to societal resources. Their only hypothesis in relation to the development of an SMS (which is their only index of whether or not a social movement is developing) is that it increases with the rise of discretionary income. It is here that we are left with an unresolved theoretical contradiction. Are we to assume that if a social movement sector expands then discontent is increasing? If that is assumed, then McCarthy and Zald are in the position of stating that discontent increases only when things are getting better economically. This is certainly contradicted by the Polish workers movement of the summer of 1980, when the shipyard workers of Gdansk struck over an increase in the price of meat. We might also point out that the French Revolution of 1789 began over the rise of the prices of bread beyond traditional levels. Thus, McCarthy and Zald's hypothesis seems patently absurd. But suppose the expansion of the social movement sector does *not* indicate an increase in discontent. We must then assume SMOs have absolutely no relationship to discontent or social crises; those organizations are nothing more than charities. This problem cannot be solved by adding more hypotheses about the development of SMSs, e.g., "The greater the discontent in a social order the greater the expansion of the SMS." Since the expansion of the SMS would be the prime indicator of the increase of discontent, the hypothesis would be tautological. The problem reverts to defining social movements idealistically in terms of discontent without addressing the question of social action. The authors have reified the concept, rendering it meaningless. Who in American society is not discontented, including the rich? Who doesn't want an alteration in the calculation of rewards (whatever that is, since it covers both the desire for class privilege and an egalitarian society without classes) that increases their benefits? According to such a definition, all of America, with the possible exception of a few eccentrics, mental retardates, and a small minority of self-satisfied fat cats, are members of social movements!

What McCarthy and Zald have attempted, and what resource mobilization theory tries to do in general, is render social movements—which are, by their very nature, disjunctive with normal society—understandable using concepts that apply to the normal appearances of society; which as Levi-Strauss (1966) and Touraine (1977) have pointed out, appear more cohesive than they really are. In so doing, they have distorted the phenomena of social movements to the point of unrecognizability. To McCarthy and Zald, social movements are sectors of the economy relegated to the fringes, dependent on discretionary income for their growth and development. The phenomena of social movements, such as strikes, riots, property destruction, marches, and sit-ins are viewed as epiphenomena and the problem of the relationship of social movements to social relations is not even attempted. By assuming that the core of a social movement is necessarily formal-organizational, which has been refuted by the experience of the 1960s everywhere in the Western world, and focusing on the relationship between those organizations and their "task environments" (to use a term coined by organizational theorist William Dill, [1958]), questions of causality are begged and social-movement phenomena that define them as distinctive are ignored. More insidiously, social-movement behavior is viewed as the consequence of competition between various SMOs as they calculate and execute actions that give themselves notoriety and increase membership in exactly the same way a corporation would engage in advertising campaigns to increase sales and profits: "Treating SMO target goals as products . . . and adherence as demand, we can apply a simple economic model to this competitive process. Demand may be elastic, and its elasticity is likely to be heavily dependent upon SMO advertising" (McCarthy and Zald, 1977:1229). Given the resource mobilization model proffered by McCarthy and Zald, social movements can only mirror social relations in the larger society. Since this is a capitalist society, social movements (presumably even when opposing capitalism) can only adhere to a capitalist model. Even goals are commodities!

McCarthy and Zald tend to take a highly simplistic model based on utilitarian economics and organizational theory; a much more complex approach is taken by Charles Tilly. He is by far the most sophisticated of the resource mobilization theorists. First, he is extremely well read, and second, he knows history, especially that of eighteenth- and nineteenth-century Europe. Tilly's theoretical work has, as its central focus, collective action, which

> . . . consists of people's acting together in pursuit of common interests. Collective action results from changing combinations of interests, organization, mobilization, and opportunity. The most persistent problem we will face in analyzing collective action is its lack of sharp edges: people vary continuously from intensive involvement to passive compliance, interests vary from quite individual to nearly universal. . . . Our chief effort, then, will flow along the lines going from organization to mobilization to collective action to revolution. Especially from mobilization to revolution. [1978:7]

Tilly notes that it is very difficult to build causal models that take into consideration interests, grievances, and aspirations (1978:6). This is indeed true, especially when "collective action" takes on the characteristics of the forcible assertion of antistructure by dissidents. Aspirations skyrocket, grievances multiply, and interests intensify within the process of collective action. Such phenomena are impossible to predict, especially from ahistorical probabilistic models such as relative deprivation. Therefore, Tilly focuses on the processes of organization and mobilization in relation to collective action. Tilly's main concerns are "What are the determinants of collective action?" and "How is collective action transformed into revolution?" We will be more concerned with the former question herein.

Why does collective action become the critical concept for Tilly? Strangely, the reader is not apprised of his reasons. It is assumed, a priori, that collective action is worth studying. We are told, however, that there are risks involved: Everybody's an expert, the subject matter is highly volatile and political, and the concept straddles a chasm between causal and purposive explanations. Causal explanations are those in which an actor's behavior can be predicted by his situation. Purposive explanations attempt to uncover rules that underlie action and constrain alternative behaviors. Tilly, therefore, attempts to achieve the best of all possible worlds through synthesizing the two explananda. The question of "Why study collective action?" has not been satisfactorily answered. Although it has a certain heuristic value—that is, it can be measured—its substantive significance as a sociological or historical concept is quite limited. As Tilly himself admits in the quotation above, it has fuzzy edges. The definition, as in the case of other definitions of social movements (cf. Blumer, 1948; McCarthy and Zald, 1977), is overly inclusive. It includes all political action engaged in by any identifiable social grouping, including the state. Implicit in Tilly's use of the term is the notion of action against the state. Included in the definition is both routine and "nonroutine" action, ballots and bullets, lobbying efforts and revolutions. Though these disparate categories of action may be lumped together for the purposes of counting, the reliability (i.e., internal consistency) of the concept as a variable is highly questionable. Tilly's perspective is problematic in that the focus is collective because it can be treated as a dependent variable in a multivariate analysis. In his section concerning the measurement of collective action, he gives examples of how such collective action as strikes could be assessed on such dimensions as size, duration, and frequency (1978:90-97). This introduces another ambiguity in his scheme. Are strikes, riots, and civil disorders collective action or indicators of collective action? If the former is the case, then the term "collective action" is not a variable at all, but rather a loose category of a whole variety of specific actions, some of which may be unrelated to others, thereby undercutting the unidimensionality that is necessary for variable analysis. If, however, collective action is a set of specific behaviors that can be ranked on a scale in terms of increasing intensity, conflict, or violence, then the issue shifts to what is being measured, collective action or qualities of collective action (e.g., incidence of violence). This may seem to be an exercise in hair splitting, but it has important consequences for the development of theory. Tilly states:

> . . . [T]he accumulating literature of collective action offers an inviting terrain for theoretical exploration. My plan here is to draw on it in proposing general concepts and hypotheses for the study—contemporary or historical—of concrete cases of collective action. We return to some

of the problems posed, but not resolved, by Marx's analyses of nineteenth-century political conflicts: how do big structural changes affect the prevailing patterns of collective action? Among the big changes, I want especially to inquire into the effects of urbanization, industrialization, state making, and the expansion of capitalism. Among prevailing patterns of collective action, I would particularly like to know what kinds of groups gain or lose the capacity to act together effectively, and how the forms of action themselves change. [1978:49]

The central assumption of Tilly's theorizing about collective action is that there is continuity between open conflict and routine collective action. At this point, Tilly is asserting that collective action is a continuous variable. We must ask ourselves if an understanding of collective action is sufficient to answer the questions he poses, especially when he insists on making no qualitative distinction between routine and nonroutine collective action. Although size, duration, and frequency may be indicators that something serious is occurring, we do not know the nature of the process without some sort of historical analysis and awareness of the underlying social relationships that are manifested in the collective action. The notion of collective action may be helpful in understanding the "natural history of a social movement" (Rule and Tilly, 1972), but it is insufficient without sociological and historical analyses, which raises the question of its marginal utility—that is, its sufficiency becomes suspect.

Tilly expressly avoids the social movement perspective because of the underlying assumption of social-movement theorists that the nature of their subject matter is nonroutine, discontinuous behavior. He also notes that the social-movement perspective evolves out of the Weberian's concern for charisma. Though this is only partly true, it provides the basis for the comparison of the collective action and social-movement perspectives.

In its sociological form, the social-movement perspective is something to be avoided because of its lack of a sufficient definition, also a problem with Tilly's perspective. It has been ahistorical and psychologistic. The Weberian conceptualizations have been criticized above as overly concerned with organization and leadership and lacking sufficient definition. Moreover, the issue of discontinuity is central to the problems inherent in Tilly's paradigm. First, there is a qualitative difference between routine and discontinuous collective action that is obliterated in Tilly's perspective. Some collective action leads to further action, some does not. Some alters the consciousness of the participants significantly, some does not. Some collective action is part of an ongoing social force, some is merely episodic. Some is dissident, some is counterdissident. Without an analysis of social relations and historical processes, these important distinctions are washed away. Collective action is torn from its social and historical context and strapped into a stochastic procrustean bed of variable analysis. It is indeed ironic that Tilly can sing the praises of Marx's analyses of the Revolution of 1848—which is a natural history—and claim the red flag of pro-Marxism, while taking a Marxian perspective and forcing it into an overgeneralized positivistic model of relations between variables.

The confusion found in *From Mobilization to Revolution* seems to stem from an internal contradiction in Tilly's theorizing. He tends to waffle from positivistic to historical explanations of collective action. (The term "collective action" itself has a positivistic tinge to it, since it can be considered a variable that can be easily enumerated and subjected to multivariate analysis. It is also devoid of historical context.)

Perhaps this point can be illustrated from his earlier major research efforts. In his exceptionally subtle and complex study of the causes of the counter-revolution in France in 1793, in *The Vendée*, he apprises the reader of his intention to focus on the urbanization process as a causal factor in the counterrevolution. Thus, the reader is braced for Durkheim and anomie theory. Tilly, however, unexpectedly launches into an analysis of the political economy of social relations. Urbanization, it turns out, is the attempt by the Parisian bourgeoisie, fresh from their success of taking over the state, to impose bourgeois social relations in the rural territories. Tilly stated that the opposition took a religious orientation because the revolutionary government removed the *curés* from positions of local power—politically and economically—by substituting a secular officer of the government to oversee political relations, selling off church lands (of which the bourgeoisie was the most prominent buyer), and making *curés* employees of the state. Those *curés* that did not comply with the changes were removed from office and state-approved ones were installed in their places. Thus, local *curés* were subject to control by the newly bourgeois centralized state. Once the bourgeoisie took control of church lands, they subjected them to capitalist "rationalization" and rack renting. Thus the residents of the Mauges were subject to a new, more alien, and harsher form of domination and exploitation than before the revolution. When war broke out between France and Prussia, the Patriots attempted to conscript from the countryside, exempting themselves. This was the precipitating cause of the counterrevolution as residents of the Vendée took up arms against the government, led by local nobility and anti-Patriot clergy. Of course, local nobility and exiled clergy had very good political and economic reasons for struggling against the revolutionary regime. So did the peasants, who were being taxed by the state for an unpopular war and also were called upon to fight it. There was also unrest among the artisans who were dependent on the bourgeoisie for work and were suffering from a crisis in industrial production. Thus Tilly began with Durkheim and ended up with Marx. Urbanization, introduced as the major concept, receded as Tilly examined the underlying social relationships between the major identifiable classes and status groups. Urbanization, then, could not be separated from the political economy of social class relationships, since it became an artifact of class action. The counterrevolution in the Vendée was not a consequence of the breakdown of traditional relationships and a consequent vacuum of leadership, leading to meaninglessness, aimlessness, and anomie, but a reaction against the imposition of a new and alien set of relationships. Marx won, Durkheim lost. The explanation rang of the analysis of the historical development of social relations between classes.

Whereas *The Vendée* is a natural history of a social movement, *Strikes in France*, by Tilly and Edward Shorter, is much more positivistic, inquiring into the alterations in strike behavior from 1830–1968. Tilly introduced his concepts of competitive, reactive, and proactive forms of collective action, noting that strike activity developed from a spontaneous, unorganized activity into that which became less violent and more planned and organized. This work is of less interest to us than Tilly's *The Rebellious Century*, with Richard and Louise Tilly.

The Rebellious Century represents a gearing up for *From Mobilization to Revolution*, which is the most complete statement of Tilly's theory of collective action. *The Rebellious Century* examines the sequence of collective action in three European states—France, Germany, and Italy—between the years 1830 and 1930. The book begins by noting that for the three countries, the hundred-year period studied had high levels of collective action. All three countries—even though Germany and Italy were not unified states at the time—were shaken by the Revolution of 1848, Germany and France were struck by the Revolution of 1830, with Italy having delayed rebellions in 1831. Italy had a particularly violent decade between 1860 and 1870, beginning with revolts in the south in 1860, shifting to the north in 1866. Following the First World War, Italy was again subjected to increasing violence until Mussolini's fascist takeover in 1922. France's history throughout the nineteenth and twentieth centuries has been fraught with insurrectionary violence—in addition to 1830 and 1848, there was unrest in 1871, 1907, 1919–20, and 1936–37. After the Second World War, there were revolts in 1947–48, 1950–52, 1955–56, 1958, and of course 1968. Although Germany has experienced less violence, there was a rash of strikes between 1909 and 1913, mutinies and the Spartacist Revolt in 1918–19 and nearly continual street fighting between 1931 and 1933. The Tillys felt that the countries and the period were quite fruitful for the comparative study of collective action. The analysis was focused on the question "Does collective action occur because of a breakdown in social order or because of the increasing solidarity of dissident elements within the system?" Thus, we are again given a choice between Durkheim and Marx.

In all fairness, the Tillys noted that the answer to the question was fraught with subtle distinctions and could be seen as the same phenomenon viewed from different perspectives. In an attempt to answer the question, they analyzed collective action in terms of who was rebelling against whom, proximate and long-term causes of the conflict, and the nature of the revolt. They concluded that if one must take sides, solidarity theory is a better explanation than the Durkheimian breakdown theory. First, they noted a qualitative change in the nature of collective action over the period studied, which indicated that rebellion began in the form of competitive action in which no political orientation could be discerned and tended to take the form of brawls between youth gangs of neighboring towns. Collective action entered an intermediate phase of reactive behavior, in which spontaneous mobs would rebel against an aggressive action by a dominating group. Rebellions in which tax collectors were ridden out of town were of that order. As the century matured, so did collective action. Dissidents were banning together and organizing in formally constructed associations. In addition to reacting against imposition of authority, they began to hold forth alternative programs, plan strategy, and engage in forms of protest that required discipline and ongoing organization, such as the mass strike. Second, the Tillys noted that there were three basic situations that led to collective action: economic crises, state-building activities, and industrialization. Only economic crises could be associated with the breakdown of social order. The other two are characteristics of the imposition of new social orders. Also, the unique histories of the countries have implications for the onset of collective violence. For example, France and Italy experienced heightened levels of violence during the periods of industrial spurts, whereas Germany was relatively quiescent during its industrialization period, but experienced greater levels of violence prior to industrialization. Collective violence tended to be located in the countryside at the beginning of the century and relocated in the cities at the end. Throughout the period studied, there was increased evidence of the participation of the proletariat in collective violence. The Tillys concluded:

> If we must choose between breakdown and solidarity theories, we have to take solidarity. If we have a chance to revise existing theories, we must build in representations of mobilization, contention for power, and repression. Instead of a direct line from "change" to "protest" through "strain" or "hardship," we discover multiple lines. The rearrangement of everyday life transforms the organization of collective action. [1975:269-70]

Is this to be taken as a victory of Marx over Durkheim? Although there is certainly an attempt to focus on the historical relations between classes, the within-class relations are treated as a black box. That is, what are the *subjective* elements within the experience of the conflict groups that lead to the development of solidarity, or in Marx's terms, when is a class in itself transformed into a class for itself? The reader is given a sense of the historical shifts in class relations. What is not given is how these shifts influence the daily lives of potentially dissident elements within the social order. The treatment of collective violence by the Tillys, when compared to, say, Marx's own analyses of the Revolution of 1848, is bloodless. However, what is even more important is the apparent lack of concern for the subjective elements in collective action. This oversight is apparently responsible for Charles Tilly's movement into the resource mobilization camp in *From Mobilization to Revolution,* in which, in the absence of data, Tilly opted for a utilitarian model of motivation for collective violence. In his introduction to *From Mobilization to Revolution,* he stated that he had produced "stone soup." He was more correct than he thought: utilitarian motivation theory stones in a Marxist soup. The stones are indigestible and the soup is thin. When researchers assume that participants in collective action engage in a calculation of potential costs against potential benefits, they are distorting the reality of social action. It may even be true that certain forms of collective action or violence during a certain historical phase may be characterized by rational calculation on the part of the participants. Is one to assume that the tremendous continent-shattering revolts that shook Europe between 1848 and 1850 were the result of the rational calculation by dissidents who saw that they could achieve short-run gains through their rebellion? The problem with such conceptualizations is that when a social movement is in progress, the locus of motivation is subject to alteration to the point where dissident collectivities see rebellion as the only alternative to capitulation. Rational calculation, which underlies the utilitarian's theory of motivation presupposes that all people adhere to conventional reality at all times. Even Max Weber and Gustave LeBon understood that this was not the case! It is especially true that the domination of the hegemonic ideology loses its potency during times of social upheaval and that during such periods, the rules of the game change (see Chapter 6, "Disalienation"). It is truly disheartening to see such a talented and scholarly researcher as Tilly repudiate the notion of the subjective leap

and eschew social-movement theory for collective action theory, lumping qualitatively different types of social action together in a homogeneous whole while
relegating social movements to "waves" of collective action. Such recent experiences as the social movements of the 1960s in the West and the Cultural
Revolution in China should clue us in to the differences between routine and
sporadic collective action and that which constitutes social movement behavior.
In 1968, one was either part of the problem or part of the solution. Middle-
class youth were "crazies on the loose" experiencing the "reality gap" (see
Foss, 1972, for an elaboration of the subjective elements of social-movement
behavior). The common threads running through RM theory are the (unproven)
assumptions that (1) social-movement behavior is subject to rational calculation
on the parts of the participants, (2) the efficacy of a social movement is based
on the qualities of leadership and formal organization, and (3) social movements
can be understood using concepts that also apply to ongoing social relations.
Underlying these assumptions is the presupposition that social movements can
be controlled by leadership from within or without. Though they may be popular
among sociologists who desire to subject social movements to "rational" or
"scientific" analysis and radicals who see themselves as vanguards, they have
failed to prove that such analysis provides superior understanding to the historical record. This is especially true of Tilly's work.

Conclusion

There are serious shortcomings associated with RD and RM theories that
undermine their ability to apprehend and understand the complex phenomena
of social movements. First, they tend to underplay the so-called "spontaneous"
aspects of social movement behavior. This is because they tend to analyze
social movements using categories and concepts drawn from ongoing social
structure, thereby distorting the social reality of social movements to fit into
preestablished categories, making them banal, as in the extreme case of
McCarthy and Zald (1977). Such trivialization tends to overemphasize formal
organizations and their impact on social-movement behavior. Second, hierarchical aspects of social-movement structure are overemphasized, whereby the
actions of leadership strata and movement "superstars" are accorded powers
they simply do not have. Third, they tend, with the possible exception of Tilly,
to ignore historical forces in the generation of social movements. Thus, the
models of social movements tend to be static, as in the case of McCarthy and
Zald; reductionistic, as in the case of Gurr; or inadequate to differentiate
movement periods from periods of social quiescence, as in the case of Tilly.
Finally, none of the theorists attempt to examine the problems of the underlying
consciousness of social-movement participants as they engage in praxis, deepening their understanding of the social order and calling forth new repetoires
of behaviors in line with their new interpretations of how society works. This
is because, especially in the cases of resource mobilization and relative deprivation theories, the emphasis has been on studying phenomena that can be
measured and subjected to variable analysis, i.e., political violence and collective action. Neither term is sufficient to distinguish routine, normal, and
episodic dissidence from that which builds upon itself and takes the form of
nonnormal dissidence, that is the hallmark of the social movement.

Notes

1. The title was unfortunate, since it was published at the very time that *women* in the Western world were rebelling against masculine domination and the very sexism implied in Gurr's work.

2. Although Gurr claimed in his introduction that his theory is about as useful for rebels as establishmentarians, we regard this as sophistry. His theory presupposes a large social-scientific establishment to collect and analyze data concerning the potential for violence by a particular collectivity. As we will demonstrate, movements are not "built" but develop on the basis of their own internal laws of motion given the historical conjuncture. Therefore, such information becomes useful only for those who wish to forestall movements.

Chapter 3

The Reproduction of Social Privilege

In our language a herd of sheep is called a flock, a herd of lions is called a pride, a herd of baboons is called a troop, and a herd of humans is called a society. The herds of other species are perpetuated on the level of biological reproduction, including the transmission of genetically encoded instincts and learning capacities whereby subsistence is appropriated, mates found, and danger surmounted or evaded. The reproduction of society, by contrast, involves four levels, each in partial combination and partial contradiction with all the others such that the precise reproduction of the social formation as a whole is inevitably rendered problematic. These levels are:

1. The level of biological reproduction. This includes behavior necessary for the physical subsistence of the members of society, such as eating, excretion, or sleep; the procreation and nurturing of the young; and activities necessary to the maintenance of people in a condition of somatic and psychic health, including shamanistic ministrations, individual and group expressive behavior, play, and most sexual behavior.

2. The level of material reproduction. This includes the making, maintenance, and consumption of products, used or possessed by society as a whole or by any individual, group, or category therein.

3. The level of cultural reproduction. This includes behavioral norms, the techniques of production, shared beliefs about the nature of the universe, social relations, "human nature," etc., or ideology, and shared conceptual categories that define "meaning."

4. The level of political reproduction. This includes, besides the reproduction of the form of the polity itself—where it is differentiated from society as a whole—the reproduction of patterns of domination and authority relations throughout society.

Our purpose in this section is to analyze the reproduction of social privilege in its historical context. We begin with the analysis of the material level of reproduction, since biological reproduction is dependent on the social formations generated by the other levels of social reproduction. Access to the necessities of subsistence and satisfaction of basic human needs depends on the relation of a particular social formation to the physical environment, which is often conditioned by such historical forces as colonization, conquest, and epidemics. Within social formations there is obviously inequality in the accessibility of need-satisfying activities and products. At the material level of social reproduction, we will explore the evolution of exploitation. At the cultural level, we will examine hegemony. At the political level, we will examine the process of domination.

It is herein that we lay the theoretical base for the study of social movements. We assume that the basic etiology of social movements resides in the process of the reproduction of social privilege and that social movements, regardless of the subjective awareness of the participants as to their purpose, are attacks on the maintenance of social privilege.

Society is an organic unit that alternates between periods of social quiescence and social movement. Although our major focus is on social movements, it is our purpose to understand what happens during the longer intervening periods of peace that lead to the forcible assertion of antistructure (cf. Turner, 1969) by dissident collectivities. Our major focus is on the reproduction of social privilege in bourgeois societies, but it is important for us to distinguish between the bases for the maintenance of privilege between bourgeois and prebourgeois societies. By taking the historical and comparative view, we can examine the ways in which problems within the relations of exploitation, domination, legitimation were improved upon by bourgeois elites. In so doing, we are also able to analyze the historical development of capitalist society and the emerging problems within capitalist social formations. By gaining an understanding of the forces of development of contemporary capitalist society and the maturation of contradictions within it, the periodicity, social categories, forms, and "issues" of the next social movement in the capitalist West can be understood.

The Material Reproduction of Society

A material object becomes a product when it is consciously modified by the direct or indirect (through animal traction or machinery) application of physical human energy (labor) for a preconceived end. Direct appropriation of nature may occur without the use of products, as when fruit is plucked off a tree or a prey animal is killed with a rock found on the spot. Products do, however, enter into the picture when the fruit is sliced off the tree with a sharpened object or the rock is preshaped to render it more lethal. Food itself becomes a product when derived from a domesticated plant or an animal species. Cooked or otherwise prepared food is likewise a product.

Material reproduction requires the simultaneous and continuous operation of the processes of the fabrication and repair of objects. That is, the production and the using up, possession, and accumulation or hoarding of products, subsumed under the term "consumption." Products are obviously consumed in the process of producing other products and must be periodically replaced to ensure continuing production. New production is also called forth by the perception within society or a portion of society that existing products are worn out, depleted, or used to capacity. The definition of "capacity use" or "depletion" may involve levels of social reproduction not yet discussed: A pyramid, for instance, was deemed to be used to capacity when the monarch it commemorated was entombed within it; though the object itself would endure for millennia, it nevertheless devolved upon the succeeding ruler to commence constructing his own. It should be added that the process of production, even under capitalist conditions, presupposes the expectation of consumption. However, capitalism—in contrast to all preceding social formations—presents the recurrence of production outstripping society's ability to consume (cf. Marx, 1973).

Material reproduction does not require that products be consumed by the same people who produce them or even consumed within the same society. Products may be exchanged for other products or for a medium of exchange. They may also be produced consciously and explicitly for sale as commodities to unknown—but necessarily anticipated—ultimate consumers in an anonymous market. Moreover, there are in every society persons who—even if by virtue of infancy—consume products but do not produce them. When an entire section of society systematically consumes products produced by the labor of another section of society, does not produce products by its own labor in exchange, and possesses access to means of dominance sufficient to ensure the regular delivery by the producers, then an exploitative relation is said to exist between social classes.

The difference between the material product required to sustain the entire population at a material standard of living conventionally defined (or historically determined) as mere subsistence and the total product produced by the exploited class or classes is the surplus regardless of by whom it is consumed. By virtue of the vagaries of nature such as weather and soil fertility, their own efforts and ingenuity, or the special favor or slackness of the exploiting class or classes, a portion of the exploited class or classes enjoys a material standard of living above the level of "subsistence" as conventionally understood. The difference between this relative material prosperity and the subsistence level represents the *unappropriated* surplus as well as—if they are indeed fortunate—part of the *redistributed* surplus. The aggregate product consumed by the exploiting class or classes constitutes the *appropriated* surplus, whether consumed in private luxury or in the performance of their public duties. Their hangers-on and minions who ensure the extraction of the same product from its producers in appropriate volume and regularity are compensated out of the appropriated surplus.

Material Reproduction in Prebourgeois Society

Prior to the advent of bourgeois society there was no exploiting class that directly and systematically intervened in the labor process. Exceptions occurred only for relatively brief periods of apparent dearth of productive labor power. The particular appearances of prebourgeois exploiting classes depended rather on two factors: first, the relative magnitude of the appropriated surplus; and second, those activities represented as the occupations peculiar to that class or classes exempt from productive labor, such as war (with an important difference arising here between commanders of soldiers and knightly warriors),[1] civilian administration, religion, law, scholarship, cultivated leisure, pomp and ceremony, and the like. The second factor thus represents the mode of absorption, that is to say, consumption, of the appropriated surplus. Different prebourgeois exploiting classes supported by the same relative magnitude of appropriated surplus could and did adopt quite various styles of life and occupational specialties. A classic case is that of Egypt, where the labor process involved irrigated flood-plain agriculture, which had been substantially developed by the second millennium B.C. This form persisted until the incorporation of the Nile Valley into the capitalist world market in the nineteenth century, when the large-scale cash-crop cultivation of cotton was introduced. During this long period the exploiting class was altered in its appearances—and this was the "coloration" imparted to society as a whole. This occurred many times under successive native regimes and those of assorted conquerors, including Asiatic and Libyan nomads, Nubians, Assyrians, Persians, Hellenistic Greeks, Romans, Byzantines, Arabs, Mamluks, and Ottomans. Where these regimes— especially the latter two—intervened in the labor process at all, the result was disruptive. In Roman times Egypt supported 7.5 million people, a figure not reached again until the last century.

Prebourgeois exploiting classes were essentially parasitic. Their primary need was for elite consumption, including the means of violence. As the latter guaranteed the production and hence the consumption of all other varieties of elite products, the thrust of their ambition was toward the maximization of military power, either through the incumbency of key offices in state-type polities or through the accumlation of military might on the spot in feudal-type polities. It might be conjectured that the easiest and most immediately rewarding policy for any prebourgeois exploiting class faced with the ever-present threat of an absolute or relative decline in the magnitude of the surplus was precisely the perfection of the means of violence and the social relations of violence: Absolute declines occurred through demographic disasters such as famine, natural calamities, epidemics, or invasions causing gaps in the ranks of subsistence-level producers subject to exploitation. Prebourgeois exploiting classes were rarely capable of innovation in either labor-saving technology or in the labor processes with which existing technology was used, though they were quite capable of systematizing labor processes and the machinery of surplus extraction. Thus the Romans generated treatises on estate management in addition to their achievements in the spheres of administration and law, but were quite unable to find practical applications for Hellenistic science. Meanwhile, fundamental innovations in iron production and agricultural technology were being made by German and Slav "barbarians." The means of violence could be used and were in fact used to tie the scarce laborers to the spot; labor-saving devices were most commonly introduced when these were not only ready at hand, but also when the machinery for the coercion of scarce laborers had broken down or become ineffectual.[2]

The alternative predicament was the tendency of the relative magnitude of the surplus to decline due to population increase once the basic forms of the means of production, the labor processes associated with them, and the level of development of the human subject, the ensemble of these comprising the "forces of production," had attained a relatively fixed or final pitch of apparent perfection. The human subject includes every possible manifestation of human individuality, especially the capacity to innovate in any sphere of activity. It must never be forgotten that the level of development of the human subject is itself part of the "objective conditions" in any social order; however, the degree of this development is determined—not precisely, but within certain broad limits—by the relative magnitude of the surplus, both appropriated and unappropriated. Under these conditions it was normal for prebourgeois exploiting classes to employ the means of violence to not only maintain but actually *increase* the absolute magnitude of the appropriated product: Apparent superfluities of labor were turned to the advantage of the exploiting classes by compelling the exploited to accept more abject servitude in preference to starvation or hopeless revolt. Pools of unappropriated surplus were mopped up; material living standards of large sectors of the exploited class were pushed below *absolute* subsistence levels, that is, to the point of interference with the biological reproduction of society; and the politico-military apparatus of the exploiters was streamlined to facilitate the preceding.

Moreover, for any prebourgeois exploiting class the use where practicable of military force for accumulation through annexation, plunder, or levying of tribute constituted an attractive supplement or alternative to exploitation. The latter is most evident in those types of feudal polities in which the effective means of violence are widely distributed through various hierarchical levels of subpolities, since society as a whole was under such conditions. A home front was maintained in a perpetual state of mobilization for a war of all against all. Peasants had to be relied upon for emergency corvée labor in transport, fortification, and so forth. The exploited could even under favorable conditions be used as troops and thus hope for mobility into the exploiting class. Thus it may be noted that until the fourteenth century—when the legitimacy of the Catholic hierarchy first became seriously eroded—the clergy had long been more conspicuous than the lay lords in maximizing the revenue from their estates. Most notable among these were the monasteries, from the Benedictines in the sixth and seventh centuries to the Cistercians in the twelfth and thirteenth.

To repeat, the material reproduction of prebourgeois class societies was characterized by the primacy of the needs of consumption in calling forth production; that is, there were no "laws of motion" intrinsic to the processes of production that required perpetual activity on the part of the exploiting classes to dispose of an ever-growing volume of products. Rather, it was production, not consumption, that was problematic. Exploited classes produced their own subsistence and were additionally made to produce the upkeep of essentially parasitic exploiting classes as well as that of various apparatuses of enforcers, collectors, overseers, and ideological specialists who ensured the production and delivery of the appropriated surplus. Relations governing the appropriation of the surplus were thus relations of surplus absorption, that is, of the consumption of part of what was produced, and not "relations of production," since the exploiting classes did not continuously intervene in the labor processes. Indeed, it was entirely characteristic of these societies that the absolute magnitude of the appropriated surplus tended to remain fixed for long periods without reference to productive capacity or labor supply, to the advantage of those—especially peasants—who managed to raise output or install labor-saving contrivances or otherwise produce unappropriated surplus. Of course it was greatly to their disadvantage in times of crop failure, famine, flood, or invasion.

Material Reproduction in Bourgeois Society

If prebourgeois exploiting classes are comparable to parasitic organisms (see William McNeil, 1976; McNeil calls them "macroprasites" by contrast to organisms causing infectious disease, or "microparasites"), then the bourgeoisie is a *carcinogenic agent*. Marx (1967) aptly remarked, in volume 1 of *Capital*, that when viewed from the outside capitalism appears as "a system of production for production's sake." By virtue of the "laws of motion" of the capitalist "mode of production"—bourgeois society's peculiar arrangement for getting products produced—the material reproduction of society is interfered with unless it takes place on an ever-expanding scale. The particular form in which the surplus is appropriated is the value of the surplus product produced by laborers over and above the value of the product necessary to reproduce their labor power at a level of subsistence appropriate for the time and place. The objective of the bourgeoisie as a class and as individuals, in fact the very purpose of life in bourgeois society, is "the endless accumulation of abstract exchange-value" (Marx, 1973:409-410), that is, the limitless piling up of claims on society's ability to consume or, vulgarly, getting rich.[3] If the system is in that condition which the bourgeoisie has traditionally called "sound," this may be most predictably accomplished by the consumption of the appropriated surplus in the expansion of productive capacity, including the purchase of additional labor power, but in such a way that the savings of the bourgeoisie increase faster than does the wage income of the proletariat. The resulting chronic imbalance between society's ability to produce products and its ability to consume them leads not only to periodic crises—whether in the form of the old-fashioned "trade cycle" or in the more contemporary guise of "belt tightening" contrived and administered by the state—but additionally to ferocious marketing pressure on the part of the bourgeoisie. This includes the progressive dominance of marketing considerations over product design (extending in our times even to military weaponry), ever more sophisticated marketing techniques, and systematic inducements to consume new products and new models of existing products before the products already sold have been fully used up (see Baran and Sweezy, 1966).

Capitalism is the first true "mode of production." The "dominant relation" of bourgeois society—the capital-labor relation—is in fact integral to the labor process: Since labor power, the source of the surplus appropriated in the process of production, is bought and sold as a pseudocommodity—"pseudo" because however much the laborers may self-consciously develop "marketable skills" or are regarded as "hands" by the bourgeoisie, the labor power is not really separable from the living beings of the laborers—it follows that, from the standpoint of capital, the cost of labor is always too high. This represents the equivalent of a permanent dearth of labor even in the presence of substantial numbers of "unemployed" persons, thereby inducing the bourgeoisie to, first, continuously intervene in the labor process, and then, ultimately, to seize control of the labor process in every detail (see Braverman, 1974).

The mode of production is thus in a sense society's relatively self-contained device for getting products produced in ever-growing mass; "relatively," because it must among other things rely on the state—ultimately on the means of violence—to guarantee the conditions of accumulation. It tends to focus new needs and capacities—which emerge with the increasing development of the human subject—rather narrowly in terms of products. By its example it induces socialist societies that emerge from revolution against it to define their *raison d'être* in terms of catching up with it. Possibly most disturbing, and as Marx (1973:410) foresaw, every hitherto autonomous domain of social life becomes coerced into conformity with the dictates of the mode of production.

A condition of the existence—or reproduction—of the capitalist mode of production is the reproduction of the bourgeoisie as a class. But this in turn requires the reproduction of the bifurcation of this class into entrepreneurs—who are themselves increasingly reproduced in the subcategories of owners and employee managers—and politico-military specialists. The latter guarantee the conditions of the accumulation carried on by the former.

The reproduction of their division of labor derives from the unprecedented character of capitalism as a mode of production. Marxian theory has traditionally concentrated on the role of the state in securing the conditions of accumulation by ensuring exploitation through the forcible suppression of the proletariat and championing the "right of poverty" generally. Some writers, like Gramsci (1977; and, more recently, Miliband (1969), have considered the role of the state in reproducing the cultural and ideological hegemony of the bourgeoisie. O'Connor's recent works (1973, 1974) deal largely with the significance of state subsidies—"indirect surplus value"—and redistributions of income in the performance of the "accumulation function" and the "legitimation function" of the state in bourgeois society. What is thus far lacking in Marxian theory, however, is a comprehensive analysis of the process of the capitalist mode of production, the inner logic of which is "production for production's sake," the using up of the products produced, that is, consumption. Capitalism has never, at any time, relied exclusively on the combination of the household consuming retail merchandise and the capitalist consuming the means of production. It has always depended heavily on elite extravagance—especially in the earlier phases of bourgeois society, when this was marvelously effective in concentrating hordes of parasitic consumers around courts and aristocratic establishments. Commodity production was stimulated and market relations were developed. Later capitalism depended even more on collectivized military (comprising war, preparation for war, and colonial expansion) and civilian consumption by the state. This is apart from the importance of war as an alternative to the trade crisis in accomplishing the massive devalorization of capital through military devastation: From the standpoint of the capitalist system as a whole, World War I was a lousy war in that the territory subject to devastation was negligible. Technological advances made during the war were, moreover, not readily usable in civilian industry in part because too much existing plant remained undestroyed. A major European state had been knocked out of the world market yet was manifestly too weak to represent a plausible excuse for continued "preparedness." This should be borne in mind when pondering the magnitude and persistence of the slump of the 1930s. World War II was by contrast a wonderful war from the same point of view; even for Germany it was more economical. It pulverized a much vaster area into ruins thereby both requiring and permitting several major states to reconstruct their heavy-industrial base almost ex nihilo—prompting some representatives of the British bourgeoisie to regret publicly in later times that the Luftwaffe had not done as thorough a job on their own country as the Allied forces subsequently wreaked upon the Germans—making room for enormous new civilian industries. As a bonus the political results of the war legitimated a high level of pump-priming militarization ever since.

The process of capitalist consumption necessarily involves many things that the rationally accumulating entrepreneurs might never countenance if left to their own devices. The entrepreneurs, from their own perspective, denounce them an egregious waste out of hand; nevertheless, should they come to savor the accumulation-promoting fruits of these policies—be they war or "do-good" social reform—they inevitably adapt themselves. Accordingly, overall political direction—including custody of the means of violence—in bourgeois society is systematically entrusted to what might be called *consumption formations*, which are typically distinct in style and mentality from the entrepreneurs themselves, however much they are, together with the entrepreneurs, integrally part of the bourgeoisie. The consumption formations retain their distinctiveness apart from the entrepreneurs although individuals may pass from the entrepreneurial category to enter electoral politics and career military men may become corporate officers. The division is reproduced with the reproduction of the bourgeoisie as a class.

Beginning with Marx himself, the Marxian tradition has been bedazzled by the twin manias of the entrepreneurial category for production and accumulation. Consequently, it has long been handicapped in the analysis of consumption formations and the process of capitalist consumption as a whole. Marx, for example, was faced by the persistence of the British "landed gentry" in control of the state apparatus of the world's leading industrial power in his day. The landed gentry, moreover, often lacked pecuniary wealth commensurate with their prestige, social status, and access to the leading posts in the state. Were they capitalists specializing in the agricultural branch of production? A precapitalist survival? A class unto themselves? In the famous chapter 52, "Classes," of volume 3 of *Capital* (1967:885-86), Marx gave his last word on that subject (or any other, for that matter). He decided that they were indeed a class, with their own unique relationship to the means of production, that is, they lived off the rents accruing from landownership. But he apparently decided almost immediately that this was silly and stopped writing altogether. "Here the manuscript breaks off," Engels noted.

Another case concerns the millions of people found in every corner of bourgeois society working in offices. They are remunerated out of *redistributed surplus*, that is, out of profit as understood by Marx. They proliferate in part because it is impossible to determine with any precision their quantitative relation to the cost of doing business or to the performance of any administrative services; on the other hand, it is perfectly clear that their employment involves the consumption, rather than the production, of products. Their role in the material reproduction of society, both on and off the job, is in consumption, hence we choose to call them "the surplus-absorbing strata" and "dependent consumption formations." The main Marxist schools of thought, however, perversely choose to quibble about their "relation to the means of production," and hence whether they represent a "new working class," the position of the

French Communist party, or a "new petite bourgeoisie," the position of Poulantzes (1975), or a heterogeneous category occupying a variety of contradictory
positions in the class structure (Wright, 1978).

In bourgeois society the labor process and the techniques of production tend
everywhere toward uniformity and differ only as to the degree of introduction
of the latest and most advanced labor-saving productive processes. Among the
countries of the capitalist core area, however, aside from differences in relative
magnitude of output, there are striking differences in the appearances of society
traceable to the process of capitalist consumption, which subsumes the uses
to which appropriated, unappropriated, and redistributed surplus are put. The
preceding does not refer to the so-called "distribution of income" as much,
since this is only an appearance of the overall process of capitalist consumption.
The major variants are:

1. Export-led growth. This version, currently exemplified by Japan (as previously by the United States in the 1920s and by Britain in the nineteenth
century) requires that a major part of the appropriated surplus in the form of
products be used up in other countries, whether as means of production or as
household-consumption goods. (The Japanese will sell you a $1 billion cement
plant as easily as an $80 TV set.) Such exports may be only marginally prof-
itable, but they do make possible the continuity of a high level of production
while the remainder of the appropriated surplus is consumed as yet more
advanced means of production, which makes possible a still larger volume of
production of even cheaper products for export, and so on. The domestic working
class is meanwhile spared not only the difficulties of periodic layoffs, but also
the corrosive effects of excessively high living standards upon industriousness
and subservience.

2. Household-consumption-led growth. This was to some extent characteristic
of the United States in the 1950s and much of the 1960s; it is today perhaps
best exemplified by West Germany. This variant requires that much of the
appropriated surplus product be used up by a substantial fraction of the mass
of the population. This in turn implies the retention of a substantial amount
of unappropriated surplus—as income exchanged for the surplus product consumed—by the upper stratum of the working class, to the intense displeasure
of the local entrepreneurs. Even more, it implies a massive reliance on dependent consumption formations, including office workers and administrators,
servants (who reappear, e.g., as waiters and cab drivers, as "service industry
employees," lumped together with altogether different types of labor), sales
personnel, professionals, semiprofessionals, etc., all of whom are supported
out of redistributed surplus. The profitability of this variant appears at some
points to be integrally related to ever-rising material standards of living; but
if these should rise too high too fast for too many it has been demonstrated by
the experience of recent history that the cultural and political reproduction of
society (see later in this chapter) is interfered with. Another difficulty arises
when the surplus redistributed to the dependent consumption formations is
rising faster—by reason of the mounting systemic pressure for ever-higher levels
of consumption—than it can be appropriated from the direct producers and
consequently appears to threaten the nominal rate of profit (as defined by the
entrepreneurs), thus promoting a general rise in prices—or "inflation"—and
inroads upon sales by imports.

3. Military-collectivized-consumption-led growth. The clearest historical example of this was Nazi Germany in the 1930s and 1940s, but the United States during the Civil War and World War II also illustrates this variant quite well. Moreover, it represents a built-in feature of capitalist accumulation in the "advanced countries"—exclusive of Japan—of the capitalist world as well as the socialist world) as a whole at this time. Its essential feature is the reliance on the state to superintend the consumption of a major part of the surplus product in the form of military goods, related equipment, and means of production for manufacturing the same. This may take the form of consumption in war, storage of the products in question until they become obsolete and more elaborate products then built, providing free military assistance to client states, or even furnishing foreign aid to a newly defeated enemy to repair the damage recently wrought as it is to the advantage of capitalism as a whole—as opposed to any particular state—that the late foe consume the means of production required to restore the war-ravaged economy as quickly as possible.

4. Civilian-collectivized-consumption-led growth. Historically, the Swedish road to capitalism, it is now characteristic of the United States and increasingly of Europe. In the United States it evolved out of variant 2, possibly as a response to the threat to the social order represented by excessively high material standards of living for too much of the population. Accordingly, it differs from variant 2 in that consumption within bureaucratic apparatuses continues to increase or increases at a faster rate, whereas household consumption is held constant or either declines or is maintained on credit. An obvious drawback is that this variant is no less "inflationary" than variant 2. Also, since the leadership in the expansion of collectivized consumption passes from "private enterprise" to the "public sector," the entrepreneurs chafe at the exactions of the "politician" fraction of the bourgeoisie and rouse popular support against their colleagues.

5. Luxury-consumption-led growth. Historically, this has been the French Road to capitalism. This variant is now obsolete, but traces remain in France, which boasts a distribution of income that would make the United States look egalitarian.

Bourgeois society, dependent as it is for stability on an expanding level of production, has developed and expanded consumption formations that consume the surplus product. Central consumption formations are the household, the entrepreneurial strata (including corporations), and the state. The extravagant consumption of the bourgeoisie is insufficient to maintain an expanding economy. Therefore, greater sectors of the population are employed in consuming the surplus. The upper middle class is the most obvious social category that composes the constituency of consumption formations, consuming on the job as well as off in their roles as volatile consumers.

The Level of Cultural Reproduction

Cultural reproduction involves the inculcation, perpetuation, and transmission of, first, that body of shared or stored things done and made in society, that is, behavioral norms and the prevailing *techniques* for appropriating nature (as opposed to the *process* of material reproduction). Second, it involves shared ideas, beliefs, notions, theories, and narratives concerning the origins and history of the universe (comprising both the extrasocial—"nature"—and social components, with the latter definable as including the dead, the unborn, the reincarnated, the good and evil spirits, the divinities, the manipulable cosmic forces, etc.). This includes the significance of customary behavior and technique, the quality and sources of right and wrong (or health and sickness, success and failure, etc.), how the universe (including the social universe however understood) operates both ideally and actually, why some people in society are better than others, why other societies are different and inferior, and so on, all of which may be subsumed under the term *ideology*. Third, cultural reproduction involves shared conceptual categorizations of the universe, which give rise to thought forms characteristic of the culture and which unite individual, social unit, society as a whole, and nature in a "totalization" (cf. Levi-Strauss, 1966) whereby social life, individual life, and the universe as a whole are all implicitly understood as what is in common parlance called "meaningful." This third dimension of culture listed here is most elusive to cultural insiders, who in times of the failure of its reproduction seek out "meaningful work," "meaningful relationships," and persons who may be hired to "put meaning back" into their lives. It is most difficult for them to apprehend that "meaning"—whatever is meant by that—is implicit within the thought forms that the collectivity imposes upon itself, and that said imposition is efficacious to the extent that there is scant evidence of people "looking for meaning."

Cultural reproduction systematically reproduces the conditions for the disruption of its own continuity. First, culture is objectified in social structure. In primitive societies the social structure is routinely subject to disruption from without (cf. Levi-Strauss, 1966, "diachronic discontinuity," and Douglas, 1966) by perils of natural and human origin. They are also subject to disruption from within by contradictions within the social structure. Douglas points out that pollution taboos, rituals, and myths tend to coagulate at points where the social structure is exposed to external threat and where it is subject to internal contradiction. An example of such disruption is illustrated by Turner (1969) in his analysis of Ndembu ritual. The Ndembu exists in social units in which there is a contradiction between rules of residence and rules of descent. Within the ritual, they symbolically harmonize the contradictory principles of matrilineality and virilocality. Second, the products of primitive societies, being nonstandardized, each in part represent the objectification of the direct producers' esthetics and are subject to incessant change in style, form, and even level of technique. Language, in its form as a shared system of behavioral norms, changes at a rate that is fairly constant; this makes possible the science of glottochronology.

False Consciousness and Alienation

To Levi-Strauss the necessity for "synchronic systematization" requires an incessant struggle against the consequence of "diachronic discontinuity" by calling upon the sphere of ideology as myth, to which—in accordance with Mary Douglas (1966) and Victor Turner (1969)—could be added rituals, pollution taboos, and the interpretation of these things formulated by the primitives themselves. The result is the imposition by the collectivity upon itself of an ideological assertion of a greater degree of solidarity, continuity, and absence of contradiction that in fact prevails, or at least is deducible from the analysis of the inner logic of the social structure. This is, therefore, *false consciousness*, which is, accordingly, a component of the ideological formulation generally accepted within even primitive societies and not limited to those characterized by relations of class exploitation.

The same may be said for *alienation*, which inevitably accompanies domination even though exploitative class relations may not necessarily be present. Alienation is the appropriation of certain human capabilities as the exclusive possessions of a social category and their denial to the dominated, who, correspondingly, render psychic tribute to the dominators for possessing what has been appropriated. Alienation is literally a reward paid by the victim to a successful rip-off artist. Alienation permeates not only the ideological sphere but also the system of conceptual categories according to which the perceived universe is organized; that is to say, the sphere of "reality" and meaning. Say that, in a sentient sexually dimorphic species, in the absence of domination, reality may be either male or female. Yet by virtue of domination he makes what makes sense to him make sense to her. The species is named "man," implying that he is normal and she is deviant to pathological. The masculine principle is given pride of place over the feminine in the categorization of the universe. But, as Mary Douglas points out, with the exception of empirically very rare societies where the social structure is such as to render patriarchy unmitigatedly absolute, the abstract dominion of the masculine principle will be disconfirmed by actual social life and the system of categorization is consequently "at war with itself." Reality leaks. Ideology is called into play (as myth, ritual, taboo, rationalization, etc.) when the organizing principles of "reality" contradict one another, leave things out, or leave loose ends hanging.

The ramifications of false consciousness and alienation obviously become much more pervasive in societies characterized by exploitative class relations. The exploited class is made to produce the material support of a specific ideological apparatus—or of ideological specialists who overlap here with the polity, there with organized religion, or even with both—which explicitly and systematically affirms the nonexistence of a class contradiction. Their existence reinforces the self-evident, eternal, and categorical character of the lodgement of alienated human capacities within the exploiting class in general and within themselves in particular.

In prebourgeois society the principal visible role of the ideological specialists was not the legitimation of exploitation—although this was occasionally done—but the personification of reifications (abstractions regarded by the collectivity as if they had independent, that is, thinglike, existence), which are themselves expressions of alienation, such as "the arts," "spirituality," "thought," "learning," "law," "philosophy," "ideas," "perfection," "virtue," and so forth ad infinitum, and even those ultimate reifications, Faith, Truth, and Tradition. As the embodiments of such things, living or dead (and often the longer dead they were, the greater their importance), they served the exploiting classes implicitly by imbuing them with conviction and confidence. This occurred to the extent to which exploiting classes were enabled to reproduce within themselves the explicit conviction—or even better, the unconscious assumption—that class society had a "higher purpose" outside the material reproduction of society, which made it a "civilization." The ideological specialists (in material terms parasitic off the exploiting class) thus facilitated that class's own parasitism by inverting it into a resolve to defend civilization, uphold civilized standards, or some such mystique. The latter was of course invariably propagated to the exploited classes whether or not it was likely to be plausible to *them*.

One of the consequences of the reproduction of the ideological specialists was, accordingly, the reproduction of the distinction between them and the exploiting class itself. A little distance was functional from the perspective of the long- or even medium-run interests of the exploiting class (and derivatively of the ideological specialists themselves) since this was conducive to the evolution of a code of conduct for the class as a whole. Thus, exploitation could be limited short of the point where it led to class suicide by way of revolution, interference with the biological reproduction of the laboring population or its flight and dispersal elsewhere, or the incitement of foreign aggression by the conspicuous display of indolent luxury. Generally speaking, the more gruesome the exploitation the greater was the distance. The Confucian scholar, for instance, displayed his integrity in retiring from public life during the corrupt and declining phase of a dynasty, but would rush to serve the state when a peasant revolutionary or crude general seized the throne and required assistance in promoting reform. When the exploiting class comprised savage Dark Age warriors, the ideological specialists were found exclusively in Benedictine monasteries. The perpetration of aristocratic hedonism in famine-ridden societies such as India or the Roman Empire practically dictated the emergence of the most extreme asceticism. Occasionally, ideological specialists served the exploiting classes best by getting into trouble or getting killed: Their fates served to develop or invigorate standards of class conduct and restraint. Almost the last thing they contemplated was the end of exploitation, which implied the end of the redistributed surplus that supported them. In any case, only a very select few ever attempted to appeal to the mass of the exploited directly, and if they did so the message was one of justice, compassion, righteousness, humility, saintliness, goodness, peace, love, brotherhood, patience, conscience, charity, benevolence, enlightenment, and so forth. In short, they legitimated exploitation by proclaiming its cosmic irrelevance, by formulating an idealized representation of it, by advocating limits to it wholly dependent on the goodwill of exploiters, and by inducing the exploited to believe that— in modern parlance—"the system still works."

The formulations of the ideological specialists, at least during periods of social peace, entered by a "trickling-down" process into the sphere of the hegemonic ideology. The term "hegemonic ideology" was evolved by Gramsci (1973) to comprise the interpretations of society imparted to the social order as a whole, which reflected the predominance of the exploiting class by way of the polity, organized religion, and other apparatuses that are at its disposal or that it subsumes. These ideas are not, in any class society, even bourgeois society, found in a state of formulation reflecting any intellectual sophistication or profundity and orderliness of thought. This was true even among typical members of the exploiting class. Yet they constitute a set of commonplaces shared by all classes about how social life is carried on both ideally and practically. This could change dramatically during social movement periods when these formulations were vehicles of ethnic and/or class conflict. We therefore see in the Roman Empire the Monophysite heresy expressing the resentment of Syrians and Egyptians against the ruling apparatus; Donatism that of the Africans; Pelagianism of the British; and Arianism the manifestation of the exclusivism of most of the Germanic tribes while fighting Rome and, subsequently, as rulers of the conquered Romano-provincials.

Hegemony in Prebourgeois Society

The hegemonic ideologies of prebourgeois class societies differed widely from place to place and period to period in their detailed elaboration, but were essentially similar in those features bound up with the reproduction of false consciousness and alienation:

First, the ordained purpose of the producers of the surplus was to make possible the mode of absorbing the surplus practiced by the exploiting class. The cake, in other words, existed to support the icing, which, in its decorative splendor, represented what the cake was all about. It was understood that the consumption of the surplus animated the social collectivity as a whole. This principle was normally so self-evident that its overt statement was necessitated only by the possible failure of the reproduction of exploitative relations. The Confucian sage Mencius, who lived in the fourth century B.C., during the "Warring States" period, wrote, "...[I]t is said, 'Some labour with their hands, and some labour with their minds. Those who labour with their minds govern others. Those who labour with their hands are governed by others. Those who are governed provide food for others. Those who govern are provided with food by others.' This is universally regarded as just" (Dobson, 1963:117). But this was said in a context in which the ruler was admonished to rule with "benevolence," that is, to restrain his greed for troops and taxes, lest the cultivators desert his territory for his enemy's or revolt against him. The Roman historian Livy (1962:92-93) recounted a legend associated with an episode in 493 B.C., when the debt serfs of early Rome defied their masters by collectively refusing to supply the produce due to them. The Senate, according to the story, thereupon sent an orator who likened the nobility to the stomach of a body and the laborers to the limbs. If the limbs did not continue to supply nourishment to be digested by the stomach, they would themselves cease to move.

Second, the exploiting classes were everywhere understood as qualitatively superior beings set apart from the exploited by a distinction that invoked the alienated supernatural, whether by direct descent from the deities (preconquest Mexico, the aristocracies of the pre-Christian Germans, Homeric Greece); by association with clergy entrusted with the study, ritual invocation of, or direct experience of the supernatural, or merely suited by character, intelligence, and skill to serve the Divine Ruler (pharaonic Egypt, Hellenistic monarchies, the Roman Empire of the third century); the Successor of the Prophet (Arab Empire); the Lord's Annointed (late Roman/Byzantine Empire, Carolingian Empire); the Son of Heaven, who holds the Mandate of Heaven by right of a successful uprising led by himself, or an ancestor (China). In other words, everywhere prebourgeois societies fall under the sway of territorial states or feudal polities there was to be found nobility.

Third, again following Gramsci, there was a pervasive tendency in pre-bourgeois society toward the autonomy of the reified sphere of "the law" or "positive law." The legendary—even if historical—Great Lawgiver was a recurrent figure: Hammurabi, Moses, Solon, Manu, Huang Ti, Yao, Shun, Yu, Wen, Wu, the Duke of Chou, Justinian, Muhammad, Alfred the Great. By projecting "the law" as a reified entity outside of and "above" the exploitative class relation, the exploiting class sacrificed some gains accruing from indiscriminate predation, but secured long-term strategic advantages: (1) It collectively protected itself against mutual predation and expropriation by its own members who, as individuals, might lose sight of the class interest. (2) It had custody of "the law" in written form, which is no small advantage where most are illiterate and the script consists of pictograms, ideograms, hieroglyphs, cuneiform, complex syllabary, or Inca quipu. When the script was alphabetical it might turn out that legal proceedings were kept in a dead language, such as church Latin for the canon law and "legal French" for the English common law. (3) It collectively acquired, via the mediation of the polity, the ability to legislate. Custom is notoriously more conservative of the interests of the exploited than is legislation, even where the exploited are nominally represented within the polity. (4) Most important, as Gramsci pointed out, awareness of the existence of legal protection—as opposed to knowledge of the content and specific applicability of this protection—enforced by a judicial machinery that is apparently impersonal and that does not present itself in class terms (at least in theory), serves within the hegemonic ideology to convince the exploited that society is just, fair, and reducible to orderly and logical principles; that there is a limit to the exactions of the exploiters the transgression of which is in principle remediable; and that which they possess is somehow safeguarded and cannot be taken from them "lawfully."

Fourth, religious beliefs propagated within the sphere of the hegemonic ideology tended to include at some point the claims of the exploited if the latter were exceptionally harshly treated. Unstinted divine benevolence did not shine upon the exploiting class once it had gone too far, though this might be very far indeed. There was consolation for the poor not only in the transmigration of souls or in life everlasting, but also in tales of mighty sinners, evildoers, and wicked oppressors brought low by the wrath of the gods. Those faiths that did not accomplish this (such as the cults of the Greco-Roman gods, the Teutonic gods, and the Shinto gods) tended to make way for those that did. Religious beliefs redefined excessively in favor of the exploiters would periodically be corrected by subcults, schisms, and heresies—often first popularized within the exploiting class itself—which worked in the opposite direction.

Fifth, the hegemonic ideologies of prebourgeois society, in considerable relative contrast to those of bourgeois society, tended to be upheld with great rigor at points manifestly quite remote from questions touching on the legitimacy of exploitative class relations or of the polity. This rigor can perhaps be interpreted as reflecting a need, deriving from the level of the material reproduction of society, for maintaining the integrity of culture hardly less strong than that found in preclass "primitive" societies: (1) Given the absence of standardized production, every product necessarily represented an immediate objectification of culture on the part of the cultivators and fabricators, much as in primitive society. (2) Again, as in primitive society, the domains of the interpretation of "social reality" and the categorization of "cosmological reality" were very closely mapped onto each other. (3) The exploiting class was most imprecisely depicted and legitimated within the hegemonic ideology as a hereditary or otherwise privileged status group (e.g., the medieval order of celibate clergy) understood as intrinsically superior, with this superiority reflected in its mode of consumption of the appropriated or redistributed surplus.

Therein lay precisely what was problematical in the hegemonic ideology of prebourgeois society: In the event of social conflict the exploiting class qua privileged status group was invariably held up to its own idealized standard. Its claims to intrinsic superiority and to privilege as a hereditary or otherwise closed order were vitiated by evidence of its members' contemptible personal character and their incapacity for their high station; and, moreover, this evidence tended to accumulate the more the dissidents were motivated to look for it. The latter might then either insist that the exploiting class enforce upon itself a nobler or holier manner of consumption or conclude that the class as a whole was superfluous, i.e., "When Adam delved and Eve span/Who then was a gentleman" (Cohen, 1961), so that the issue had to be settled by violence.

Within the sphere of the hegemonic ideology, however, potential dissidence could normally be fended off by ideological outworks, permeating the everyday lives of the mass of the exploited, which focused the attention of the latter upon their own moral and characterological deficiencies and upon their own invidious distinctions whereby they were split into a multitude of fragments along lines of legal categories, ritual purity and other forms of petty hereditary privilege, petty relations of exploitation, longstanding kin-group quarrels, and minute gradations of wealth and status. The exploiting class, contrarily, was observed in distorted perspective, normally in the context of spectacles, rituals, and the performance of ceremonial courtesies; quite often a foreign or dead language was spoken or intoned or else a class-specific dialect or accent was used. The exploited would have no a priori knowledge of what was frivolous or corrupt. Consequently, only the most serenely confident—or suicidal—of prebourgeois exploiting classes would have countenanced untrammeled speculation within its own ranks—let alone its inferiors—as to the necessity of its rituals, manners, theology, esthetic style, or monumental consumption (that is, edifices such as tombs, palaces, fortified residences, statuary, cathedrals, frontier fortifications, which were built by the labor and or at the expense of the exploited class to the greater glory and eternal memory of the exploiting class. The beginning and end of prebourgeois hegemonic ideologies is the reproduction of the mode of consuming the surplus.

Hegemony in Bourgeois Society

Of all historic exploiting classes the bourgeoisie alone is continuously present in the labor process. This class, initially finding the labor process in its "naturelike" condition and subjecting it to the capital-labor relation, proceeded to incorporate into itself the sole power—appearing as the sole *capacity*—to make innovations in productive technique and to set the labor process in motion. (Consider the likelihood, given the sway of bourgeois relations of production, that the members of a United Auto Workers local would believe that they are capable of operating the factory without the presence of management, let alone introduce automated productive technique, which would eliminate their own jobs.) Consequently, the bourgeoisie, in contrast to all its predecessors, has legitimated itself and has induced the reproduction of this legitimation within the hegemonic ideology of bourgeois society as *productive* on two principal counts: (1) It calls attention to the tremendous productive forces it has unleashed, both in terms of ever-more advanced technique (progress) and in terms of the ever-mounting magnitude of products that it orders produced for sale (delivering the goods). (2) It emphasizes the terrible burdens (responsibility) of administering the labor process (management) and ensuring the realization of surplus value (hustling, meeting the payroll, the bottom line). The illusion is that because the bourgeoisie (or at least part of it) is a hardworking, that is, a *busyness* class, it is also a *productive* class. But historically, the reproduction of this illusion has taken different guises. Through Marx's day and perhaps into the early twentieth century, the specific reward of capital, personified as the owner, was represented as taking the specific form of profit, whereas that of the laborers was understood as taking the specific form of the wage, that is, a given quantity of money per time units worked. The whole of the profit, less the relatively minuscule expenses of doing business, was quite visibly at the disposal of the owner for accumulation less luxury consumption.

In any case, it is clear that the classical entrepreneurs were visibly privileged in that they were conspicuously exempted from the discipline of the labor process. Aside from the characteristic monumental architecture of this epoch, the ornate railroad station, the bourgeois of the Gilded Age comported themselves much as had their predecessors: They spent vast sums on town houses, country seats, vacation villas, private railroad coaches, lavish formal entertainment, art collections, bejeweled women of exquisitely delicate complexion and refined manners whose obligatory frailty required them to be prone to fainting spells, sumptuous yachts expensive beyond price ("If you have to ask what one costs," said J. P. Morgan, "then you can't afford one"), and, of course, armies and hordes of servants.

The second epoch has witnessed the emergence of a bourgeoisie of dual character, that is, as "investors," or owners of capital, and as employee managers, that is, as administrators of capital. Some entrepreneurs are exclusively the first, that is, rentiers, speculators, and idle rich; some are exclusively the second, that is, executives headed for the top whose salaries are not yet high enough to permit them to invest; but most combine both functions. The increasing specializaton of the managerial function corresponds to the share of the profit, i.e., redistributed surplus, received for the exercise of this function disguised as a *pseudowage*. For this pseudowage the top executive must not only work long hours but must also *appear* to do so. This is epitomized in the monumental architecture characteristic of the epoch of monopoly capitalism, the corporate headquarters and other office buildings. Here the bourgeoisie conspicuously consumes the services not privately of domestics but rather collectively of subaltern bureaucrats and clerical workers whose total consumption on and off the job derives from redistributed surplus. These expenditures are "necessary" to the cost of doing business in much the same way as domestics were "necessary" to the "proper" style of life of the Victorian bourgeoisie. The contemporary bourgeoisie is, therefore, at least in *appearance*, subject to the discipline of the work place; the older image of the idle-rich squanderer has been ideologically downgraded. So thorough is this change that the Prince of Wales and future Charles III of England has been taken to task in the British news media for lacking "a career" or even "a steady job."

Unlike the historic predecessors of the bourgeoisie, who asserted claims to privilege as hereditary or otherwise closed status groups, the bourgeoisie denies that it is one even though it is. More correctly, the denial of the existence of hereditary privileged (or disprivileged) status groups within bourgeois society, except possibly as anonymous vestiges, is systematically reproduced within the hegemonic ideology of bourgeois society. The privilege of saving an increasing portion of income—once that income exceeds a certain determinate point—and thereby accumulating sizable wealth plus the additional right to transmit said wealth to posterity intact are guaranteed by law (if only by way of subterfuges and loopholes) in every capitalist core state. Also, whereas in former times there was no precise correspondence of privileged status and the exploitative relation, it is most difficult to "have money" in bourgeois society without owning, however indirectly, some entitlement to surplus value. In the ideological sphere, however, the question of hereditary privilege is never broached directly, barring a systemic crisis. Instead, the principal consumption formation (the state) is given considerable autonomy in objectifying the abstract principle of "equality" in protective legislation replete with administrative apparatuses to enforce it. "Equality" is thus successively redefined: first, negatively, as "equality of rights," by the suppression of the special privileges of the former aristocracy and established church; second, "equal justice under law," or the protection of rights in property equally for great owners, small owners, and owners of none at all; third, "democracy," or the extension of nominal rights of representation in the polity to all adults, at least in principle; fourth, "equal protection of the laws," the abrogation of the formal persecution of certain categories of citizens by means of legislation; fifth, "equality of opportunity," or the abrogation of the right of private citizens to persecute others de jure; finally, "affirmative action," the symbolic effort to provide certain limited advantages to select numbers of those groups or categories whose persecution in the past has been found irremediable in the present.

The concept of equality is never systematically reproduced within the hegemonic ideology so as to signify or imply "equality of result." It is objectified and operationalized so as to systematically reproduce all the material inequalities that are officially deplored. Nevertheless, it does facilitate the mobility of highly talented individuals into the bourgeoisie, which is thereby strengthened, from the dependent consumption formations ("the middle classes," "the consumers") and into the latter from the working class. In the latter case, the position of the dependent consumption formations is strengthened as an *employed* status group interposed between the employed bourgeoisie and the working class, thankful that it is employed. This is no small factor in the protection of the bourgeoisie from the working class, though the bourgeoisie may not necessarily be protected from the dependent consumption formations themselves. Bourgeois society has displayed a historic tendency to emancipate itself from behavioral norms and institutional patterns not immediately derived from the capitalist mode of production itself, as are industriousness (the work ethic, which Marx considered an artifact of the system of commodity production) and, simultaneously, hedonism (the American standard of living, which he interpreted as an artifact of the incessant pressure to expand markets for products). Also tied to the mode of production is the reproduction of the segregation by class of the rearing of the young as well as the segregation of mental life in general. (For instance, the top 1-2 percent of U.S. households by income, that is, the bourgeoisie proper, watch television the least; cf. Mander, 1978.) In institutional patterns not integral to the mode of production but dependent on it, capitalism has, for example, demonstrated the capacity to revolutionize the form of the family—the conditions of biological reproduction—not once but twice: It first generated the substitution of the nuclear for the extended family, accompanied by a sharp increase in birth and fertility rates; it is presently engaged in the substitution of the modular[4] for the nuclear family, accompanied by an even sharper drop in these same rates.

The entire domain of mental life in bourgeois society is likewise dependent, and increasingly so, on the mode of production proper. This is associated with the objectification of the reproduction of mental life in mass-produced products, upon which depend the vast industries of music recording, consumer electronics, publishing, broadcasting, photography, cinema, art (galleries, supplies, appraisals, auctions, criticism), "live" entertainment, and so forth. The reproduction, including the initial or "original" production, or vulgarly the "creation" of mental life, is consequently increasingly subsumed by "reproduction" in the narrow sense of the word (recordings, copies, etc., along with playback equipment), which is subject to the market forces and "laws of motion" governing the circulation of commodities and the accumulation of capital. The difference between these and "pure" commodities is that the use value of the product for the consumer inheres not in the product itself but in the musical performance or literary composition or set of ideas objectified in it.

The rise of the sheer bulk of the industrialized means of the reproduction of mental life has been concurrent with a secular decline of commitment by bourgeois society to the reproduction within the hegemonic ideology of specific ideas, doctrines, theologies, moralities, esthetic traditions, artistic forms, and other aspects of cultural expression. In this bourgeois society differs markedly from its predecessors, wherein states would routinely wage war using such matters as ostensible grounds, and entire classes might occasionally go down to irreversible defeat. (Thus, for example, the Byzantine Empire was extinguished by refusing to accept as the price of military assistance the doctrines of papal supremacy and the double procession of the Holy Spirit.) To sustain the extended reproduction of the products objectifying mental life, as well as that of products in general through the development of new human needs in strict association with products corresponding to them, it is necessary to periodically smash and recycle all sorts of cultural forms and ideologies, including the "end of ideology" ideology. Stagnant pools resisting cultural change are mopped up. Whole peoples are stripped of ancient traditions, which may then be repackaged and resold; thus the Jews are first assimilated so that their descendants may consume neoorthodoxy as an "alternative life-style." Marxism emerges as a tool for career mobility and even dominates the intellectual life of major countries such as France, Italy, and Japan without the slightest evidence of any adverse effect on the reproduction of the bourgeoisie as a class. (Marx [1973:410ff] foresaw much of this. It may be doubted that he could have predicted that his picture would adorn a parlor game called Class Struggle.) The specific representation of the above in the bourgeois hegemonic ideology is the notion of "freedom" (or human rights), wherefrom the United States named its world order "the free world." Like "equality," "freedom" has proved susceptible to broadening as new "freedoms" are defined. Thus, to the traditional "four freedoms" (of speech and religion, from want and fear) have in recent times been added, e.g., "academic freedom" (the right to advance one's career by advocating the subversion of the state by which one is employed), "freedom of expression" (the right to profit by the publication, exhibition, or display of quondam "pornography"), "freedom of sexual orientation" (the right to participate in homosexuality without loss of social privilege), and possibly even "freedom of life-style experimentation" (the right to be publicly intoxicated on substances other than alcohol). "Intellectual freedom" is of course welcomed under the conditions of the "free marketplace of ideas." The only ideological use of the word free that is categorically suppressed is in the sense of "without pecuniary cost," i.e., freedom from bourgeois society itself. (Hence the absurdity of the militaristic advertisement calling for greater military expenditure that was painted on bus-stop benches in Los Angeles, a center of U.S. armaments production: *"Freedom is not free!"*)

Unlike its predecessors, bourgeois society does not reproduce a single, relatively compact community of ideological specialists committed to the intellectual and stylistic integrity of "civilization." C. P. Snow's notion of the *Two Cultures* vastly understates the situation, for there are several: (1) the academic "hard" scientists; (2) the extra-academic "hard" scientists and engineers; (3) the academic humanist-generalists; (4) the extra-academic humanist-generalists, including the "literary world" and cinema critics; (5) the academic humanist-specialists, subdivided by discipline; (6) the political intellectuals, including social scientists who write and lawyers; (7) the psychologist intellectuals; (8) the Marxist intellectuals, subdivided by profession and orientation; (9) the feminist intellectuals; (10) the "art world"; (11) the assorted devotees of "serious music," subdivided by the period of its composition; (12) the theologian-moralists; and so forth. In most of the foregoing, careerism dictates a quest for controversy or at least the appearance of originality. Even the professional critics of the various arts are essentially paid to disagree with each other, thereby collectively inducing their readership to resonate to the issues over which they debate. Moreover, the former "folk culture," which had subsisted in a "naturelike" state prior to its liquidation at the hands of the industrialized reproduction of mental life (cf. Ewen, 1976) (or its subtle transformation from within by the invention of a major-label recording contract and other forms of availability to extra-folk marketing), now becomes the domain of critics and connoisseurs within the cultural elite. Even the most commodified and industrialized cultural products, such as comic books and bubble-gum cards, in part precisely because they had previously been "low culture" now become the objects of sophisticated analysis, with elaborate esthetic systems devised to apply to them by professional critics. But this proliferation of cultural elites coincides with a new departure in bourgeois cultural reproduction.

Historically, the reproduction of the bourgeoisie as a class had always been accompanied by the systematic reproduction of a formation that might be called the cultural counterbourgeoisie, and that is perhaps best remembered as "bohemianism." Comprising a mixture of political and esthetic dissidents, highly stratified by wealth and fame (or notoriety), this formation was united by its location in a metropolitan zone such as the Rive Gauche or Greenwich Village, but even more by its overt contempt for whatever in mental life appeared to be labeled officially bourgeois by virtue of its respectability. If the bourgeoisie fancied classicism, the bohemian became romantic. When that caught on, the counterbourgeoisie affected realism. With the prevalence of that style, the opposition tried impressionism, cubism, anything to *épater le bourgeois*.

During periods of social upheaval the cultural counterbourgeoisie tended to tag along behind the crowds or to run for cover: Their intention was to shock and scandalize in an individualistic fashion, not to engage in overt conflict and certainly not to submerge their individuality dictated by the emergent pattern of class and bureaucratized dissidence. Nevertheless, in times and places of especially stifling cultural conformity or ideological censorship, they appeared from the outside—and even from the inside—to be fully merged with the whole of the political opposition and were persecuted accordingly.

The cultural counterbourgeoisie was thus systematically reproduced through the 1950s—the beat generation in the United States, the angry young men in Britain, etc.—until, during the social upheaval of the 1960s, the bohemians became the new masses, recruiting millions of people. In the 1970s—through devices discussed at length elsewhere—the boundary setting off the counter-bourgeoisie was liquidated, whereas all sorts of cultural and ideological diffuseness were introduced into the bourgeoisie itself as well as its subaltern strata: "We have no intellectuals in the Bay Area," said the editor of the *Yoga Journal*, "only creative people."

The upheaval of the 1960s did represent, while it lasted, the conscious interference, on the part of diverse and mutually hostile cultural oppositions, with the systematic reproduction of cultural and ideational patterns understood as characteristically bourgeois, even if in such vague and nonsensical language as "middle-class conformity." Yet in earlier social movement periods parallel developments occurred—e.g., in the 1930s, when a substantial part of the cultural counterbourgeoisie espoused one or another variant of Marxist doctrine—only to be reversed in the ensuing conservative periods. This time the change appears permanent. Whether this represents the culmination or logical conclusion of a secular trend in bourgeois society, or else whether it represents some emergent failure in the reproduction of the bourgeoisie as a class due to underlying structural contradictions of capitalism, or even, possibly, whether it represents *both*, must await clarification by events yet to come.

Political Reproduction

The Forms of Political Relations

Regardless of whether power exists in its "raw" form, with the means of violence openly displayed, or as so-called legitimate authority (classified by Weber into traditional, charismatic, and legal-rational variants), there are in class society three basic styles of wielding it outside the household:

1. The patriarchal. In this type of relation one party is unmediatedly, that is, personally and directly, dependent on the other for subsistence or possibly future reward or both, and the dominant party is meanwhile reciprocally dependent on the subordinate for labor, military service, or other contribution; the relation may actually involve real, adoptive, or fictive kinship. A distinction should perhaps be made between patriarchy as an institutionalized authority relation and patriarchy as an ideological representation: The latter is a convention of hierarchical systems where the topmost levels are unseen and remote from the bottom, as when the traditional Russian peasant alluded to the faraway tsar as *batyushka*, little father, although the local administrators of the state exercised despotic control over him. Likewise, exploiting classes habituated to the command of forced labor affected a guise of patriarchal relations unless, of course, they encountered insubordination, at which time the despotic essence of the relation became manifest (at least to the laborer).

Patriarchal relations are commonly found in association with petty exploitative relations in societies where the main axis of exploitation lies elsewhere; that is, for example, between rich peasant and poor peasant, or between master craftsman and journeyman, or between ward heeler (or the "Godfather") and recent immigrant. They are also typical of exploiting classes organized into great households competing for power: The Roman aristocrat thus employed his dependents and hangers-on upon whom he relied for political support. The Germanic chieftain was accompanied by his following of armed warriors who anticipated reward in the form of landed property.

2. The despotic. This type of relation implies the ability of the dominant party to command the subordinate party under the threat of summary forcible sanctions in case of refusal. It is commonly accompanied by arbitrary acts of force and violence—ranging from insults to destruction of possessions, mutilations, lynchings, and massacres—against members of the subordinate category or specially targeted fraction thereof, which have the effect of reminding the subordinates of the irremediable character of their subjection.

Despotic relations must enter at some point into any system of class exploitation, either as part of the process of appropriating the surplus or as the guarantee of the conditions of exploitation or both. In state-type polities despotic relations are, moreover, the essence of the social organization of the effective means of violence.

3. The collegial. In relations of this type a body of individuals, defined for this purpose as peers, collectively render a decision by some procedure whether personally, as in a meeting, or impersonally, as in an election or in the classical market mechanism, which is to be accepted as binding upon all. Collegial relations should not be confused with "democracy," especially in prebourgeois society, when they were invariably expressions of privilege: The members of the electoral college of the Holy Roman Empire, for example, were despotic rulers in their own principalities. The imposition of collegial relations upon an exploited class could moreover represent the intensification of subjugation for the purposes of more ruthless exploitation; hence, Russian landowners imposed the redistribution of lands upon village communes to preclude the emergence of a rich-peasant leadership in their villages (cf. Blum, 1961).

Of all forms of class society only bourgeois society possesses a genuine "mode of production." Within that mode of production, as Marx (1973:239-75) understood, the capitalist labor process itself involves despotic relations, which appear to be entered into voluntarily by the laborers in accordance with collegial processes that determine the price of labor impersonally by the supposedly competitive actions of capitalists and laborers alike. The realization of surplus value likewise occurs via the market mechanism involving the appearance of impersonal collegial relations among manufacturers and consumers whereby the prices of commodities are determined.

These authority relations are paralleled in the idealized image of the polity, whereby the social collectivity, through its representatives elected by collegial procedures, that is, by "equal" citizens, governs a centralized administrative apparatus whose means of enforcement are ultimately despotic in character.

The actualities of authority relations underlying the appearances of both the economy and polity, however, are, in general, the prevalence of a combination of collegial and patriarchal relations within the bourgeoisie and its subaltern strata, and the exercise of despotic relations by the bourgeoisie over the working class as a whole, which single out the most submerged and marginal strata of the working class for exemplary treatment.

The perpetuation of the political reproduction of society, which requires the continued reproduction of manual toil, must be taken into consideration when, during the past decade, the bourgeoisie responded to the rise of energy costs not by a still faster introduction of capital-intensive technique, which might have led to the technically feasible possibility of permitting the whole of society to engage in office work; but rather, to a switch to *labor*-intensive technique (see Rothschild, 1981, for data). From the standpoint of the level of the political reproduction of society it is no more possible for the bourgeoisie to imagine life without a working class than it was for a debt-ridden antebellum Virginia planter to imagine life without slaves.

Bureaucracy is the contemporary mode of social discipline within bourgeois society. The idealization of bureaucracy represents it as applying uniformly to all ranks, strata, and classes, uniting them all in either a Parsonian or a Marcusean totality; but this misrepresents the difference within the bureaucratic edifice in those authority relations that prevail for the bourgeoisie on the dependent consumption formations (i.e., the "middle class," whose labor consumes rather than produces material objects) on one side and those that apply to the working class on the other. It is after all the production workers, of all the bureaucratic strata, who alone are excluded from the corporate headquarters office building. One might hazard the guess that one of the most important, if not the paramount, aspect of the social privilege enjoyed by the surplus-absorbing strata, that is, the dependent consumption formations, consists of their exemption from the rigors of the authority relations imposed on the working class. What is more, given that it was perhaps the extremely rapid numerical and income growth of these surplus absorbers relative to that of the working class that emboldened the younger ones to rebel in the 1960s, one might ponder the possibility that the technically—and even, possibly, economically—irrational perpetuation of manual toil at its present levels is in part dictated by the necessity for the reproduction of the awareness within this stratum of its social privileges, thereby precluding it from similar adventures in the future.

The State as Alienated Authority

Alienation on the level of material reproduction is above all *exploitation*, that is, the alienation of the human capacity to labor in the working up of material. Alienation on the level of cultural reproduction is above all *false consciousness*, the alienation of the human capacity to interpret society subsuming the individual in society. Alienation on the level of political reproduction is above all *domination*, the alienation of the human capacity for government.

(Alienation on the level of biological reproduction is subsumed in the whole of patriarchal relations such that the species is understood as Man.) Government is the capacity of society to take care of itself. The caring function implies a limited despotic relation for its exercise: parent-child, shaman-patient, professional-client, defenders-defended, and so on. Where government becomes alienated, it is by consequence of the concentration of the means of violence in the polity. In preclass society such concentration may be wholly subsumed in the level of biological reproduction. In class society the polity is found either as the state, an organization that monopolizes the effective means of violence in a given territory, or as feudalism, in which the means of violence are accumulated by all levels of subpolities locally and wherein the hierarchical levels of subpolities are mutually dependent such that effective coercive power is not deductible in a logical and determinate fashion from rank.

The state, which in class society may be commonly called "the government," tends to maximize the accumulation of the means of violence at its disposal and therewith the generalization of despotic relations both within itself and in society as a whole; thus it is the ultimate guarantee of all relations of superordination and subordination. At the same time it tends to minimize the caring functions that it proffers. The alienation of government eventuates in a double-edged fetishism: First, the state and reified notions of power and dominion are worshipped so as to imply the diminution of the remainder of society on which the state is materially parasitic. Second, there is propagated a fear of chaos, invasion and plunder at the hands of criminals or subversives in the absence of the coercive power of the state and the despotic relations upon which this is founded and which it presupposes—as in the labor process—which are summed up in the overtones of the word *anarchy*.

In prebourgeois society the characteristic or ideal vocation of members of the exploiting class is that of the politico-military specialists. The maximization of wealth is subordinated to the means of the acquisition of the means of violence or access to the control of the means of violence. This is true despite the fact that exploitation is a presupposition of domination. Prebourgeois society lacked a "mode of production," that is, a relatively self-contained set of relations whereby it was ensured that products got produced. There was instead a situation of, materially speaking, large scale consumers producing nothing, for whom production was problematic and had to be ensured by some threat of force on the spot. This in turn fostered an effort to cast the exploitative relation with an aura of patriarchalism however despotic its actual conditions. It likewise fostered an effort to represent the proper sphere of life of the exploiting class to be rulership or the tendering of spiritual guidance or administrative services to the same. For prebourgeois exploiting classes solvency was never the critical virtue; lavish and magnificent consumption and redistribution were instruments for maximizing politico-military power. The very transition to capitalism was itself marked by a historically unprecedented preference for pecuniary income over territorial power or state office.

The bourgeoisie as a class is reproduced as entrepreneurs (combining the owning with the managerial functions) and politico-military specialists. This bifurcation is preserved such that in appearance there is continuous tension between these two sectors of the bourgeoisie. One manifestation of this tendency is the perpetual reluctance of the entrepreneurial sector to sanction the expenditure of funds upon the upkeep of the politico-military specialists. In classical early-nineteenth-century bourgeois ideology there was an animus against a large and expensive state apparatus (however much it may actually have been growing in size and cost at the time). The state was to be the mere guarantor of property, that is, of the exploitative relation, the "night watchman" as the famous metaphor has it. Characteristically, the state was stripped of such caring functions as had survived from the Old Regime; assistance to the poor or unemployed was to be withheld except by way of persecution (cf. Polanyi, 1961). Caring functions were readopted by the politico-military specialists in the course of their exercise of the caring function on behalf of the bourgeoisie as a class: So-called "social reforms," such as measures for the protection of labor or the sanctioning of trade unionization, were always forced upon reluctant entrepreneurs (to refrains of "creeping socialism," "incentive sapping," or "bleeding-heart programs") by political specialists. This was carried out in the performance of their functions in, to use O'Connor's (1973) terms, *legitimation,* or the enhancement of the ideological respectability or plausibility of bourgeois society in terms of "freedom," "democracy," "equality," "opportunity," or individual judgment according to just and fair desserts; or *accumulation,* that is, the intervention of the state in the economy so as to promote the accumulation of capital. Thus an intervention to promote an increase in wages may be an exercise of the legitimation function in that it fosters content of the workers for the regime, and of the accumulation function, whereby the market for articles of household consumption is expanded to the further general welfare of business, whereas the workers on their own may have lacked the strength to prevent the share of profits increasing faster than wages and thus to a slump. Latterly, the state has appeared as the consumer of last resort, performing the accumulation function by collectivizing consumption; and performing the legitimation function, however perversely, by precluding the subversion of capitalism by excessive household consumer affluence;[5] this we call the *scarcity-simulation* function.

The politico-military specialists exercise a caring function for the bourgeoisie as a whole not only by saving the entrepreneurial sector from political, economic, and social disasters that would otherwise be logical consequences of its inclinations; but also in military affairs, external relations, and all activities associated with these. In so doing they discipline the entrepreneurs to think of the class as a whole in terms of this or that country, which, if only for reasons of geography, has this or that national interest not reducible entirely to those dictated by the accumulation of capital. The politico-military specialists may use this understanding of national interests to influence the level of expenditure on the means of violence, which progressively influences the accumulation of capital as a whole. The sophistication of the means of violence in terms of the training of soldiers and the cost and complexity of weaponry rises in tandem with the level of scientific technique. Due to the position of the state as a monopsonist (monopoly consumer), it is not subject to the same degree to the cost-cutting imperative imposed on industries producing goods for household consumption or means of production. The military establishment itself fosters the temptation—understood as the *duty*—of the politico-military specialists to act on their interpretation of these national interests to involve the entrepreneur in military adventures that they would rather have avoided as unpopular or unprofitable (or restrained them from popular or profitable wars that were "not in the national interest"). At times the politico-military specialists may see fit to impose a dictatorship or lesser restraints on the bourgeoisie as a whole in order to carry out a war policy or to preclude the abandonment of one already embarked upon. In so doing it may also promote the plausibility of the motive of pecuniary gain as a human ideal by requiring at least the appearance of the suspension of that ideal for a "higher" or "patriotic" interest; promote unwittingly the function of war in the devalorization of fixed capital through destruction, conversion, reconversion, or obsolescence of military equipment and the means of production used in producing it (or accomplishing the same thing without war as in Japan by the devalorization of fixed capital by administrative decision); and promote the hegemony of the bourgeoisie of one country over that of others.

The entrepreneurial sector of the bourgeoisie, in short, cannot take care of itself. It is required from time to time and sometimes decisively to hand over its destiny to the politco-military sector, which is under some ideological inhibition in understanding or at least in publicly defending its mission in crassly economic terms. It may act in contradiction to the accumulation of capital (e.g., in 1975–76, when Gulf Oil was trying to do business with a regime that the CIA was trying to overthrow in Angola). Alternatively, the politico-military sector may promote the accumulation of capital pervasively, over the long term, and in a fashion not fully understood by either sector, as in the fostering of military Keynesianism or the women's movement.[6]

The geographical units wherein capital was accumulated were historically smaller or larger than the territorial units governed by states; the latter have at times developed national markets out of local ones or at other times competed for hegemony in a single multinational market. Yet it remains that the control of the effective means of violence has been distributed in territorial-state "national" units in the bourgeois core, whereas the countries of the periphery and semiperiphery have come to rely wholly or in part (and in some cases not at all) for their internal as well as external security on the states of the core. It is this pattern of the distribution of the means of violence that ultimately guarantees bourgeois social relations in all their ramifications on all four levels of social reproduction and that must inevitably become the focus of social conflict. That is, efforts at the collective forcible assertion of antistructure interfere with the political reproduction of society. Where relations of domination—authority relations—are interfered with momentarily in the street, in the university, in the household, or in the factory, the resumption of their routine reproduction must be enforced by the state, failing which the interference with political reproduction tends to become generalized. Ultimately, the question may be posed of the interference with the reproduction of the polity as a whole and, most concretely, the reproduction of the means of violence themselves.

Where interference occurs with the reproduction of the means of violence themselves, as when troops refuse to fire on a crowd and instead join it, the generalization of interference with the political reproduction of society as a whole occurs much more rapidly and thoroughly than it does when the political reproduction of society is interfered with in "everyday life," that is to say, outside the polity and specifically outside the military. This represents the difference between what is merely a social-movement period and a period fraught with what is called "social revolution."

The Provenance of Social Movements: State and Society; Core and Periphery

Social movements always focus on geographical units defined by states (leaving feudal polities aside), as these ultimately guarantee the whole of social relations pertaining to the material cultural, and political levels of social reproduction and thereby, indirectly or even directly, exert influence on the biological level of social reproduction as well (in terms of the birth rate, life expectancy, and general somato-psychic well-being of the population). States, as organizations wielding monopolies of the effective means of violence in their respective geographical units, are inevitably the foci of attention in social movements in that the latters' development entails the forcible assertion of antistructure. This may involve the failure of the regime to employ the means of violence contrary to prevailing assumptions as to the nature and workings of "social reality"; or, conversely, a precipitate resort to their employ contrary to the same sort of assumptions. A temporary local defeat of, or successful resistance to, the employ of the means of violence may generalize resistance. In rare cases, the apparatus by which the political regime wields the means of violence is destroyed and therewith the state itself.

Yet forms of society do not coincide with geographical frontiers: A given polity such as Nigeria may embrace several, ranging from the preclass to the peripheral-capitalist; the Roman Empire may have been still more diverse. Alternatively, medieval society—or "Christendom," as it was locally known— could display considerable homogeneity of technique throughout its agricultural and industrial core area, though with considerable local variation in the character of the exploitative relation and the degree to which the polity was more of the state type or of the feudal type. Similarly, bourgeois society, core or peripheral, embraces two-thirds of the human species and still decisively determines the character of the development of the socialist countries.

It should therefore not surprise us that social movements appear to come in waves which transcend political frontiers however they may be focused on particular states. In some periods this was attributable to structural conditions common to regions much larger than political frontiers: For example, in the upheavals of the early fourteenth century, especially in the period 1333–43, there was as a common background of rural overpopulation and soil exhaustion; stagnating markets for urban products partly attributable to limited rural purchasing power and partly to the onset of the Hundred Years' War; and state building accompanied by mounting elite consumption—including that of the church, despite its waning political influence—at the expense of rural and urban producing classes. In the late fourteenth century and through the period of the Hussite Wars, social movements had as their structural background a generalized labor shortage caused initially by the bubonic plagues and subsequently abetted by predatory interstate and civil wars induced by the urge and ability of the greater magnates to resort to plunder to compensate for revenues unobtainable through exploitation of scarce labor power. A cultural crisis centering on the declining ideological hegemony of the church and the demoralization of the great feudal magnates (for the latter, cf. J. Huizinga, *The Waning of the Middle Ages*); and the obsolescence of the feudal cavalry corresponding to the revival of the infantry arm, such that Swiss or Czech peasants could prevail against the German chivalry.

In modern bourgeois society the rule is that upheavals in capitalist core countries rapidly spread to other core countries and to the periphery, though immense social movements in the periphery do not necessarily find echoes in the core countries if these are in a period of social quiescence. A dramatic illustration of this occurred in 1848, when the February Revolution in France was imitated throughout Germany beginning with the key states, Prussia and the Hapsburg monarchy; and then in non-German Hapsburg-dominated areas including Italy and Hungary; with lesser degrees of social conflict becoming manifest in Rumania, Scandinavia, and even the United States (as a recrudescence of antislavery agitation, albeit short-lived, 1848–50).

A contrast between the 1960s and the 1970s should establish the point: The former decade was one of social movements in the core countries practically without exception. The events of 1968, partly inspired by events in the core, included the overthrow of a political regime in Czechoslovakia and the occupation of university buildings by students in Turkey, Poland, and South Korea; student dissidence in Mexico was bloodily suppressed in the Plaza of Three Cultures; the toll exacted by the Mexican military has been variously estimated from 500 to 3,000. By the end of the decade there were "Black Panthers" in Israel protesting discrimination against Jews of non-European descent; and untouchables *(dalits)* in Bombay, India, were organizing the Dalit Panthers.

The decade of the 1970s was quite turbulent in the periphery and semiperiphery (Portugal, Spain, Greece, and Turkey). To take the semiperiphery first: There was a complex political and social upheaval triggered by a military coup in Portugal, which lasted through most of 1974 until late 1975. Basque nationalism has been rife in Spain, with less intense working-class dissidence. In Greece, passive resistance among ordinary soldiers contributed to the fall of the regime of the Colonels (1967–74). Religio-political dissidence and counterdissidence in Turkey culminated in pogroms perpetrated by Sunnis on Shi'ites from December 1978 through January 1979. To consider the periphery: There was a full-scale revolution of the "classical" type—as reproduced within the military—commencing in February 1974. Protracted wars came to victorious conclusions in 1975 in Cambodia, Vietnam, and the counties of the former Portuguese Africa. Guerrilla warfare steadily intensified for several years in Zimbabwe, until the negotiated settlement establishing the Black-dominated Mugabe regime. In 1979, there were revolutions in Iran and Nicaragua. These are merely some of the more dramatic events.

Contrast this with the capitalist core in the same period, where the picture is one of social somnolence tending toward political reaction: Elections in France, Italy, Great Britain, Canada, and even Sweden gave victory to the Right. In the United States, the manifest and growing incapacity of successive heads of state, partly personal and partly political in origin (since presidents structurally lack the capacity to do very much about domestic issues of concern to the electorate, though they wield vast power in the international politico-military sphere), have thus far not led the citizenry to question the iron necessity of staggering or lurching through the day one way or another. But this might change, as part of the periphery is so situated geographically that its upheavals have the capability to cause the American way of life to run out of gas.

Notes

1. This represented a difference in vocational outlook of the most profound importance in terms of the *appearances* of prebourgeois society, which, e.g., was easily appreciated by a monk chronicling the deeds of William the Conqueror at Hastings: "But it would have seemed shameful and slack to William to take on the role of general in that conflict in which he crushed the English if he had not also done his duty as a knight, as had been his custom in earlier wars" (Lyon, 1967:98). Where a prebourgeois exploiting class legitimated its existence in part by its monopoly of the martial arts, it sometimes paradoxically maximized its military power by consigning itself to permanent weakness vis-à-vis external enemies rather than countenance changes in military technique, which might have involved the arming of the exploited class. Hence the suicidal behavior of the French nobility in the Hundred Years' War (until divine intervention appeared in the suitably incongruous guise of Joan of Arc); the disarmament of the Hungarian peasantry by the nobility following the revolt of 1514 and the refusal of the nobility to rearm them at the time of the German Peasant War (1525) and on the eve of the Turkish conquest at Mohacs (1526); and the preference of the Japanese nobility to seal the country off after 1600 rather than permit the introduction of firearms to change the rules of samurai warfare.

2. This in fact was precisely the difference between the late Roman Empire following the demographic catastrophe brought on by epidemics of smallpox and measles in the third century and Merovingian Gaul following the equally horrendous epidemics—principally of bubonic plague—in the sixth century and afterward.

3. A funny thing happened to the word *rich* on the way to capitalism: It is derived from the Old English *rice*, meaning kingdom or rulership; thus a *cyning*, that is, a member of the divinely descended lineage eligible to rule, was said to "feng to rice"—come into the kingdom or take power—when his reign commenced. Similarly, French *riche*, German *reiche*, and Spanish *rico* all derive from cognate words in Teutonic languages akin to German *reich* and Old Norse *riki*, both meaning state or dominion (Sweden/Sverige = Sve + Riki). These in turn appear to descend from an ancient Indo-European root with the most widespread distribution of cognates, e.g., Old Irish *ri*, genitive *rig*, king; Latin *rex, regis;* Sanskritic *raja;* and possibly Russian *ruka,* arm.
  The point of this is that it was not until relatively recent centuries that it occurred to an exploiting class to conceptually separate the process of amassing material wealth by exploitation from the process of the consumption of the same in the accumulation of the means of exercising dominion, whether as magistrates and military commanders in state-type politics or on the spot in feudal-type politics. Making this point with regard to medieval society, Edward P. Cheyney (1936) translates *ricos hombres*, the appellation of the feudal-magnate stratum of medieval Aragon, as "the ruling class."
  One of hallmarks of capitalism is precisely the preoccupation of the exploiters with the accumulation of capital—as means of production and as tokens of abstract exchange (value)—to the neglect of wielding the means of violence whether in person or mediated through an apparatus by virtue of holding a magistracy of state. Yet a curious paradox emerges when bourgeois society is contrasted with its predecessors: In Roman times the agricultural core of classical society lay in Egypt with secondary cores emerging in Sicily and Africa (Tunisia); its commercial and manufacturing core lay in Egypt, Syria, and Asia Minor; but its politico-military core migrated successively to Italy, Spain, Gaul, and Illyricum (Yugoslavia). The agricultural core of medieval society was in northern France, southern England, and western Germany; its primary industrial core

was in the low countries, with secondary cores in Italy and the Rhineland; its commercial and financial core was in Italy; but its politico-military core—depending on the fortunes of state building, war, and hereditary succession—could be found in various times in Germany, England, France, or briefly even in the papacy. In bourgeois society, contrarily, it has been that the rise of a new center of developed production in a state previously peripheral had not been followed within a few years or at the most decades by an effort on the part of the state in question to elbow or shove its way into the politico-military core of the state system.

4. By modular family (easy disassembly, easy reassembly), we mean the form that is supplanting the nuclear family in which minimally one partner has been married at least twice, having had progeny from the former marriage. As divorce *and* marriage rates increase per capita, the modular family emerges as the characteristic type among certain sectors of the surplus absorbing strata. Between 1960 and 1973, marriage rates rose from 8.5 to 10.9 per 1,000 (an increase of 22 percent) and divorce rates doubled from 2.2 per 1,000 to 4.4.

5. By this we mean that as the level of the aggregate surplus swelled in the post-World War II period, it was more or less democratized in the form of increasing household consumption, especially in the surplus-absorbing strata, interfering with the reproduction of the rational accumulator. In the minds of a significant sector of the surplus absorbers—youth—it became evident that material scarcity was at an end. This meant, to them, that society could relax, life no longer needed to be harnessed to the market mechanism, and the species could turn its attention to concerns of a "higher" order, namely subjective development and self-actualization. Bourgeois relations were attacked as a fetter on such development.

6. By sponsoring a denatured corporate feminism, creating opporunities and increasing aspirations of women, capital increases competition in the labor market, effectively cutting the price of white-collar labor.

Chapter 4

The Intensification of Conflict

Morales said to me, "It is strange—isn't it?—the process of the Revolution." El proceso de la Revolucion is a phrase constantly on people's
lips, one which usually makes them pause, for it makes it possible
for them to stand off and look at what has happened to them in a few
years. "In 1958, I told a fellow student in the Movement that I expected
our Movement would establish a decent constitutional government and
he said to me, Is that all you think this enormous effort will accomplish? It was then I got my first suspicion of the process set in motion.
Who would have thought that it would take us to socialism and me to
the Party!" (From a 1967 conversation with a Cuban doctor in José
Yglesias, *In the Fist of the Revolution*, p. 68)

According to the anthropologist Victor Turner (1969), just as there is an
evident human need for social structure whereby the reproduction of society,
in particular the level of material reproduction, is promoted, there is also a
universal need to periodically express—or indulge in—an antistructure whereby
the social structure is periodically suspended such that the statuses of the
workaday world are abolished or reversed, and the collectivity experiences a
moment of exaltation that he calls "communitas." He illustrates this in his
analysis of the rituals of the Ndembu, a people thus far denied the blessings
of class exploitation. The level of cultural reproduction, in effect, provides for
the suspension of the levels of material, cultural, and political reproduction
on ritual occasions, thus having the contrary effect of reinvigorating the social
structure between ritual occasions. Turner points out obvious parallels in the
class societies of the Mediterranean and India: the Mardi Gras and Holi festivals. He evidently intends his model to apply to social movements in class
societies, though his examples are drawn from religious movements that explicitly renounced overt social conflict. There is, nevertheless, no denying the
element of celebratory euphoria associated with social upheavals: In July 1967,
for example, Governor Hughes of New Jersey, having denounced Newark as
"a city in open rebellion," proceeded to deplore the "carnival atmosphere" in
the streets. It was difficult to tell whether he was more shocked by the breakdown

58

of order or by the festivity of the rioters. However, "communitas" need not assume the guise of shared grim determination or sacrifice; so it is probably idle speculation to distinguish between "instrumental" and "expressive" social movements. Indeed, there is in all authentic contemporary revolutions, no matter how serious their style, euphoria at the decisive moment, as in Portugal in April 1974 and Iran in January 1979, when the troops of the regime stuck red carnations in their guns.

If social structure is *eo ipso* painful among preclass societies such as the Ndembu, it must be doubly painful in class society, where, after all, the exploited pay the upkeep of the group that does the "civilization," a second group that ensures the continuity of the payment, and a third that explains why all this is desirable and inevitable. Excellent reasons for social dissidence are always present, which will not be set aside by Mardi Gras playacting. After all, there is no evidence that the material well-being of the average human anywhere was improved by class society before 1800 (cf. Braudel, 1973), and there is plentiful evidence that since that date the material improvement in the capitalist core countries—which of course does not correspond with any precision to nonmaterial improvement—systematically entailed the deterioration of material conditions for the vast majority of humans in the periphery (cf. Amin, 1974).

Hypotheses as to macroeconomic conditions that instigate social movements have led to no definitive conclusions, perhaps because these generalize from a few "great revolutions" while ignoring dissidence with less spectacular consequences. The old-fashioned "immiserationist" perspective once looked to economic depressions and declining living standards as especially conducive to revolt. More recent notions look to periods of prosperity as more likely to generate upheaval because of "revolutions of rising expectations," or "relative deprivation." That is, an illusion of perspective on the part of people on the rise, who believe that they should be rising even faster, and consequently feel that they are declining. Other recent explanations include "social strain," or the dislocations and antagonisms among the various social categories due to unaccustomed affluence, and "status inconsistency," or the unease of long-established status groups at the prospect of the newly affluent rising above their station. Sophisticated wrinkles include attributing movements to long periods of improvement followed by sharp declines, as may have been true of the French Revolution; or, contrarily, to long depressions followed by sharp upswings, as may have been true of the revolutions of 1848. One cannot rule out the possibility that any sort of macroeconomic change or even no change at all—in effect, prolonged boredom—may serve as the background to social upheaval. Focus on political and ideological trends, that is, on "legitimacy," has led to no more clear-cut results except insofar as it clarifies the situation leading to the initial demands (the developments Professor Stone [1965] calls the "precipitants" and "triggers").

We may consequently generalize about the development of social movements only once they have emerged. They display the development of the three ongoing, simultaneous, and mutually reinforcing processes mentioned in Chapter 1, "The Guises of Social Movements." We will now examine the phenomenon of the *intensification of social conflict*. This refers to progressive departures from the routine of "politics," under the customary rules, as well as to departures from formally sanctioned types of conflict, such as strikes for higher wages or lawsuits. It is necessary to stress that the period in which these innovative departures occur and develop, followed by the usually much briefer period during which they subside, together define the temporal extent of the movement, and that this is the case irrespective of the institutionalized consequences, if any, of the movement. That is, the movement must be understood as temporally limited to the conflict period whether it eventuates in the total transformation of social relations, palliative reforms supplemented by modest reshuffling of the governing circles, no change at all, or a counterrevolutionary regime that is more oppressive than the initial situation.

We understand social movements, on the basis of all the historical evidence known to us, as limited temporally to periods of a few months or years, and that the duration of such periods may be delimited in terms of ongoing and intensifying *overt social conflict*. Without this pivotal criterion, all distinctions among social movements, general social change, and cultural, intellectual, or artistic movements would be—as we find they generally are in the sociological literature—hopelessly muddled.

Social-movement periods have *always* alternated throughout history with periods of social quiescence, which are usually longer in duration. In the analysis of preindustrial social movements there is substantial agreement among historians and other social scientists as to the length of social-movement periods. With the development of bureaucratized dissidence (i.e., social movements characterized by formal-organizational cohesion) in the nineteenth century, the analytic problems became more formidable for social scientists principally because of the persistence of bureaucratic entities such as political parties and trade unions, which continued to call themselves "the movement" despite the absence of indices of true social movement activity such as rapid increases in membership and escalating turmoil in the form of strikes, riots, demonstrations, insurrections, and so forth. The movements of the 1960s were, moreover, fertile ground for still other analytical errors because of their characteristic *subcultural cohesion*. Some social scientists denied them the status of social movements altogether because of the relative absence of the familiar type of bureaucratized dissidence recalled from the past, e.g., the 1930s. Others on this same ground subjected these movements to simplistic analyses. Still others, identifying with these same movements, were led astray by the fact that the subcultures of the dissident groups persisted after the overt social conflict itself had become sublimated either into general change or into routinized "radical" intellectual activity or both.

These departures from social quiescence include innovations in conflict behavior, in the social categories appearing autonomously in the arena of conflict, and in the location of the terrain of conflict. We see the development of conflict within social movements as following three laws: (1) the Law of Mounting Stakes, (2) the Law of Emergent Contradiction, and (3) the Law of Shifting Terrain. The remainder of this chapter will analyze these laws in detail.

Innovation in Conflict Behavior, or the Law of Mounting Stakes

This level of development is most clearly visible in situations wherein a certain modicum of low-level routinized dissidence is tolerated or sanctioned by law. When the possibilities of open and secret negotiation, as well as whatever is meant in practice by the freedoms of speech, press, petition, and assembly have all been exhausted, then some act of forcible defiance elicits a mass response by way of support and imitation. Forcible defiance means, at minimum, placing one's body in some spot where by law or custom it does not belong, whether spontaneous (as in Rosa Parks's action of sitting on a whites-only seat in a crowded Montgomery, Alabama, bus in 1955 because she was "tired") or contrived (as in the first "sit-in," February 1, 1960, in Greensboro, North Carolina, when four Black college students, impeccably dressed in conservative suits and ties and reading Bibles, vainly awaited service at a whites-only lunch counter until beaten up and arrested). Both sides may then proceed to the use of mounting levels of force in response to each other's raising of the stakes, culminating in "political" strikes, riots, arson, looting, and ultimately insurrection on the one side and employment of the effective means of violence, such as the standing army, on the other. One variant proceeds along lines of rising levels of "nonviolent" force employed by the dissidents, e.g., from hunger strikes to self-immolation to efforts at disrupting the regime by such means as masses of people lying across the railroad tracks, in accordance with Mohandas K. Gandhi's doctrine of *satyagraha*. This, however, presupposes not only traditional religious self-discipline among the dissidents, but also either self-restraint on the part of the regime deriving from a tradition of "fair play" that limits the ferocity of its response or an equivalent restraint in the guise of adverse media coverage of repressive measures taken openly. The absence of such restraints on either side can lead to the immediate transition to violent forms of force.

The historian Flavius Josephus (1970) in recounting the historical background of the revolt of A.D. 66–73 against Roman rule, recounted a quite sophisticated use of nonviolent resistance against the Roman governor Pontius Pilate in A.D. 32: When the latter sought to comply with an order to install Roman eagles in Jerusalem (a sacrilege to the Jews), a crowd said to number 30,000 converged on the governor's residence at Caesarea and in unison presented their necks as if for decapitation, maintaining that death was preferable to tolerating the presence of the heathen eagles; Pilate had them removed. However, Pilate next confiscated the sacred Temple treasure to finance an aqueduct to improve the Jerusalem water supply. A peaceful protest took place outside the Roman garrison in Jerusalem, but Pilate secreted in the crowd a number of soldiers in disguise armed with leaden truncheons; on Pilate's signal they proceeded to break heads. One Jew, who appears in the Gospel of Mark under the name of Barabbas (literally, "son of his father," or "Joe Blow"), under sentence of death for "sedition," managed to kill a Roman soldier. Consequently, when the next preacher of nonviolence came to town and got into trouble with the regime, the Jews of all classes preferred Barabbas.

In much the same way, when neither the nonviolent disruptions inspired by the teachings of Dr. Martin Luther King, Jr., nor adverse media coverage had much impact on the ferocity of the repressive measures employed by the Birmingham, Alabama, Police Chief, Eugene "Bull" Connor, in May–June 1963, a riot broke out in the Black ghetto of the city, where much of the populace was not under the discipline of traditional Black Christianity. In this riot, which set a precedent for those of 1964–68 in the North, the police were driven off the streets by missiles thrown by the crowds at their vehicles. It was in fact this event that was decisive in prompting the Kennedy administration to force a settlement, for which Dr. King was given full credit.

In another variant, the regime is so repressive that the most modest act of dissidence, even if formally legal, is punished with immediate repression to the point of summary execution. The regime may err on the side of stringent repression to the point of summarily executing persons suspected of dissident ideas or those thought to be friends or acquaintances of suspected dissidents or, indeed, for no specific reasons at all. The late Iranian monarchy provides an example. In such a situation, dissidence, if it is to emerge at all, must begin at an advanced stage of the use of force, as the only basis of confidence for the dissidents is the certainty that there are too many of them to all be summarily executed. In a variant of this variant, the regime is apparently wholly successful in stifling any possible dissidence within civil society, but reproduces within the effective means of violence on which it relies the same contradictions that exist between itself and civil society. In such situations revolutionary forces may be unleashed when crowd action suddenly manifests itself and intensifies in tandem with the progressive disintegration of the armed forces (Russia, March 8–12, 1917). Alternatively, a spontaneous crowd action signals a military coup on the part of a section of the armed forces (e.g., Addis Ababa, Ethiopia, February 14, 1974, when a taxi driver, protesting a state-imposed increase in the price of gasoline, drew a spontaneously riotous crowd, which in turn prompted a military coup, which overthrew the monarchy). The emergent contradictions within civil society are then reflected in a succession of military coups and revolts (as in Ethiopia, 1974–77). Yet another possibility is that a section of the armed forces, detached for a prolonged period from the political and ideological ambience of civil society, constitutes itself as a dissident social category, and overthrows the regime (Lisbon, Portugal, April 1974); subsequently the emergent contradictions within civil society are strictly harnessed to the polarizations within the military itself (whence the Portuguese revolutionary slogan "Army and People!"), and the ultimate social and political settlement in civil society is a reflection of the outcome of a succession of coups and countercoups along political and ideological lines. In the Portuguese case, the ultimate coup led to the dictatorship of the conservative General Eanes from late 1975. This personage became the duly elected president of a bourgeois constitutional republic whose parliament was initially numerically dominated by a coalition of socialists and populists. In late 1978, General Eanes finally dispensed with Soares, his socialist prime minister, and replaced him with a man of his own political persuasion, Nobre de Costa, a conservative described as a "nonpolitical technocrat." The Portuguese revolution was somewhat exceptional in that the armed forces were throughout to the left of the fascist regime they overthrew and continued to move to the left through the initial series of coups. Perhaps more "normal" was the behavior of the French army in Algeria, which in 1958 replaced a conservative republic with a reactionary but pragmatic dictatorship and then in 1962 sought to replace that with a fascistic regime.

As part of the intensification of social conflict, participants in a social movement as a rule innovate new channels of lateral (that is, interdissident) communicaton as well as vertical (that is, between themselves and the leaders of the movement) communication whereby they supplement the usual channels of communication flowing downward from the regime or the exploiting class as a whole. This may involve the innovation of wholly original media (alternative or "underground" presses, *Samizdat*, wall posters, graffiti, etc.) and interpersonal contact (telephone trees, networks, cells, affinity groups, consciousness-raising groups, "soul sessions," ad hoc meetings, periodically assembling groups with the most rudimentary formal structure). In addition, dissidents may divert to social-movement uses communications techniques never before employed in this way: In Iran, for example, we have the instance of a country in which the whole of the press and broadcasting industries were a cartel monopoly of the royal family and the state. Iran was plentifully supplied with the household luxury consumer goods of the advanced countries. Consequently, ingenious use was made of the cassette recorder. In the first place, it was used to copy inspirational messages and calls to arms from the exiled symbolic leader of the revolution, Ayatollah Ruhollah Khomeini, who perhaps was the logical leader of the diverse opposition precisely because he was in exile, his social program was nebulous, and he was head of the faith that embraced nearly the whole of the population and that by tradition accorded at best conditional legitimacy to the secular ruler (since the latter was not of the house of the Caliph Ali, assassinated A.D. 661, and his son, Sharif Husain, assassinated A.D. 680). Khomeini's voice could be taken as the closest thing to a direct revelation from God (*ayatollah*—reflection of God), and as the movement gained in momentum, ever-greater numbers were moved to take his equation of the regime with Satan, a being of Persian invention, quite literally. During the actual street demonstrations, moreover, cassette recordings were made of gunshot noises and, following the dispersal of the demonstrations, these tapes were played back through high-wattage stereo systems to confuse and disorient the armed forces.

As conflict intensifies, dissident collectivities develop innovative modes of collective action. Additionally, new social categories are called into the conflict. This, we call the Law of Emergent Contradiction.

Innovation in the Players of the Game, or the Law of Emergent Contradiction

It is a well-known feature of social movements, most conspicuous in revolutions, that as the intensity of dissidence rises there occurs a simultaneous development of the autonomous identity of social categories, which, usually of lower social rank than the original champions of the movement and at first subsumed in the united opposition under their leadership, come to articulate their own demands and interests in contradiction to policies pursued by their social betters or in rejection of settlements these had previously regarded as final. One commonly finds that the emergent categories are structured in an exploitative class relation with the earlier dissident vanguard, or that they are otherwise subject to neglect, injury, contempt, or persecution at the hands of the "natural leaders" of the "people." What is more, their appearance as *historical subjects* is unprecedented and had not been entertained as a serious possibility during the preceding period of social quiescence. Indeed there is a pattern in social movements, repetitive to the point of monotony, whereby the initial dissidents assert the universal validity of collegiate relations (that is, "participatory" or "democratic" procedures) in wielding power, but understand tacitly that this applies to themselves alone or to relations between themselves and the embattled regime; simultaneously, they insist on the reproduction of exploitative relations at the level of material reproduction, despotic or patriarchal authority relations throughout civil society, and the continued exclusion of the lower orders from the blessings of collegial procedures that they have achieved within the polity as their pride and joy. The contradiction between abstractions and everyday practice readily conduces to suspicions among the multitude that their superiors are not merely prisoners of ideological self-deception, but are positively hypocritical, and that their manifest caution in prosecuting the common cause reflects not mere pragmatism, but treason and accommodation with the enemy (which often proves to be the case). Hence we find those successions of movements within movements and revolutions within revolutions that, as in Crane Brinton's *Anatomy of Revolution*, are often perceived by outsiders as transitions from the "moderates" to the "radicals" or "extremists."

As a case in point we may consider the English Revolution, whose initial leadership was described previously in the context of its placing itself at the head of society in opposition to an unpopular regime: Recall that the united opposition had initially envisaged little more than denying to the monarch the fiscal and political means for the erection of a continental-style autocratic despotism. Charles I oscillated wildly between inconclusive concessions and inept repression, leading the gentry opposition in Parliament to make political demands beyond its original intentions, including the claims of exclusive control over the armed forces (which could not be reconciled with the original ideological posture of defending the traditional English constitution). These events took place under the noses of the inhabitants of the City of London. As vividly described by Zagorin (1976), these swept aside the entrenched oligarchical government of the municipality, with its intimate financial ties to the crown, replacing it with a more broadly based local government, with effective control of the streets and the local militia vested in a provisional Committee of Public Safety. (Revolutions are notoriously traditional in their nomenclature, whence the reappearance of this appellation in the French Revolution to designate the Robespierrist regime of the Year II.) The aroused populace, under the leadership of the London bourgeoisie, was then able to throw its weight behind the gentry opposition in the crisis that brought about the execution of Strafford (political pillar of the regime and organizer of the remaining armed forces prepared to fight for Charles I against Parliament) and subsequently in the civil war itself. Zagorin emphasizes that the open appearance of the urban bourgeoisie as a political force was quite contrary to the custom of the period (except, of course, for those of its members who as individuals had acquired the landed property, style, and outlook of the gentry).

With the outbreak of the civil war, the command of the armed forces of Parliament was given to titled noblemen, and political leadership as a whole was vested in a landed faction sometimes known to history by reason of their religious views as the Presbyterians. (That is, they favored the Scottish system of church governance, whereby the church officials were selected by collegial procedures among the clergy and important laymen, but the clergy themselves were appointed; the right of appointing the parish clergy was in many places an attribute of landed property at this time.) This faction, which was quite comparable in its social conservatism to the enemy it was fighting on the battlefield, was charged with considerable justification of being loath to bring the war to a victorious conclusion. Consequently, there occurred the episode of the "purge," whereby the more vigorous commanders and organizers of the New Model Army, whose leader was Cromwell, expelled the earlier leaders from their army commands and from Parliament itself. Power was now vested in the Independents, a coalition of the more radical gentry and the urban bourgeoisie, whose religious policy was "Congregationalist." (That is, the validation of the claims of the clergy to inclusion among the saints by reason of the inspiration by divine grace was to be determined by collegial procedures within the congregations.) This power was henceforth exercised through the army command.

Social movements, in accordance with the Law of Emergent Contradiction, display the developing *vertical* spread of collegial relations in society, that is, downwards to more exploited and dominated social categories, and their *horizontal* spread, that is, to wider and more encompassing functional areas of social life (as opposed, say, to their confinement to episodic encounters with the formal procedures of the polity as on Election Day). But revolutions, or at least all historic revolutions to date, are defended by despotic relations, specifically those authority relations implanted in the hierarchical structure of the armed forces loyal to the revolutionary regime and implicit in the organization of support activities associated with a war effort of any complexity and sophistication. (For possible exceptions to this generalization one might have to go back, say, to fourteenth-century Switzerland.) There consequently comes a point in the development of a social movement that has eventuated in revolution where the means of violence at the disposal of the revolutionary regime, whether of its own creation or the preexisting but undismantled military apparatus, arrests the momentum of collegialization and reverses the process. In the English Revolution this moment had come by 1649: The Levellers, based socially on rich peasants—who as a status group were known as "yeomen" and urban artisans, were as numerous as ordinary soldiers in the ranks of the New Model Army (moreover having, while fighting the civil war, been systematically defrauded by their officers of their claims to purchase confiscated lands [cf. C. Hill, "The Agrarian Legislation . . . " 1958]). They had come to suspect (rightly) that Charles I was plotting further civil war and, by implication, the motives of Cromwell and the other senior officers in refraining from abolishing the monarchy. The "agitators" (this word, like purge, dates from this period) therefore called for the abolition of the monarchy and the extension of the parliamentary suffrage to male holders of small property (though not universal manhood suffrage). As many belonged to the multitudinous competing small Puritan sects beyond the fringe of "respectable" religious life, they made a case for religious toleration (for Protestants only, of course). Their mutiny at Putney was suppressed by General Ireton. This event still more completely doomed the movement of the Diggers, landless laborers who squatted on uncultivated land and simply dug in. Nor was Cromwell's militaristic regime conducive to the development of incipient feminism. (For feminism in this period, cf. Sheila Rowbotham, 1972.) Paradoxically, with the various propertied groups split along complicated ideological and political cleavages, the only possible center of power was Cromwell and the army command, who spent several years vainly seeking to create a durable source of legitimacy and a base of popular support for themselves. Meanwhile, the propertied groups found themselves under the yoke and the taxation imposed by the very thing for which in theory they had originally opposed: that is, a centralized, despotic, militaristic, and expensive state.

Less dramatic examples of emergent contradiction may be adduced from social movements in the United States in the 1930s and 1960s. In the former period the trade unionization of the working class was initially promoted by the state in Section 7a of the National Industrial Recovery Act (1933), which by establishing the National Recovery Administration to regiment the economy along the lines of the Italian Corporate State (and itself copied by Nazi financial wizard Hjalmar Schacht) sought to eradicate judicial definitions of unions as "monopolies in restraint of trade" to procure labor representation in industrial cartels. A spontaneous popular upsurge was manifest by 1934 in the form of receptivity to unionization and mass adhesion to unions that already existed; but the existing AFL leadership, traumatized by successive defeats and a dwindling base during the period 1920–23 was unable or unwilling to respond. It clung to the obsolete policy of unionization by craft and trade, which not only precluded the unionization of heavy industry but moreover corresponded to the stratification of the working class itself into status groups related to ethnicity. (That is, the elite or skilled workers had an overrepresentation of Irish and German Catholics, Scandinavians, and Jews; ordinary workers in manufacturing, especially heavy industry, had a similar disproportion of southern and eastern European immigrants; and Blacks were assigned to the hardest and lowest-paid work or to none at all.) In the second phase, 1936–39, the "industrial unions," which had broken away from the AFL to form the more visibly class-conscious CIO, successfully penetrated such previously impregnable industries as steel and automobiles. In 1936 the UAW imitated the French device of factory occupation ("sit-down strike") in Flint, Michigan, and in 1938 fought the equally symbolic "battle of the overpass" at the Ford works in Dearborn. A simultaneous Black movement was under way, but its course was more difficult to chart: Black political action and collective-conflict action since the 1840s at the latest has displayed the alternating and sometimes concurrent—but mutually contradictory on the ideological plane—thrusts of assimilationism (the demand for the color-blind society) and nationalism (of varying content but exhibiting the recurrent feature of a suspicion of the prospects for a satisfactory alliance with any groups of whites). The assimilationist tendency was represented by the efforts of trade union leaders is such as A. Philip Randolph (for decades leader of the Brotherhood of Sleeping Car Porters; subsequently the most conservative of Black leaders in the 1960s) and Bayard Rustin (discredited as an Administration stooge in 1964) and supported by the Communist Party which was fairly successful in recruiting Black intellectuals during this period. By 1942, after the overt entry of the United States into World War II, the autonomy of the Black working-class movement was such that Randolph was able to pressure President Roosevelt—by threatening a mass protest march on Washington—into signing an executive order that banned, however ineffectually, racial discrimination in war industry. The nationalist thrust was present also, as displayed in the Harlem riots of 1935 and 1943—

the prototypes for the "long hot summers" of the middle and late 1960s—and as perhaps articulated on the ideological plane by the late Honorable Elijah Muhammad, whose Nation of Islam (now Bilalian Nation) was founded in Detroit (1931) and Chicago in the period, spreading to other northern cities.

The Black movement of the 1960s was initially led by the southern Black elite of clergy, lawyers, teachers, and entrepreneurs who had the support of that section of the urban Black working class under the sway of the pulpit and were abetted by northern white money and propaganda as well as volunteers from among intellectuals and students both Black and white. The initial objectives were wholly assimilationist in appearance, with rival groups ranging on the conservative-to-radical spectrum according to the degree of nonviolent force to which they were prepared to resort. Students and young intellectuals supplied leadership to the rural Black working-class (soon to develop its own leaders) areas of the Deep South where the Black elite was feebly developed. The assimilationist or "civil rights" phase of the movement faded out in disorientation during 1964–66, in part because the initial assimilationist objectives had been enacted into legislation, which, however, had no impact on more fundamental structural inequalities; but primarily because the leading edge of the movement had visibly passed to the Black ghettos of the northern cities, where the most depressed strata of the working class in the United States were largely concentrated. Young Black intellectuals at this time adopted nationalist postures and symbolism; this included those still operating in the South, where they developed the Black Panther symbol (in Alabama) and the "Black power" slogan (in Mississippi) and renounced cooperation with former white allies. Northern Black elites, lacking the moral authority conferred by traditional religion and having lost the political initiative, were confined to playing games of "extremists and moderates" with the state on various levels. (This is a game common to many social movements undergoing the development of emergent contradiction: "If you don't deal with me, you'll have to deal with them!" Subsequently, the visible leadership comprised young intellectuals of wholly mythic significance. That is, their authority was symbolic and derived from acts, rhetoric, style, and slogans that procured Black admiration in part by frightening whites, but whose ability and direct collective dissidence was insignificant. One might even argue that the efficacy of the often spectacular dissidence that did occur derived precisely from its insusceptibility to manipulation and prediction from within and from the absence of an organizational structure that might have been held hostage.

The movement based on white candidate members of the bourgeoisie ("youth") in the 1960s was no less of a novelty in recent history than the Black movement, but like the latter its similarities to preceding movements, including its manifestations of the laws of social-movement development, often appeared in guises equally unprecedented, if not more so. For example: There is a tendency for social movements in bourgeois society to reproduce the division of the bourgeoisie itself into entrepreneurs and politico-military specialists by developing dual and contradictory thrusts of "economic" and "political" character. (In the stereotyped working class movements of the first half of the twentieth century, this took the form of debates over the priority to be given to strikes for wage increases by the trade unions relative to that accorded pressure on the state by the party. This debate resounded with charges of "naive economism" or "parliamentary cretinism.") Thus the specific form of the economic thrust of the youth movement—during the period of greatest intensity in 1967–70—was toward the maximum possible renunciation of bourgeois social relations ("dropping out") in favor of the promotion of communist (not socialist) social relations, including demands for collegial ("participatory" or "tribal") authority relations in organizational structures impinging on everyday life or else the removal of everyday life to remote rural regions, and the production, exchange, or simple appropriation (including "ripping off") of use values. The "political" thrust took the form of confrontation with the state over, e.g., the Vietnam War, racism, and educational policy. For purposes of protest solidarity this required the dissidents' presence in the vicinity of if not necessarily enrollment in a college or university (that was *not* necessitated by the economic thrust). These contradictory thrusts were reproduced at the level of leadership as acrimonious debates between "politicos" and "druggies," though such distinctions were far less acute among ordinary participants whose solidarity rested on a common subculture and who might by turns emphasize politics, then drugs, sex, or communal living, then politics again. The distinction was certainly not made by counterdissidents, who lumped both thrusts together under the vulgar "3 P's" slogan ("Peace Pot Pussy"). And most interesting, it was the "street people"—that amorphous aggregation, so despised by the politicos, of dropouts, "spare change" beggars, drug dealers, speed freaks, burnt-out cases, hangers-out and hangers-around, and teenage runaways increasingly recruited from the white working class—who perpetrated some of the most dramatic acts of collective violence of the youth movement, e.g., in Berkeley, June 28–30, 1968.

It was precisely the subculture, with its emphases on "rediscovery of the body," "consciousness," and the intense scrutiny and forceful experience of the minute details of everyday life ("bringing it all back home"), that facilitated the emergence of a separate feminist movement in 1967–68. The story that has been handed down recounts that women in SDS chapters at that time were restive over consignment to menial tasks, whereas the male "heavies" monopolized discussions of policy and "analysis." Consequently, they formed their own groups wherein the enemy was redefined from "the straights," "the system," "the ruling class," or "establishment" to "men" or "patriarchy."

Innovation in the Definition of the Problem, or the Law of Shifting Terrain

Routine politics is conducted in terms of "issues." That is, from the perspective of the exploiting class in its day-to-day practice of formulating policies and making decisions, there appear certain options of rather narrow scope wherein the ideological premises that limit that scope are never questioned and indeed even brought to the level of awareness; much less are the structural conditions underlying the ideological restrictions ever considered. This set of options, at least in bourgeois society, is "public opinion," which unless quantitative survey research is specifically indicated, usually connotes the opinions of those strata sufficiently educated and sophisticated that they can articulate the technicalities involved in the process of the acquisition of education and sophistication: Public opinion is divided into that which is "responsible" and that which is dismissed as "irresponsible," "muddle-headed," "wooly-minded," at best "bleeding-heart," and at worst "the wild-eyed crackpot lunatic fringe." With its options "clarified"—whether by public opinion or by secret deliberation—the regime then yields, and in fact believes itself to be yielding, to obvious necessity; survey research is resorted to in the determination of whether the obvious necessity is *popular*. Routine politics in periods of social quiescence most often resembles the radio commercial wherein the consumer debates with him or herself, "Should I take something strong but effective? Or something gentle but safe?" The underlying message is that he or she must at all costs take *something*, specifically an acceptable compromise in the form of the advertised product. Occasionally, it is true, politics *does* resemble the TV deodorant commercial featuring rival crowds, one noisily championing "The stick! The stick!" while the other shouts for "The spray! The spray!" until one courageous independent-thinking leadership type pronounces for "the roll-on"; the crackpots who believe that daily baths with soap suffice are unrepresented. Advertisers are deliberate brainwashers; however, the stuff of politics is the appearances of society that accomplish their own brainwashing in the course of the routine living of everyday life.

Consider this contemporary issue: The regime has pronounced that of two wicked alternatives—either more inflation or more employment coupled with cutbacks in "social programs"—it has chosen the latter. A "conservative" opposition announces that the regime does not go far enough (although it is more conservative on this issue than the conservatives when they were last in office) and a "liberal" opposition says that it has gone too far. Yet the differences in policy represented by the rhetorical differences of all three positions can only be marginal, since both the "rate of inflation" and the "rate of unemployment" are structurally determined and reflect a contradiction between capitalist relations of production and the necessity to maintain social discipline (see Chapter 9, "Conclusion," for details). The prices of products rise because the productivity of labor does not. Consequently, to support the growing numbers of office workers and other consumption formations who must be hired to use up the products society produces, society must charge itself extra; the state appears as the consumer of last resort, since it may go into debt indefinitely. Productivity does not increase because capitalists do not invest in new productive technique. They cannot do so because they must thereby drastically reduce the size of the working class. Although they could easily hire the laid-off workers to push pencils in offices and still make money through increased exports reflecting the declining real cost of production, they will not do so because this would contradict the authority relations intrinsic to the capitalist labor process, by virtue of which the whole of the strata superior in social status to the working class understand themselves as privileged. But unemployment neither may fall too low, lest the whole of the "employed" category lose their sense of privilege with respect to that category called "unemployed," nor rise too high, lest it no longer appear plausible to most of society that a normal human being, that is, a person genuinely in search of employment, will surely find it with a little persistence. The dictates of a capitalist economy contradict those of bourgeois society as a specific form of society. The practice of the bourgeoisie is here conditioned by its experience of the decay of social discipline in the 1960s, most painfully among candidate members of the bourgeoisie themselves.

During the course of social-movement development such issues, hitherto apparently isolated, discrete, and unrelated, are generalized. That is, connections and patterns are found among them and are understood increasingly as manifestations of conflict between major social categories, the boundaries and character of which will also appear to shift in accordance with the development of conflict and consciousness. An example of the generalization of issues in the 1960s might be found in the reconceptualization of the 1960 election issues of economic growth, unemployment, and civil rights into, first, structural unemployment, poverty, and cultural deprivation, and ultimately into the issue of racism defined in social-structural rather than attitudinal terms. Another example was the generalization of numerous foreign-policy questions—including the Vietnam War, the Dominican intervention, Cuba, colonial wars in Africa, the China policy, the Middle East, etc.—into those of "the military-industrial complex," the United States as "world policeman," or "imperialism" vis-à-vis the "Third World." New "issues" appear, that is, whole new areas of social life are redefined as problematic and grounds for conflict. Examples of such new issues in the 1960s were environmental pollution, legalization of abortion and marijuana, rights of Selective Service registrants in evading induction, rights of conscripts within the military, hair and dress codes in schools, the work place, and the military, rights of defendants in the structurally racist criminal-justice system, the definitions of "pornography" and "obscenity," teenagers' rights of access to contraceptives and contraceptive information, the right of academics in the employ of the state to favor in the classroom the victory of the enemy in time of war, the right of state employees to steal state secrets in a time of war for dissemination to the public in order to undermine the war effort and the right of the press to publish the same, the rights of welfare recipients, the legitimacy of discrimination in employment on political and ideological grounds, the lengths to which the state is obliged to go to suppress or even reverse discrimination on ethnic or gender grounds that it had previously condoned, and so forth. Finally, new and previously unconsidered options are introduced into the debate on certain issues: Thus, in the opposition to the Vietnam War, grounds for opposition shifted from the pragmatic ("a mistake") to the moral ("inhuman killing") to the radical (assertion of the right of revolution against the United States) to the revolutionary ("Bring the war home!"). "Pragmatic" perspectives yielded support for policy options such as a negotiated peace short of victory or the end of the bombing of North Vietnam on the grounds that it was ineffectual. Moral opposition promoted options implying the recognition of the defeat of the United States, such as calling for the withdrawal of the U.S. troops from Vietnam to preclude their further perpetration of genocidal acts or dying in the commission of genocidal acts implicit in the pursuit of military victory; or else calling for the cessation of the most genocidal acts—such as the bombardment of North and South Vietnam, Laos, and Cambodia—which logically implied a negotiated surrender. Radical opposition called successively for (1) victory for the NLF/PRG in the belief that it was an independent force desiring and capable of sustaining a separate socialist-neutralist regime in South Vietnam; and (2) victory for the DRV regime in Hanoi. Revolutionary opposition, of course, called for imitation of the actions of the enemy on the battlefield "in the belly of the beast" to destroy the systematic promotion of "imperialism" at its source (e.g., the position of the Weathermen, subsequently the Weather Underground). The entire landscape of political categories thus, during social movements, is transformed until it becomes entirely or at least partially incomprehensible in terms of the political language and categories prevailing in the immediate premovement period. But this shifting terrain is itself closely tied to the development of consciousness, which subsumes the reinterpretation of social reality and the human being.

Summary

We began this chapter by noting that inherent in the human being is both the need for structure and antistructure; that in so-called primitive societies this latter human need is satisfied through the ritual suspension of structure. In class-based societies the suspension of social structure takes the form of social movements that alternate between usually longer periods of social quiescence.

Our focal point has been the primary evidence that a social movement has occurred: the intensification of conflict, which delimits the boundaries of a social-movement period. We maintain that the intensification of conflict occurs according to three basic laws:

1. The Law of Mounting Stakes. Once the routinized modes of dissidence have been exhausted, social-movement participants will engage in innovative modes of conflict that elicit mass support and imitation by other potentially dissident collectivities. It forces the regime to resort to increasing levels of force, and ultimately to violence, to maintain control, which in turn demands new tactics.

2. The Law of Emergent Contradiction. Social movements often begin with conflict between categories of elites. As the intensity of conflict increases, the autonomous identity of the social categories emerge, the usual case of which members of ranks lower than the original leaders articulate demands of their own. Either through conflict or within daily life the abstract ideological interpretation of what is right and correct are undermined by actual practice. This is reflected in the normal course of revolutions as they move from the moderate to the radical stage.

3. The Law of Shifting Terrain. Social movements begin with the routine issues that evolve around with the appearance of social relations. As conflict intensifies, issues heretofore seen as isolated, discrete, and unrelated are generalized into a comprehensive analysis of the relations between major social categories. This phenomenon will be considered in greater detail in the next chapter, in which we will analyze the process of the reinterpretation of social reality.

Chapter 5

The Reinterpretation of Social Reality

In all social movements we find an ongoing process of the reinterpretation of social reality, comprising the interference with the reproduction of the "hegemonic ideology" (see Chapter 3, "The Reproduction of Social Privilege,") and its increasing replacement among dissidents by new formulations as social conflict intensifies. At the outset of a social-movement period, society is pervaded by a conventional interpretation of reality imposed on all classes (which are themselves mediated by the appearances of other systems of social categorization at best only vaguely corresponding to classes) by routine practice within the confines of relations of exploitation and prevailing authority relations. The formulations of the hegemonic ideology are conducive to the reproduction of the exploiting class, the regime, and the apparatuses of exploitation and domination, and fortified by the possibility of the preceding resorting to force in defense of what is seemingly inevitable, right, and proper.

The hegemonic ideology (or conventional interpretation of social reality) may in part be formulated into abstract theories or idealizations of the practice of the exploiting class or the regime (e.g., Social Darwinism for nineteenth-century capitalists or Official Nationality for the regime of Nicholas I in Russia), but, more important, it is found at the level of commonsensical assumptions and folk wisdom about how society works, how and why it was put there, what the functions of the appearances of society in the various groupings and social types are supposed to be, the legitimate, that is, the idealized bounds of exploitation and domination, the nature and source of reward for virtue and chastisement of wickedness throughout society, and the appropriateness of the prevailing appearances of the exploiting class as status groups (e.g., warriors, leisured landowners, clergy, managers, and experts) for the proper running of things. The hegemonic ideology (or the conventional interpretation of social reality) need not possess the coherence and order of formal logic, so long as the exploited and dominated are content to "make sense" of society and of themselves in the language and from the perspective of the exploiters and dominators.

When collective dissidence arises, the participants come to reject ever-larger portions of the hegemonic ideology. Social relations previously accepted as reasonable, inflexible, inexorable, and primordial now appear as contrived, unnatural, substantively irrational, parasitic, and senseless. Their own subsumption within relations of exploitation and domination, formerly accepted as part of the natural order of things, is repudiated as unjust, arbitrarily imposed and void of moral sanction. The panoply—that is, the trappings, pageantry, and other badges of status, self-serving rationalizations, snobbery, and the various apparatuses of the exploiting class and the regime—is denounced as illegitimate, and even the idea of the necessity for social hierarchy yields to progressively more egalitarian notions. As conflict intensifies and their numbers swell, dissidents discern that the very nomenclature and linguistic structure of common speech embody assumptions about their innate inferiority, inevitable subordination, and social invisibility. Thus, for example, the French Jacobins transformed the nomenclature of dates and places; the Russian Bolsheviks abolished the obsequious form of address, the "-s" suffix; and U.S. feminists promoted the replacement of the element "-man" in titles and job designations by that of "-person" and rendered problematical the generic "he" without any definitively correct usage having yet replaced it.

The dissidents simultaneously reinterpret social reality such that their own insurgency "makes sense" to them. This may involve, at first, a mere modification of the hegemonic ideology; but as social conflict intensifies and their numbers and self-confidence (individual and collective) grow, the reinterpretation of social reality tends to become more sweeping. Thus the positions taken by the New Left in 1962 appear in retrospect as a humanistic gloss on the New Frontier liberalism of the time, whereas, the condemnation of bourgeois social relations in 1969 by youth-culture "freaks" (including the overlapping categories of drug dropouts and New Left politicos) were infinitely more far-reaching.

In the most intense phase of a social movement the reinterpretation of social reality may have proceeded to the point at which, to the movement participants, the wider society appears to make no sense at all or, at best, a wholly negative sort of sense—as a vast and malign conspiracy. For example, the "underground" newspapers published by "freaks" during 1967–70 portray all conventional social relations with a mixture of surrealism and disgust.

Nonsocial Movement Reinterpretations

This social-movement reinterpretation must be distinguished, first, from ideological changes imposed by new regimes that nevertheless leave the exploitative relation and indeed the contours of the social structure as a whole unscathed. Under this heading we may certainly place the substitution of Christianity for paganism by Constantine the Great in the fourth century and possibly also the substitution by Arab conquerors of Islam for variants of Eastern Christianity (Orthodox, Monophysite, Nestorian, Monothelete), Zoroastrianism, and Buddhism in the seventh and eighth centuries. In recent times parts of bourgeois society have been dressed up in assorted officially imposed doctrinal guises, both in the core (National Socialism, fascism) and, more often, in the periphery as for example, African Socialism (Kenya), Arab Socialism (UAR/Egypt), Peronismo (Argentina), Personalism (Diem's regime in South Vietnam),

National Populism or "Sun Yat-senism" (China under Chiang Kai-shek), the "socialism" of Lee Kuan Yew in Singapore, and of course the late and unlamented "White Revolution" of the Iranian monarchy.

Second, it is necessary, as noted in Chapter 1, "The Guises of Social Movements," to distinguish this process from recurrent cultural, artistic, religious, and intellectual movements, even where these, as in the French Enlightenment, may be demonstrated to have furnished ideological ammunition for subsequent collective dissidence. Such movements are part of the normal process of cultural reproduction in all forms of class society and even perhaps in preclass society. Their association with social movements proper is not determinate, that is, they may be confined exclusively to the level of cultural reproduction or even to the froth and foam of the intellectual stratosphere that is today the quarry mined by graduate students and professors. As stated in Chapter 3, "The Reproduction of Social Privilege," it was in a sense the duty of prebourgeois ideological specialists, and still more of the "intellectuals" at the summit of the former cultural counterbourgeoisie, to stand somewhat apart from the hegemonic ideology in its most conventional guise.[1] Thus Socrates was condemned to death by the Athenian landowning class collectively for teaching doctrines that overtly cast doubt on the existence of the gods. Probably few if any of the 500 jurors were sincerely pious, but it was nevertheless reproduced within their hegemonic ideology that faith in the gods (especially by their social inferiors and slaves) was inseparable from the stability of society and the security of the state; the naivete and obsolescence of this proposition obliged Socrates to courageously repudiate it openly. Similarly but even more, the "intellectuals" of bourgeois society were routinely expected to criticize the abuses of the bourgeoisie (especially of its politico-military sector). As noted above, provision for this was made in the bourgeois hegemonic ideology as manifesting the "freedom" of society. Of course, some of the "intellectuals" did, and still do, idealize and extol the bourgeoisie and bourgeois society to an even greater extent than prevails in the hegemonic ideology itself, e.g., "neoconservatism," but then, that is implicit in "intellectual life." Nevertheless, movements on the purely cultural level, whatever their content, *eo ipso* affect the structural foundations of society only in the reproduction of alienation and false consciousness. That is, there is always an implicit claim advanced for the innate superiority of spiritual guides, "thinkers," and "creators" over workaday people and for at least a modicum of social privilege wherein this alleged superiority is objectified. By implication, this argues for the entire system of social relations in which the elite realms of cultural reproduction are embedded and by which they are supported, since these are understood as the adornment of the social order, the "higher things in life," even though the content of particular "creations" may disgust "decent people," thereby reinforcing the faith in the "ultimate significance" of these things by their proponents.

Social Movement Reinterpretations

In our characterization of the reinterpretation of social reality, we intend to emphasize the mental life of ordinary participants in social movements. This can *never* be identified with the ideological statements made by intellectuals, whether as oratory and recorded by scribes or tape recorders on the spot, or as written or otherwise recorded documents; it cannot be easily identified with the recollections in the form of oral history subsequently taken from participants who have lovingly recounted their experiences and actions in great detail. The introduction of new conceptualizations of social reality into the mental life of the dissidents may, for example, arise from ordinary participants who thereby become intellectuals. But these new conceptualizations may themselves reflect the structured conservatism of the thought forms underlying the everyday use of language, and may consequently understate the degree to which the mental life of the dissidents has already been transformed by new *expectations* and *understandings* that dissidents cannot yet verbalize but of which they are conscious as subtle emotional states. In such situations "objective" and "scientific" outside observers—including professional revolutionaries and counterrevolutionary intelligence agencies, as well as experts in the social sciences—can make and have made serious errors in evaluating the vehemence and determination with which dissidents will act on the basis of "hard empirical evidence" elicited verbally. Consider the following examples:

1. L. D. Trotsky, in his *History of the Russian Revolution*, demonstrated—on the basis of documentary evidence such as leaflets, as well as oral accounts taken from participants in the street action—that the Petrograd Bolshevik organization systematically sought to *restrain* the insurrection of March 8–12, 1917 (the "February Revolution," which overthrew the monarchy) for fear of official repression, refusing for instance to distribute weapons after the point at which victory was probable. All that Trotsky could say on behalf of the Bolsheviks on the spot was that the organizations of the other opposition parties gave an even worse account of themselves. Far from seeking to cast aspersions on the "revolutionary vanguard" theory, Trotsky was merely villifying his subsequent political enemies such as the "mere college boy" Molotov; but he was nevertheless obliged to resort to a strained and tortuous explanation *ex hypothesi*, not supported by historical evidence well known to himself, whereby the Bolsheviks could be given credit for the February Revolution on the basis of the preceding period in which they were supposedly leading and indoctrinating the masses (of which there is no evidence given), despite the failure of the local committee in its mission of scientifically determining the balance of forces at the critical moment.

2. The great proving ground of applied social science in the contemporary period is the U.S. intelligence apparatus, especially the CIA, which has at its disposal far greater and more sophisticated means to forestall social upheaval than those available to professional revolutionaries to foment it. The apparent failure of the CIA even in its intelligence-gathering function, whereby it has time after time failed to give advance warning of the intensity of dissidence in various countries (notoriously, for example, in Cuba, 1957–61), has consequently been blamed on the error, incompetence, and careerism of operatives on the spot or upon the mismanagement of the CIA Director. This recurrent pattern was repeated once again in connection with the Iranian Revolution.[2] Thus: "In August, months after the first riots had broken out, the CIA in a top-secret intelligence assessment advised the White House that 'Iran is not in a revolutionary or even a pre-revolutionary situation' " (*Newsweek*, January 29, 1979).

Although Marxist-Leninists are presumably biased in favor of what it is the mission of the CIA to oppose, we have an interesting specimen from that quarter of a failure of equal magnitude in predicting the Iranian Revolution: Fred

Halliday's *Iran: Dictatorship and Development*. Halliday was in Iran as late as September 1978 and, though calling the situation a "crisis" for the regime, located it in the historical perspective of five prior crises since World War II that the shah had withstood without a scratch if not with enhanced power. In any case, he was grossly mistaken as to the outcome, possibly due to the Marxist-Leninist proclivity to rationally calculate the "correlation of forces": On the one hand he was impressed by the bulk and ferocity of the repressive apparatus, that is, SAVAK and the military, it having not yet been revealed that the latter would not fire on anything capable of firing back. On the other, the Marxist-Leninist bookkeeping showed a glaring deficit of anything that could be taken for a serious vanguard party of the working class. And, of course, atheists tend to expect little of revolutionary consequence from the clergy.

Halliday belittled the Ayatollah Khomeini, whose "intransigent demands" he saw as playing into the hands of the shah. Similarly, he belittled the Mujaheddin and Khalq-e-Fedayin guerrillas, subsequently major political forces, for their "restricted cultural level." The author's "realistic" speculations as to the final crisis of the regime indicated its advent as no sooner than the early 1980s, with its most likely scenarios being military coups either outright or in the name of Crown Prince Reza.

3. In late 1966, the eminent sociologist Seymour Martin Lipset announced to an audience of 2,000 at Syracuse University that, according to the most recent and authoritative surveys of U.S. students' political attitudes, there was no evidence of any significant change in the results of such surveys between the late 1950s and mid-1966. Does our knowledge of subsequent history invalidate this conclusion? Yes and no: Attitude surveys presuppose the persistence of ideological conceptualizations and underlying thought forms characteristic of a period of social quiescence. They are, moreover, conducted by persons who adopt the "objective" mind-set, wherein the assumptions reproduced within the hegemonic ideology as to the limits of the possible are embedded. The respondent must assume the mind-set in order to communicate; that is, the respondent must adopt "realistic" notions of the limits of the possible. If the respondent's understandings of the limits of the possible are undergoing change, but such understandings are perceptible only as subtle feeling states whose implications are not understood by the respondent, who is, in addition, unsure as to whether these are at all widespread in their distribution, the respondent is left with no alternative to replying in "realistic" terms. If the survey is, furthermore, taken in a period of "sociocharacterological revolution" (which was exemplified by the 1960s in the United States, with certain striking parallels to early-seventeenth-century England), the breakdown in assumptions as to the limits of the possible may not be confined to the rather restricted terrain of policy issues on which "liberal" or "conservative" responses may be rendered.

Consider the folk-ideological usage of the term "bullshit" in the youth movement of the 1960s. There was, first, the traditional meaning of "lies" or "duplicity." Second, "bullshit" could denote statements that, taken individually, may be demonstrably true, but that lack substantive importance even if true, while in the aggregate amounting to ideological deception. Hence, "Everything you learn in school is just bullshit brainwashing." Third, "bullshit" denoted something understood as substantively irrational whose substantive irrationality the speaker lacks the conceptual apparatus and thought forms to articulate. Hence, "a bullshit nine-to-five job." Fourth, "bullshit" denoted contradictions between intellectual articulations of "radicalism" and the condition of being behaviorally enmeshed in bourgeois social relations. Therefore, for example, a professor who was an avowed Marxist revolutionary, yet who upheld academic discipline and standards while condemning drugs and untidiness, was accused of "Old Left bullshit." Similarly, in 1968, the "action faction" in an SDS chapter (as at Columbia or the University of Michigan) would accuse the entrenched leaders, who argued for the importance of "analysis," of "rhetorical bullshit." In short, "radicalization" implied an *emotional* rejection of the conventional interpretation of social reality as "bullshit"—with this rejection manifested through behavior or "action," i.e., "putting your body on the line"— rather than in subscribing to a fully conceptualized reinterpretation whose forthcoming was, in any case, not all that crucial. The "movement" subculture in fact relied heavily on the intensification of feeling states from whose perspective bourgeois social relations could be critiqued as "bullshit"; for this reason we have used the term "subjectivist ideology" in connection with it. The prevalence of subjectivist ideologies in the social movements of the 1960s was in part dictated by the diffuseness of specific ideational content in the bourgeois hegemonic ideology deriving in turn from the conditions of cultural reproduction in contemporary bourgeois society.

The reconstruction of the reinterpretation of social reality from oral histories taken from participants after the fact is also fraught with possible sources of error, such as: (1) the owl-of-Minerva syndrome, (2) illusions of nonparticipants and counterdissidents, and (3) postmovement adaptation illusions.

1. The owl-of-Minerva syndrome. This is named after Hegel's maxim "The owl of Minerva takes wing after the shades of dusk have already fallen," in other words, the development of consciousness receives its definitive theoretical formulation only after its possibilities for further development have already been exhausted. Thus, where the reinterpretation of social reality is formulated as abstract theories or doctrines bearing something of an "official" stamp, that is, endorsed by recognized leaders and intellectuals of the movement, former dissidents may be tempted to read this back into their own recollections of what they did, felt, and thought during the actual events. Hence, they may claim for themselves a precocious apprehension of and subscription to the "official" version of the reinterpretation of social reality as stated in the form that has been handed down to history. Otherwise, or additionally, they may simplistically reconstruct the process of the reinterpretation of social reality so as to delineate with spurious clarity the stages of individual or collective experience and development that culminated in the official version while bypassing or downplaying the complex currents and cross-currents of mental life that were actually present though in retrospect are inadmissible.

The Puritans of the English Revolution have come down to history as a stolid, abstemious, and self-disciplined lot, fighting for godly virtue against sin in church and state. According to Hill, this stereotype ignores the orgiastic side of the movement associated with the Ranters:

"Religion is now become the common discourse and table-talk in every tavern and ale-house," men were complaining as early as 1641. "Ale-

houses generally are . . . the meeting places of malignats and sectaries,"
a preacher told the House of Commons in 1646. . . . "Eat of Christ,
therefore, the tree of life, at supper, and drink his blood, and make you
merry, John Eacherd, a Suffolk parson who spoke up for the common
soldiers in 1645 . . . Thomas Edwards reported an "antinomian preacher
in London, who stated that 'on a fast day it was better for Christians to
be drinking in an ale-house, or to be in a whore-house, than to be keeping
fasts legally.' . . .

The analogy of modern drug-taking should enable us to understand
that—in addition to the element of communal love-feast in such gath-
erings—the use of tobacco and alcohol was intended to heighten spiritual
vision. Some years later the millenarian John Mason was excessively
addicted to smoking, and "generally while he smoked he was in a kind
of ecstasy." (Tobacco was still a novel and rather naughty stimulant,
though by 1640 it had risen to first place among London's imports.) In
New England, Captain Underhill told Governor Winthrop "the Spirit had
sent into him the witness of free grace, while he was in the moderate
enjoyment of the creature called tobacco." Was it in a tavern, or at a
religious meeting, that Captain Freeman declared that he saw God in the
tableboard and the candlestick? . . .

At one Ranter meeting of which we have a (hostile) report, the mixed
company met at a tavern, sang blasphemous songs to the well-known
tunes of metrical psalms and partook of a communal feast. One of them
tore off a piece of beef, saying "This is the flesh of Christ, take and eat."
Another threw a cup of ale into the chimney corner, saying "There is the
blood of Christ." Clarkson called a tavern the house of God; sack was
divinity. Even a Puritan enemy expresses what is almost a grudging
admiration for the high spirits of the Ranters' dionysiac orgies: "they are
the merriest of all devils for extempore lascivious songs . . . for healths,
music, downright bawdry and dancing." One of the accusations against
Captain Francis Freeman was that he sang bawdy songs. . . .

"Unity with the creation," tobacco "a good creature," parodying holy
communion: we should never fail to look for symbolism in what appear
the extravagant gestures of seventeenth-century radicals. Ranter advocacy
of blasphemy, it has been well said, was a symbolic expression of freedom
from moral restraints. Abiezer Coppe was alleged on one occasion to have
sworn for an hour on end in the pulpit: "a pox of God take all your
prayers." An obsessive desire to swear had possessed him early in life,
but he resisted it for twenty-seven years. Then he made up for lost time.
He would rather, he declared, "hear a mighty angel (in man) swearing
a full-mouthed oath" than hear an orthodox minister preach. "One hint
more: there's swearing ignorantly, i'th dark, and there's swearing i'th
light, gloriously." Even Joseph Salmon, from the mystical and quietist
wing of the Ranters, was also in the habit of using "many desperate
oaths." [Hill, 1973:198-202]

For recent parallels in restrospective oversimplification one need only reflect
on the aftermath of the 1960s youth movement: Those who, in the 1970s,
continued to regard themselves as "radicals" detected as the central thread of
the movement's reinterpretation of social reality the development of the awareness of the implications of anti-imperialist and antiracist struggle among "serious" people, that is, those not wholly taken in by the drug-crazed spirit of
the times, whereby many of them were drawn to variants of Marxism. For those

who, alternatively, identified with the New Age subculture, which comprises Eastern spiritual disciplines, new psychotherapies, "holistic" medicine, natural foods, environmental concerns, and "alternative" uses of technology (e.g., in the fields of architecture, energy, and computer software), there is a tendency to identify the 1960s as the beginnings of a *cultural* movement of consciousness exploration and development of alternative social relations, whereby the social-conflict dimension of the youth movement is deemphasized or disowned (cf. Satin, 1978). This division represents the prolongation of the reproduction within the movement itself of the bourgeois categories of the "political" and the "economic," as noted in Chapter 1, "The Guises of Social Movements." The same process is evident in feminist recollections of the youth movement, especially in its sexual aspects, as a sexist plot promoted by males to devalorize women in the sexual marketplace by increasing the supply relative to the demand, thereby precipitating the feminist revolt.

Another example of the owl-of-Minerva syndrome may be suggested but not proven (since any documentary evidence that might tend to support it has either been destroyed or is kept top secret by the USSR regime): It is an article of faith in all variants of Marxism-Leninism that the Bolshevik party had forged an organic bond between itself and the Russian working class by, at the very latest, the period between the February and October revolutions in 1917. The empirical evidence for this assertion is usually provided in the form of a citation of a tenfold increase in party membership during that period (that is, from 25,000 to a quarter million), but a breakdown by occupation is not provided—though this could easily be done from the CPSU archives—so there is no telling how many of these were workers and how many were intelligentsiya, that is, nonmanual employees and professionals. What is certain is that they did enjoy limited popular support prior to the July Days (a popular insurrection in Petrograd aimed at the overthrow of the provisional government and the Menshevik-SR leadership of the soviets) because of their posture of resolute opposition to the regime's policy of fidelity to the Allies. This they apparently lost when, because of their ambivalence over whether or not to lead the manifestly futile revolt, they compromised themselves with both sides. It is equally certain that there was no mass street action during the October Revolution (November 7)—the work of the numerically insignificant party militia—such as that of February (March 8–13). There is no convincing evidence that the working class was under the guidance of *any* political party between "July" and "October": The substitution of Bolsheviks for Mensheviks in elections to the soviets in this period may be plausibly attributed to the well-known preference for the "lesser evil." Trotsky, in his *History* (1957), indicates that during the period of waffling prior to the October Revolution the workers were paying increasing attention to "anarchists," but these are not described as a party. The working class was in any case acting on its own account in class-conscious but "anarchically" antiauthoritarian actions such as food riots and the takeovers of factories from employers. Evidence for *real* mass popularity in the working class for the Bolsheviks comes only with Lenin's legalization of the factory takeovers *after* the October Revolution and during the ensuing civil war (1918–21). With the end of the civil war came popular chafing at the rigors of the Bolshevik revolutionary dictatorship: This was expressed in antiauthoritarian terms (e.g., "Soviets without Communists!")—generically stigmatized as anarchist—during the Kronstadt Rising of 1921 and the wave of strikes during 1921–22; but such traces died out with the return of social quiescence and the onset of the New Economic Program (NEP) period. After this time foreign observers sympathetic to the revolution ceased to report any disagreement with the version of the history of the revolutionary period promoted by the victorious regime on the part of ordinary members of the working class. (In 1918, Emma Goldman had been shocked by the Cheka's extermination of nests of anarchists in Petrograd on grounds of debauchery and armed hooliganism; but there is no telling whether such people were in any way representative of ordinary members of the working class.)

2. *Illusions of the nonparticipants and counterdissidents.* Nobody in society is *entirely* unaffected by a social movement, which everywhere promotes both a subtle psychic disorientation and a corrosion of social control. The degree to which a social movement thus affects the thought and actions of nonparticipants, especially those outside the visibly dissident social categories, is almost by definition beyond their awareness at the time, and may be at best partially reconstructible later only with the assistance of diaries, documentary records, and statistical evidence.

One obvious and historically recurrent form of this is the disorientation of the *regime*. The latter, albeit the real threat to itself and the social order as a whole may be minimal, may overreact and panic itself into persecution. In this it may either orchestrate or be swept along by the hysteria of counterdissidents, whose fears are equally exaggerated or misdirected. At the other extreme, and typical of the onset of major social upheavals, the regime underreacts; indeed it appears that the whole of ruling circles have gone into a species of hibernation born of either fatalism or fatuity or both. Thus, for example, Charles I of England was described in 1637 as "the happiest king in Christendom" (Wedgewood, 1955). Similar dream worlds at the top are associated with the French, Russian, and Iranian revolutions.

Another aspect takes the form of acts of omission or commission, usually of the petty sort, involving breaches of social discipline but not consciously articulated by the perpetrators as motivated by broader social conflict. Such acts may be widespread within social categories apparently characterized by nondissidence or counterdissidence as well as within the dissident categories. For the former, however, these acts do not lend themselves easily to ideological interpretation, for example, Jerry Rubin's statements in 1968 that "drugs *are* political" and "long hair is the most emotional political issue in America today"; or the Livingston College student's excuse for tardiness in handing in his term paper in May 1970: "I was too busy fighting the revolution." These actions will rather be explained in terms of situational, intrapsychic, interpersonal, or perhaps even meteorological ("a lousy day" or "too nice a day") factors.

Working-class and lower-surplus-absorbing strata ("lower middle-class") whites, for instance, were associated in popular stereotypes in the United States in the 1960s with nondissidence (e.g., support by the trade unions, both leaders and members alike for the Vietnam War) or counterdissidence (e.g., "hardhats" roughing up antiwar demonstrators or making lewd or provocative gestures at suspected feminists; the "white ethnic" racism of Imperiale in Newark and Rizzo in Philadelphia). Obviously, it was these whites who constituted the backbone of the forces of repression—the local police and the National Guard—

deployed by the authorities on the front lines of social conflict. Nevertheless, in industry the 1960s were notoriously a period of worker absenteeism, especially where the union provided a modicum of protection against summary dismissals. Hence it became a commonplace at this time that one should preferably buy a car assembled on a Wednesday and under no circumstances purchase one put together on a Monday or a Friday.

Absenteeism was the fundamental form of white working-class indiscipline in the U.S. armed forces as well: According to Lawrence Baskir and William Straus, senior officials of the Ford administration's Clemency Board, for the 7,575,000 "Vietnam-era active force troops" there were recorded 550,000 "desertion incidents," that is, cases of "administrative desertion" defined as AWOL of thirty days or more (1978:115). (These figures may represent an underestimate, since some cases were probably covered up and never recorded.) The authors' social profile of army perpetrators leaves no doubt of the overwhelmingly white working-class character of this offense (though Blacks and Hispanics were twice as likely to commit it):

> If there is such a thing as a "prototype" Army deserter of the Vietnam era, he lived in a small town and grew up in the South. He came from a low-income family, often with only one parent in the home. He had an IQ of 90, and dropped out of high school in the tenth grade. He enlisted to get away from problems back home, to learn a skill, or just to find something to do. He finished advanced training and had almost two years of "good time," which often included a full tour in Vietnam. However, he rarely progressed beyond the lowest ranks. He was arrested at least once by civilian police, and he frequently committed other minor infractions against military discipline. After going AWOL once or twice, he went home to stay, usually because of family problems. Two years later, he was arrested and given an undesirable discharge in lieu of court-martial. He entered the service at age eighteen, committed his first serious offense at nineteen, and was discharged at twenty-one. [1978:120]

"Family problems": The bulk of the incidence of administrative desertion was consciously motivated neither by ideological opposition to the Vietnam War nor by fear of the battlefield:

> Every official analysis of Vietnam-era deserters has found the same thing—that the overwhelming majority were neither conscientious nor cowardly. They were men who decided simply to put their own interests over the day-to-day needs of the military.
>
> Personal and family problems accounted for almost half of all absence offenses. For most enlisted men, military life was their first experience away from home. When their grandmothers died, their mothers fell ill, or their girl friends dropped them, they often wanted to go home as quickly as they could. Frequently, the problem was financial. The military pay scales were so low—starting at $115 per month—that married soldiers sometimes had to go home just to keep their families off welfare. [1978:116]

Yet the same "personal" or "family" motives were presumably also operative in previous wars waged by the United States in periods of social quiescence but not characterized by comparable rates of long-term absenteeism:

Pentagon officials claim . . . that the rate of Vietnam-era AWOLs was no higher than that of World War II or the Korean War. They claim that there was nothing unique or extraordinary about these offenses; only about 10 percent were motivated by opposition to the war, and the rest were no different from the AWOLs that the military has always experienced.

The statistics are correct, but they vastly understate the impact of Vietnam. Only the rate of short-term AWOL (less than thirty days) was comparable to that of earlier wars, and short-term AWOL almost always involved petty misbehavior that bore little relationship to the war. The statistics for long-term absence offenses tell a much different story. Absences of more than thirty days, administratively called "desertion," increased to an unprecedented level. In 1966, the Army and Marines reported about fifteen desertion cases per thousand troops. The rates climbed to more than fifty per thousand in 1969, and about seventy per thousand in 1972. By contrast, long-term absence rates during the Korean War were about twenty-five per thousand troops.

During the entire period of the Vietnam War, there were approximately 1,500,000 AWOL incidents and 500,000 desertion incidents. At the peak of the war, an American soldier was going AWOL every two minutes, and deserting every six minutes. This had an enormous impact on the ability of the armed forces to function. Absence offenses caused a total loss of roughly one million man-years of military service, almost half the total number of man-years American troops spent in Vietnam. The Senate Armed Services Committee estimated that in 1968 alone, well before AWOL and desertion reached their peak, absenteeism was costing the military the equivalent of ten combat divisions of fifteen thousand men each. While few of these young men were consciously voting against the war with their feet, their behavior was unmistakably connected with the unusual stress which they and the armed forces experienced during the Vietnam era. [1978:121-22]

Barring the theoretical possibility that the same cosmic "historical forces" that induced the United States to fight the war also generated the social movements that, simultaneously, impeded its ability to fight, it would appear likely that the same war (i.e., fought in the same place with the same methods under the same ideological representations by troops recruited from the same strata by the same draft) fought in a period of *social quiescence* would have yielded a pattern of military absenteeism closer to that of the Korean War than that which actually occurred (though not identical because of the impact upon morale of military conditions specific to Vietnam). It should then be in this light that one must interpret accounts of motives for desertion given by individuals at the time (or subsequently in exile, since exiles are insulated from the "post-movement adaptations" of consciousness that prevail in the domestic society; that is, they are ideologically—and perhaps, more broadly, psychically "mental museum pieces"). From this perspective, the account of a chain of incidents by a white working-class soldier that prompted his desertion for "personal" reasons, or an analogous account by a soldier of working-class Black origins of a similar train of incidents prompting similar action possibly in addition accompanied by the sudden illumination of "radicalization," should be understood as having made perfect subjective sense to such an individual at the time and in the context of a social movement period in which the threshold of insubordination is lowered. However, this may not be understood as strictly comparable to what might be required to precipitate the same action on the part of a socially similar individual during a period of social quiescence when the threshold of insubordination has once more risen to something like its former level.

3. Postmovement adaptation illusions. All social movements come to an end after a few years at most, giving way to periods of social quiescence; the fever pitch of emotional intensity and the physical dangers of social conflict—to say nothing of the more elemental problem of the regular acquisition of the means of subsistence—cannot be sustained by masses of people indefinitely. Movements that eventuate in social revolution are no exceptions to this, since weariness with social upheaval facilitates the consolidation of revolutionary regimes whose rise had been made possible by popular passion and spontaneity. In the more normal instances, which fall far short of social revolution, social life proceeds much as it had prior to the upheaval.

When a movement comes to an end, the reinterpretation of social reality—as it had been formulated by the dissidents and counterposed to the conventional interpretation at the height of the movement—becomes an incubus to most former movement participants. It has embodied visions of possibilities that could only have been actualized by social transformations that had not occurred, these visions now having become insupportably painful to people who must now return to conventional lives they had rejected. They resort to a number of options, ranging from total obliteration of their reinterpretation to efforts to preserve it in a state of unsullied purity:

a. RETREAT INTO PRIVATIZED CONCERNS. Some degree of reacceptance of the conventional interpretation of social reality as amended by consequence of the movement (especially in postrevolutionary periods) is almost inevitable; the other guys, after all, had won, and in emotional terms, *might* always makes a certain amount of *right*. (Especially poignant in postrevolutionary periods is the circumstance that some of "the other guys" were formerly "us.") The most common manifestation of this is sullen apathy in the public arena, i.e., a "realistic" acceptance of "what is," coupled with a narrowing of focus to domestic, intrapsychic, careerist, and suchlike preoccupations. Hence, following the restoration of the English monarchy in 1660, former revolutionaries ceased to believe in the possibility of objectifying Christ's kingdom in earthly society, transposing it to a wholly spiritual realm:

> "The rich will rule the world," sighed the well-to-do Richard Baxter philosophically; "and few rich men will be saints. . . . We shall have what we would, but not in this world." Not in this world: the words were often heard now. . . . After the restoration. . .Edward Burrough told Friends, "Our kingdom and victory is not of this world, nor earthly." [Hill, 1973:283]

b. DISSIPATION. This is the compulsive obliteration of social and political awareness. The succession of periods of intense social conflict by those in which political and social reaction is combined with a climate of cultural "permissiveness" are a recurrent social phenomenon: Thus the stern asceticism of the English or Puritan Revolution (1640–49) and the Commonwealth (1649–60) was followed by the indulgent escapism of the Restoration period whose tone was set by the "merry monarch," Charles II (1660–85).

Dissipation appeared in the aftermath of the youth movement of the 1960s, although in relation to a social movement in which disreputable appearance, untidy living, psychedelic drug use, and sexual openness were frequently credentials of participation, this statement may appear superficially incongruous. Yet the drug preferences of many turned to barbiturates, soporifics, tranquilizers, heroin, and alcohol, that is, drugs of "consciousness contraction." Sexual faddism flourished, divested of oppositional content.

c. ATTENUATED OPPOSITION. This is the shrinkage of the reinterpretation of social reality to the dimensions of vague notions of, for example, "change." In our example of the English Revolution, the ex-parliamentarian gentry thus became the prototypes of what subsequently—by the late 1670s—became the Whig party.

d. DISSOCIATION OF CONSCIOUSNESS AND BEHAVIOR. This adaptation is popular among privileged dissidents, whereby the conventional interpretation of social reality is accepted to the extent that the individual pursues a conventional career, especially in the professions, and settles down into a "normal life." Meanwhile, the reinterpretation of social reality is retained in a fossilized, petrified, "academic" form, and the individual may engage in "radical" activities of a routine, perfunctory, or faddish character.

e. REPENTANCE. This is the systematic and hyperconformist adoption of the perspective of one's former enemies, often accompanied by accusations of betrayal against those whom one now betrays. A classic case is that of the "professional anti-Communists" in the United States in the 1940s and 1950s, some of whom made lucrative careers out of exposing their ex-comrades of the 1930s.

f. ENCAPSULATION. For those who hold fast to the reinterpretation of social reality with all its visions of possibility and who reject "normal life" there remains this option, since an ongoing and developing social movement no longer exists; the material possibilities for social transformation are absent; and those capable of resisting the appeals of normal life are few. This may take the form, for example, of rusticated isolation or an "underground" existence possibly associated with terrorism. Alternatively, former dissidents may physically remove themselves from the scene of defeat or anticipated persecution and go into exile. In the latter case, exiled dissidents may reproduce arcane ideological divisions on foreign shores, even to the point of establishing entire communities under the guidance of dogmatic orthodoxies whose origins lay in protest against social conditions and associated ruling orthodoxies in other times and places.

We are all familiar with the story of the emigration to New England of the "Pilgrim Fathers" (1620) and the Puritans of Massachusetts Bay (1630), whose passage brackets the social movement in England in the 1620s, culminating in the Petition of Right (1629), which in a sense was the precursor of the English Revolution of the 1640s. Less well known is the emigration of Presbyterians to New Jersey following the restoration of the English monarchy in 1660.

The Presbyterians had been the most conservative (excepting of course, the ultraroyalist Roman Catholics) of all the sects opposed to the established church during the revolution. With the return of Charles II, they expected to "work within the system," as we would say, that is, obtain toleration of their creed in return for tolerating the king. The Cavalier Parliament (1661–67) was, however, packed with fanatical Anglicans who were determined to root out

Presbyterianism with stringent, repressive legislations: the Act of Uniformity (1661), the Test Act (1662), the Conventicles Act (1664), and the Five-Mile Act (1665). Consequently, in 1666, a shipload of Presbyterians left England and settled in New Jersey, naming their community Newark after the English town where the wicked King John had died 450 years before (1216), hence a possible code for "Death to tyrants!" Newark, New Jersey, remained a theocratic state under the "temporal rule" of the First Presbyterian Church until 1745.

g. CULTURAL INVERSION. This final adaptation consists of the readoption of the conventional interpretation of social reality in an unconventional setting while perhaps retaining elements of the social-movement reinterpretation in a fragmented or dissociated form. Such "cultural inversions" of reformist or radical impulses into repressive-reactionary caricatures of themselves are quite common in the wake of social conflict. Christopher Hill, for example, vividly describes the inversion of two cultural strains in the reinterpretation of social reality during the English Revolution of the 1640s, enthusiastic religion and rationalist skepticism as to the validity of received tradition, into reactionary superstition and elitist rationalism:

> Rude plebian soldiers had referred to their royal prisoner as "Stroker," "in relation to that gift which God had given him" of being able to cure the King's evil. Leveller journalists had mocked a story that Charles I's spittle had cured a sick child. But now plebian soldiers and Levellers were silenced. The tremendous ceremonial of the coronation was accompanied by a revival of "touching" on a grand scale. Charles II is alleged to have "touched" over ninety-two thousand persons during his reign, though I do not know who counted. On one occasion half a dozen of those hoping for a cure were trampled to death in the press.
>
> . . . There was a considerable literature denouncing "vulgar prophecies" among other suspect forms of enthusiasm. Thomas Sprat claimed it as the job of science and the Royal Society "to shake off the shadows and to scatter the mists which fill the minds of men with a vain consternation." Prodigies and prophecies could be self-validating by breaking men's courage and preparing them for disasters "which they fondly imagined were inevitably threatened them from heaven." This had been "one of the most considerable causes of those spiritual distractions of which our country has long been the theatre." The ending of belief in day-to-day divine intervention in politics helped to produce an atmosphere in which science could develop freely; elevation of the mechanical philosophy above the dialectical science of radical "enthusiasts" reciprocally helped to undermine such beliefs.
>
> "Fanaticism" and "enthusiasm" were the bugbears of polite and scholarly restoration society. The carefully cultivated classicism of the age of Dryden and Pope was (among other things) the literary form of this social reaction. For the radicals Latin and Greek had been the languages of Antichrist, as were the languages the universities, law, medicine, the three intellectual elites. [1973:353,355]

Similarly, the inverse relationship between antislavery and anti-Catholic sentiment in the antebellum era in the United States is pointed out by Ray Allen Billington (1964).

The aftermath of the progressive era offers another instance. Progressivism began as a liberal reform movement within the nonmonopoly bourgeoisie (i.e., the groups whose status and cultural dominance were immediately threatened by the rise of monopoly capital; cf. Richard Hofstadter, 1955). The progressive era, although a cultural unity, comprised two distinct social movements each—in conformity with the Law of Emergent Contradiction—culminating in a working-class movement: 1904–1907, possibly terminated by the Panic of 1907; and 1912–14, subsiding with the onset of the war boom. (The first period witnessed the initial prominence of the Socialist party and the IWW and the second their emergence as major working-class organizations; both were suppressed in 1917 for opposition to the entry of the United States into World War I.) Culturally and ideologically, bourgeois progressivism had been characterized by efforts toward the moral purification of government (drives against corruption; women's suffrage; technical modifications of the political process such as initiative, recall, referendum, and primary) and of business practices (antitrust legislation, regulation of child labor, consumer protection, creation of a central bank, conservation, etc.); contemporary historians now interpret the underlying dynamics of this reform at the federal level as the paradoxical consolidation of the grip of monopoly capital in the guise of regulation (cf. Kolko, 1963; and Weinstein, 1968). Simultaneously, the bourgeois progressives sought to extend to the immigrants the benefits of the dominant culture (by means of the diffusion of education, settlement houses and social work, and the beginnings of empirical sociology—among whose practitioners the Protestant clergy were heavily represented). With the end of World War I these themes emerged in the repressive-reactionary guises of Prohibitionism and nativism. Andrew Sinclair (1964) analyzed Prohibition as the pseudoreform that represented a distortion of the characteristic moral uplift purificatory thrust of progressivism. John Higham (1955) likewise chronicled the shift in emphasis from the paternalistic effort to "Americanize" the immigrants to racist and xenophobic measures to exclude them and to terrorize those already here along with racial minorities, as exemplified by the recrudescence of the KKK and its growth to 5 million members by 1925.

During the 1970s, such cultural themes of the youth movement of the 1960s, as consciousness exploration, voluntary poverty, "community," and generational revolt were inverted in some of the patriarchal or mock-bureaucratic "new religions" and some of the more authoritarian of the new psychotherapies such as Synanon, Scientology, and—to some extent—est, whereas New Leftism was inverted into neo-Leninism. The former dissident thus mimiced the social patterns in the wider society, above all in the last decade the reproduction of conventional authority relations in unconventional form, which he or she formerly rejected, while maintaining a posture of nonconflictual estrangement toward that society.

Now that the caveats have been issued and the problems of assessing the development of the reinterpretation of reality within the social movement—which are complex and manifold—we will turn our attention to the thought forms generated within the social movement.

The Thought Forms of Antistructure

The English theorist and social historian Sheila Rowbotham points out, in *Woman's Consciousness, Man's World*, that social categories victimized by the social structure are also victimized by the linguistic structure; they are handicapped in periods of social quiescence in articulating their own variant of the hegemonic ideology, since their use of their own idiomatic speech reproduces the mark of their inferior status. The "working class" is consequently "represented"—for the purpose of utilizing those narrow channels to which "politics" is ordinarily confined in bourgeois society—by persons of higher status than their own who are adept in the "standard" dialect to which "respectable" speech on "serious" matters is confined. The surrogates, also, are closer in their thought forms to those they ostensibly oppose than to those they supposedly represent, reflecting the differences in everyday-life practice between the classes. Any introductory textbook in sociolinguistics will in fact devote at least a chapter to illustrations of the general law whereby, in any stratified society, the speech of the higher strata is always defined as "better" or more "correct" than that of the lower.

Linguistic stigma only scratches the surface of the problem, since the "deep" linguistic structure, that is, the immanent cosmology at the core of society's mental life, is mapped in a complex and subtle fashion onto the social structure (see Chapter 3, "The Reproduction of Social Privilege"). Thus the terms "worker" and "working class" (though not quite as much as the obsolescent "hands" and the obsolete "mechanicks") denote both *intrinsic limitations* and *destiny*. Workers work. That is what, by nature, they do. That they also drink, swear, fornicate, and watch ball games is peripheral and comprehensible in that no better can be expected of persons properly consigned to that station. The mental life of bourgeois society thereby reproduced the mind-body dichotomy found in all class societies in the usual relations of relative prestige, with its characteristic twist: Those whose bodies were used—*employed*—by others in factories (or prostitution: High bourgeois civilization, c. 1914, was the golden age of prostitution) for pecuniary "compensation" (the latter usage positing as its presupposition that surplus value is *not* extracted) were *eo ipso* inferior to the bourgeoisie, who alternatively (1) symbolized status by their physical underdevelopment, e.g., women indoctrinated in the arts of frailty and fainting spells and men whose grotesque obesity by contemporary standards was not held against them even as candidates for the presidency of the United States (this tradition reaching its logical conclusion and termination in the person of William Howard Taft, 1909–13 whose predecessor, patron, and ultimate nemesis was an exemplar of the next alternative); or (2) did the same by spending lavishly on elite sports such as mountain climbing, sailing and yachting, horsy sports—fox hunting, polo, racing, etc.—subsuming horse breeding, training in fisticuffs ("the manly art of self-defense"), provided one did not enter the prize ring and reserved such skills for the proper occasions (e.g., defending milady's honor or smiting a socialist agitator), and sports requiring the expert handling of firearms and other weaponry, e.g., hunting, dueling, and war ("the sport of kings").

At that, "workers" in lands where the English tongue prevails are, linguistically speaking, comparatively lucky: "Work," like "toil" or "labor," is negatively loaded, but at least the same word is also used to denote a "high-culture" artifact (except in music, where the Latin singular equivalent, *opus*, is used unless the production is extroadinarily elaborate and takes the plural form *opera*). But French *ouvriers* or *travailleurs* do *travail* in producing *biens*; an *oeuvre* is something Louis Althusser may write on the subject. Likewise,

German proletarians do *Arbeit* within the *Werke*, albeit the latter word may adorn the cover of Marx's collected writings. They may, however, aspire to linguistic upward mobility by organizing a *Gewerkschaft* (trade union). In this respect the Russian *Rabochiy Klass* is in a most unenviable condition, as both *rabota* (n.f., work; obs., forced labor, from *rab*, slave; cognate to Czech *robot*, servile toil) and *trud* (n.m., toil) are so negatively loaded that neither can be confounded with the writer's *sochineniye*, the painter's *obraz*, or other *tvor'chestvo* (creation); but collectively their prospects are spectacular for they then become a *professional'niy soyuz* (trade union; *profsoyuz* for short). And this particular aspect of the classless society in Russia had already been achieved under tsarism!

Rowbotham was herself sensitized to the magnitude of the issue thanks to her early acquisition of a thick coating of Marxist theory employed in polemics among Trotskyist splinter groups during the early 1960s; as she tells it, this coating cracked apart under the impact of rock music, sex, and marijuana, whereby she arrived at the preliminary synthesis of subjectivist New Leftism; she then followed a common course of development to subjectivist feminism; and by the time of writing the aforementioned book, her first, had begun to reintegrate this with Marxist theory critiqued for patriarchal bias. Her case goes far beyond the still intractable generic third-person-pronoun problem to assert that patriarchal bias ensconced throughtout common speech systematically denies objective reality as encountered by women in everyday life, subsuming the same in patriarchal ideology represented as reality, such that everything identifiable as biologically female or culturally feminine is overcast with a patina of abnormality or inferiority.

The foregoing is by way of introducing the problem, that is, of empirically detecting and describing "the collective development of the thought forms of 'antistructure.' " As the ideological structure of the hegemonic ideology is reproduced first and foremost at the level of common speech, it is first and foremost at this level that the thought forms that posit as their presupposition the suspension by way of progressive repudiation of this hegemonic ideology must proceed: There are, first of all, "countercultures" of resistance, however unconscious; of explicit collective self-differentiation; and, obviously, of "deviance"—however this be defined by theorists in this area—or "marginality" in times of social quiescence. These each have a particular idiom, shop talk, jargon, argot, dialect (U.S. Blacks), or wholly distinctive language (European Jews); these may be supplemented in social-movement periods by wholly new subcultures, which either dissipate afterward or become encapsulated as subcultural enclaves having undergone a subtle vetting of the social-conflict dimension. Thus, whether the basis of movement solidarity is religious, ethnic-communal, formal-organizational, or exclusively cultural, a social-movement subculture is always associated with it: A preexisting subculture merely undergoes a "flowering" of its existing lingo, which is accelerated once the social category with which the subculture is associated undertakes innovative collective social-conflict action. Wholly new subcultures must collectively create a wholly new lingo, subsuming bits and pieces scrounged from the diverse origins of its members into a distinctive creative synthesis. Thus, for example, the white youth movement of the 1960s scavenged lingo from Black speech, sociological jargon, Marxist rhetoric, "folk" music, Black-based rock music,

Yiddish, and its own practice in some areas (sex, drugs, overt "politics") or vicarious admiration in others (motorcycles, guerrilla warfare). This list no doubt could be easily expanded.

Shades of meaning subtly or even drastically changed over the course of a few months or years (q.v. *relevant*). Semantics was not standardized from place to place or even person to person. New lingo succeeded the old, which thereupon became unfashionable, taboo, or even reversed in its loading (q.v. *masturbation*), requiring those aspiring to appear culturally "in" to sensitize themselves to fine changes in meaning, the introduction of new vocabulary, the discarding of "old" words due to overextension of their meanings (q.v. *freak out*, or more broadly to shifts in emphasis of the subculture as a whole (as from the *groovy*" ethic to the *together* ethic to the *mellow* ethic, which all took a maximum of three years, 1967–70).[3]

As antistructure is forcibly asserted by members of dissident collectivities, hierarchical barriers that normally separate them and call for ritualized forms of interaction are breached, allowing for this creative synthesis. One logical consequence of this breaching is that members of the more privileged sectors of the dissident subcultures begin defining their position in terms provided by members of less privileged social categories thus radicalizing their consciousness. For example, in the 1960s, hippies became the "new niggers" and students began defining themselves as "niggers" as evidenced by the popularity of Jerry Farber's book, *The Student as Nigger*, on college campuses. This intermingling of subcultures, the building (however tenuous) of solidarity between them, becomes the crucible for the fashioning of new forms of consciousness. E. P. Thompson (1966) demonstrated that the flowering of Luddism was preceded by the growth of "Societies of Correspondence" among workers of London and several places in the Midlands. The Correspondence Societies were the first working-class organizations by virtue of the fact that they broke away from the old patterns of guild organization and included workers from several types of labor (e.g., weavers, potters, stockingers, dyers, etc.). The Luddites were the first truly proletarian social movement, complete with demands that reverberated through the next 120 years of workers struggles, such as a legal minimum wage, protection for women and children, and the right to organize unions.

Along with the "democratization" of social relations among dissident collectivities comes the impulse to define society from the bottom up rather than from top down, as occurs during periods of social quiescence. There is the tendency to give primacy to "experience" over received interpretations of reality. That is, dissidents become less amenable to interpreting their experience in the social order in categories provided for in the hegemonic ideology; but instead prefer to reinterpret them in terms of the currently evolving counterreality. The reinterpretation, because of its temporal and transient nature, is capable of rapid shifts and is extremely sensitive to alterations in the conjuncture. One only has to look as far as the Iranian Revolution to note that within a few days the enemy of the Revolution changed from the shah to American imperialism, which consequently led to the sacking of the U.S. Embassy and the taking of hostages. Not only is the reinterpretation constructed out of the borrowings of the dissident subcultures and from "experience," which is the result of a new praxis and becomes nonnormal and subject to interpretation from different coordinates (e.g., theft becomes "liberation"), but is built from oppositions to the dominant ideology, as in the case of Black dissidents changing the color symbolism (black is good; white is evil).

The new praxis, whatever form it may take—and it does take new forms during social-movement periods—is fundamentally opposition to the set of social relations that pervade the social order. Thus, as dissidents struggle to alter those social relations, to which, prior to the social movement, most had acquiesced, the conception of reality is changed as a consequence of entry into the struggle. It is one thing to be a passive recipient of one's social subordination and quite another to struggle against it as part of a collectivity. Therefore, the "communitas" that is experienced by dissidents during social-movement periods provides a context in which not only new social realities can be constructed, but also offer a theraputic function in that it becomes a means whereby dissidents are able to retrieve aspects of human consciousness that were alienated from them as part of their socialization to positions of social subordination.

It has been observed that in periods of social quiescence members of subordinated social categories more or less accept their subordination, and problems of alienation and stratification are seen as "personal." During periods of social movement, they are reinterpreted as political. In the former is the internalization of the belief that institutions are objective and stand outside the individual. We might also see this process as reification—that is, that the social order seems suprahuman, having a life unto itself, and is relatively impervious to intervention by mere mortals ("The system runs itself"). During social-movement periods, a subjectivization of the social structure takes place, whereby the institutionalization is redefined as "interests." Structures are seen as serving the interest of certain sectors of society and working against the interests of others. Within the social-movement reinterpretations, then, we find the process of delegitimization.

Though many theorists of social movements claim that social movements must have an ideology, our point is that ideologies are not generally social-movement phenomena, but are reconstructed post hoc when the movement has exhausted its capacity for innovation. What social movements *do* produce, as they evolve, are visions of alternatives to conventional living, normal existence, or the quotidian, and changes in the locus of motivation of social-movement participants, which diffuse into the larger population. Sometimes these changes in motivation are so radical that we have referred to them as "sociocharacterological revolutions," since they portend the emergence of a new kind of human being, such as rise of the "rational calculator" as an important social type in the seventeenth century. Perhaps a more mundane example can be drawn from the populist movement in the United States in the 1880s and 90s, whereby disposessed small landholders and tenant farmers banded together in the Farmer's Alliance in an attempt to battle credit merchants locally and the newly emerging corporate capitalism nationally. Says Goodwyn of the movement "culture":

It encouraged individuals to have significant aspirations in their own lives, it generated a plan of purpose and a method of mass recruitment, it created its own symbols of politics and democracy in place of inherited hierarchical symbols, and it armed its participants against being intimidated by the corporate culture. The vision and hope embedded in the cooperative crusade held the agrarian ranks together while these things took place and created the autonomous political outlook that was Populism. [1978:178]

Thus it was possible for people who had perhaps never been more than 20 miles from home in their life to participate in Alliance wagon trains and attend Alliance conventions hundreds of miles from their residence.

Another aspect of the reinterpretation of reality is what we will call—after Willis (1977)—penetrations. We have noted elsewhere that a social movement begins with a critique of the manifest appearances of social relations and, as it develops, engenders more penetrating critiques and proffers interpretations of society that include aspects that were formerly hidden, obfuscated, or unseen. Again, the populist movement is instructive. It had its origins in Lampasas, Texas, in 1877 and was concerned with freeing farmers from the crop-lien system that had reduced millions of independent farmers to the peonage of tenantry. They developed their own cooperatives, giving them leverage over the local credit merchants. By 1892, they had formed the People's party, attempted to forge an alliance with industrial workers, developed the concept of the "productive classes" on which solidarity could be built in a struggle against the eastern banking establishment. The banks had created the conditions for the tenant farmer's immiseration by making sure the government paid them the debts for the Civil War on the gold standard, creating a deflation that was disastrous to the producers of wealth. The Alliance sponsored a widespread educational program with lecturers fanning out all over the South and West. They were able to tie the miseries of local farmers to national policy and the social relations of capitalist exploitation.

Perhaps another example of penetrations can be gathered from the working-class insurgencies in early-nineteenth-century England. English workers' presses published a tract by the French Jacobin Volney, originally entitled *Ruins of Empire*. An excerpt was published in a cheap paperback edition, entitled *The Laws of Nature*, in which the following dialogue occurs [Thompson 1966:99]:

People: What labor do you perform in the society?
Privileged class: None: we are not made to labor.
People: How then have you acquired your wealth?
Privileged class: By taking the pains to govern you.
People: To govern us! . . . We toil, and you enjoy; we produce and you dissipate; wealth flows from us, and you absorb it. Privileged men, class distinct from the people, form a nation apart and govern yourselves.

Thompson also reported that the recruitment to Methodism tended to be most successful in the wake of political action (1966:389). As a matter of fact, Methodist chiliasm diffused with the greatest success among the working class when their situation was most desperate, such as during the Napoleanic wars. In 1819, a year of expanding worker insurgency leading to Peterloo, the Methodist Committee of Privileges issued a circular

. . . expressing "strong and decided disapprobation of certain tumultuous assemblies which have lately been witnessed in several parts of the country; in which large masses of people have been irregularly collected (often under banners bearing the most shocking and impious inscriptions) . . . calculated, both from the infidel principles, the wild and delusive political theories, and the violent and inflammatory declamations . . . to bring all government into contempt, and to introduce universal discontent, insubordination, and anarchy." [Thompson, 1966:353]

Here we are able to glimpse at the penetration process from both sides of the barricade, so to speak. As the working class forged its own identity through its struggles with the "privileged class"—in which the clergy was included—they were villified as crazy, deluded, "anarchists," and, of course, infidels and blasphemers. As mentioned above, conventional reality is enforced. The rampaging of a peaceably assembled crowd of men, women, and children by the defenders of the order at Peterloo, was, according to Thompson, class war, with the yeomanry on mounts doing the greatest damage. Peterloo effectively ended this period of working-class insurgency.

The thought forms of antistructure are, above all, a consciousness of kind. As we have seen from historical examples, they can take on such forms as religious doctrines as in the case of Thomas Munzer and the Anabaptists or the Heresy of the Free Spirit; class consciousness; ethnic and racial consciousness; feminine consciousness; and even youth consciousness. Within the stratification system of any given society, a consciousness of kind can develop among members of any given identifiable social category based on their common position in the social relations of domination. These thought forms are subversive of the given set of social relations in which they exist. From the outside, they are viewed as sinister and dangerous. Although the reinterpretation of social reality within the context of a social movement may be extremely difficult to assess, not only because of its volatility and ephemerality, but also because dissidents use terms from common parlance that are loaded with different meanings, it may be the single most important indicator of the existence of a social movement, since it provides the basis of, and continuity between actions. Additionally, the development of the consciousness of dissidents also provides the legitimations for intensification and innovation in the means of conflict.

Notes

1. The use of quotation marks—"intellectuals"—designates members of a publicly recognized and mutually defined (that is, an "intellectual" must be accepted by other "intellectuals" as included within this category, which should on no account be identified with more inclusive categories such as writers or academics) status group that stood at the summit of the cultural counterbourgeoisie in the socially quiescent state of bourgeois society. As noted in Chapter 3, the cultural counterbourgeoisie was systematically reproduced as a distinct formation until the 1960s. The *absence* of quotation marks—intellectuals—denotes persons addressing ideological statements to dissident audiences in social-movement contexts and accepted by them as ideological formulators.

2. Seymour M. Hersh, reporting in the *New York Times*, December 21, 1978, attributed the optimistic slant of intelligence out of Iran to the agents' fears of defying the pro-shah line of National Security Adviser Brzezinski, since the careers of at least two of them had been blighted by reports of their contacts with opposition politicians by SAVAK—the Iranian secret police—to Brzezinski over the heads of their superiors.

Nevertheless, according to the same logic, one must assume that at some point the careerist motive would work in the opposite direction, that is, the operatives who failed to correctly assess what was happening under their noses would not be assured of the most brilliant prospects either.

3. A lexicon of terminology has been published by the authors in Sayres, et al., *The 60s Without Apology*, which may give some insight into the thought forms that pervaded the social movements of the 1960s in the United States. The authors' names were inadvertently reversed by the editors. Our names should be listed in alphabetical order in all our collaborative works.

Chapter 6

Disalienation

If I were a carpenter
And you were a Lady
Would you marry me anyway
Would you have my baby?

> —*Tim Hardin (1966)*

Some are mathematicians
Others are carpenters' wives
I don't know where they're all at now
Or what they're doing with their lives.

> —*Bob Dylan (1976)*

As we have attempted to demonstrate, one of the inevitable consequences of exploitation and domination is the alienation of individual capacity. Within the hegemonic ideology, it is self-evident that those at the top of society are in some way inherently superior to those below. That is, they present themselves to the lower social orders as superior by virtue of the intervention of the alienated supernatural into human affairs, such as the Brahmin caste in India characterizing itself as in a second incarnation as human beings, distinguishing themselves from "firstborn" castes by their superior level of consciousness, ritual purity, and material circumstances; alternatively, dominators can idealize themselves as superior by achievement (which may also be characterized as evidence of being God's chosen or possessing superior intellect) as the bourgeoisie has presented itself; or, most recently, as resources seem increasingly scarce, elites legitimate their domination by virtue of their access to scarce institutional resources, such as a high-quality education, information, life-enriching privileges such as trips abroad or increased leisure time, and so forth. It is this very alienation of personal capacity that, given the *appearances* of the social order, serve as prima facie evidence of the innate or structured inferiority of those of the lower social strata. In periods of social movement, dissidents attempt to reappropriate those capacities alienated from themselves as a consequence of their position in the social order. In this chapter, we will examine this process.

Learning as an Alienated Capacity

The forcible assertion of antistructure necessarily implies interference with the political reproduction of society. It therefore makes problematical the role of the polity and prevailing authority relations ultimately guaranteed by the polity in confining the self-interference of cultural reproduction to that level. In the absence of antistructure, advocacy in principle of "the unity of theory and practice" predictably has the impact of the Boy Scout oath; whereas, in the presence of antistructure its advocacy is superfluous. In the late 1960s, dissidents in the various social-movement collectivities of the time were setting about assimilating complex abstract ideas—most often, it is true, not even to the extent designated by the expression "half-baked"—in the spheres of politics, Oriental philosophy, psychology, Marxist theory, poetry, and anthropology *without* the rewards proffered by bourgeois social relations in the guise of the (ultimate) prospect for enhanced material wealth or status. Curiously, the same people might simultaneously resist the inculcation of the same ideas and subject matter in the context of bourgeois social relations as, say, by a teacher standing in front of a class, lecturing for fifty minutes, giving midterms and finals, and dispensing grades. Though an acceptable compromise might involve the same teacher adopting informal attire, bidding everyone to sit in a circle on the floor, yielding to the "group process," and promising everyone a grade of A in advance (unless the school had gone over to a gradeless system).

The relativistic attitude of the students of the late 1960s, whereby the validity of any abstract idea was inseparable from the context of social relations wherein it was presented, is an example of what we have earlier called disalienation. To elucidate slightly: When a human capacity, such as the capacity to learn, has been developed as part of the totality of the development of the human subject in history in such a way that it is represented to its bearers as having been appropriated—*ripped-off*, so to speak—by an external agency, which in turn brandishes it against its bearers as a hostile potency or weapon, as in the implicit assumption underlying the whole of the educational industry to the effect that, "you cannot learn except under circumstances wherein we teach," this was to Marx (1964) and is to us "alienation" (cf. Chapter 3, "The Reproduction of Social Privilege"). Alienation everywhere and at all times has the effect of demonstrating the inferiority of some and the superiority of others, not least to the satisfaction of those whose destiny it is to be accepted in due course into the midst of those understood as "superior." The capacity to learn by exploring the environment and the capacity to "think" are biologically determined (or "hard-wired," as the sociobiologists say), and it is just as natural for "consciousness" to become more complex as it is for striated muscle tissue to get thicker. However, it is not to "nature" or biology but to history that we owe the specific extent of the development of the capacity to learn possible for an individual in a particular social order. History determines as well the forms and constraints under which that development proceeds.

Alienation is invariably found in conjunction with false consciousness, with false consciousness positing alienation's nonexistence: One goes to school to be educated. This is not to say that utter passivity is enjoined; but rather that the education industry rewards you to the extent that your ambition, initiative, curiosity, and "creativity" motivate you in the direction in which it would otherwise push you. Those who proceed thusly are smart, intelligent, bright; those who cannot even be pushed are stupid. The categories "smart" and "stupid" are accepted in bourgeois society as self-evidently real, and not least by privileged (that is, educated) persons who have no idea what illiterate garage mechanics are doing to their cars and could not possibly figure it out. "Intelligence," as measured quantitatively, boils down to something called "cognitive skills," which in turn are those mental capacities that, all other things being equal, should result in high achievement in school, the latter by universal agreement the sole satisfactory legitimation of entry into privileged status groups below the level of the bourgeoisie and increasingly into the bourgeoisie itself by way of the increasingly fashionable masters in business administration degree. The precise relationship between the "skills" allegedly imparted by "the educational process" to the concrete practice of the privileged groups in question is never spelled out, nor is it even closely scrutinized. And this is not all: As it is increasingly accepted among psychologists that "cognitive skills" are lateralized in the left cerebral hemisphere, one wonders whether a definition of "intelligence" could be constructed around functions lateralized in the right hemisphere (in that it has been determined by the research done by TenHouten [1971] and others that certain victimized social categories, including Native Americans and Blacks, display a lesser degree of left-hemisphere dominance than that found among affluent male whites); this would go beyond the question of "cultural bias" in testing, which normally involves nothing more than testing the same left-hemisphere-lateralized functions measured by the "standard" instruments only in subcultural argot. Beyond that, one asks whether it is no more than sheer ideology that "intelligence" be identified as a property of discrete individuals competing against other discrete individuals for status places whose relative importance is normally comparable in quantifiable, that is, pecuniary terms. May we not, perhaps, posit a dialectical relationship between collective and individual learning? In this way "intelligence" would be associated with collective and cooperative practice in which mutual teaching occurs; individual learning and practice would here constitute the basis of personal contributions to mutual education.

This is not merely utopian; it is impossible, as it presupposes a situation in which what is to be learned is determined by collective and individual practice built upon what has been previously learned, which was itself freely chosen in a similar fashion, and so on. It posits as its presupposition, in other words, the suspension of the social structure such that the content as well as the proper forms, e.g., "methodology," of "knowledge" and the system of credentialing it are not dictated by the exigency of a structure of a particular kind to impose a determinate "reality" upon society as a whole. Insofar as there is a human need for structure, there is a corresponding readiness to accept the imposition of a "reality" that must be taken seriously.

Antistructure and Disalienation

But there is also—as we have posited following Turner (1966)—a human need for antistructure, though necessarily for relatively short periods (at least until such a time as production of the basic necessities is carried on by automated machinery while a prolonged vacation from social order is called). In the context of antistructure our little fantasy of disalienated learning can and has taken place. Consider, for example, one of the famous French student graffiti of 1968: "There is neither smart nor stupid. There is only free and unfree." This is about as concise a demystification of the ideology of individual intelligence as one can hope to find. There were also indications in the United States in the same period that collective mutual education could (that is, normally did not but still *could*) be vastly more efficacious in imparting social-science-type information and modes of reasoning. However, such mutual education was for the purpose of fostering the collective forcible assertion of antistructure rather than upholding the structure of bourgeois social relations. There was no reason to doubt a student in those days who, having spent a fairly brief period participating in an intense investigation by a "collective" of the workings of the Selective Service System, the bureaucratic vested interests served by it, and its relation to class, status, and ethnic stratification in society as a whole; or in tracing organizational and personal connections between university officials, trustees, and certain senior faculty to local, national, and international "power structures" announced: "I learned more in six weeks of doing this than in four years of college."

As the degree of disalienation varies in accordance with the intensity of a social movement as a whole, and as vestiges of antecedent social relations are not fully liquidated by even the most thoroughgoing of social transformations, it is hardly surprising that most students, to the extent that they approved of the slackening of the bureaucratic rigor of the "educational process" in the late 1960s, did not educate themselves in any sense, individually or collectively, except in that they further immersed themselves in the more hedonistic aspects of the "youth" culture. Sectoral ideologies asserting the self-evident inevitablility of the alienation of particular human capacities—all subsumed under the overarching hegemonic ideology positing as its presupposition the indubitable necessity for alienation-in-general—are so thoroughly inculcated in the practice of everyday life that they are *assumed*, taken for granted, and not even worth mentioning. If ever overtly stated, it is as commonplace truisms: Without the church you cannot be religious. Without the fear of hunger you will never work. You will cease working if we do not watch you. Only labor power expended in exchange for money is work; otherwise it is a hobby or housework. Without grades you will not study. Without the display of armed force on the streets there will be chaos. Without the state you will not be safe. The army makes a man of you. An unmarried woman is nothing. (This is a free country but) you can't fight City Hall. A fair day's work for a fair day's pay. Anyone who wants to work can get a job. The price of liberty is eternal vigilance.

The lessons inculcated thusly, that is, that whatever is not managed, watched, disciplined, or guarded by force of arms is dangerous; that society consists of selfish, isolated individuals who cannot be trusted; that nonhierarchical cooperative or collective activity for purposes other than getting drunk and meeting potential sex partners is a priori impossible; that invidious distinctions are eternal ("It's still the same old story/The fight for love and glory/On that you can rely/As time goes by"); that those who are not in it for the money are fools or insane; that one cannot do anything about anything except strive for upward mobility; that the human animal is fundamentally wicked, with the questionable exception of oneself; that one's hierarchical superiors *must* know what they are doing since one perforce relies upon them for what little security and sustenance there is. All these were implicit in bourgeois culture and the bourgeois hegemonic ideology and were self-fulfilling prophecies. People did steal, cheat, and fornicate when the back of Authority was turned, though by the standards prevailing since the assault upon bourgeois culture "from below" in the 1960s and "from above" in the 1970s it is remarkable how little they did so. Logically implicit was the positing of a person who, insofar as he or she was a rational calculator, played it safe and took no risks except in habitual gambling dictated by get-rich-quick fantasies and self-destructive tendencies; this person yet represented a formidable human advance over the dependent peasantries of earlier class societies. Upon the reproduction of the human being as here depicted rested the entire edifice of high bourgeois civilization and subsequent developments in the core of bourgeois society through the 1950s: This person produced with his or her life energies the surplus value by which capital was accumulated, the means of violence kept up, and the standards of decorum of the wealthy maintained. This was for Marx (1964) the most fundamental and essential alienation: The proletarian shrank as a human being *in the very act* of producing the aggrandizement of the bourgeois as the representation, the embodiment, the personification of the generalized development of human capacities and the highest level hitherto reached in the emergence of the human subject in history. To this was added further payment for the upkeep of organized religion, the entertainment industries, and other vehicles of bourgeois ideology wherewith the proletarian was comforted with the thought that life was yet "worth it," which, in objective reality quantified in pecuniary terms, it was not.

Marx (1973) foresaw that the emergence of new human capacities, which bourgeois society relentlessly fostered, was to be associated with the marketing of particular commodities or particular skills until a stage of "universal prostitution" was reached and no further human capacities could be developed without subverting bourgeois society as a whole. Then somebody—his guess that it would be the proletariat was wishful thinking—would reappropriate everything that had been sold out and thereby reconstitute the human being as a whole and on a higher level. The only sign of the imminence of such times is the fact that the concept of *together* (see Chapter 5, "The Reinterpretation of Social Reality") was developed by people who had not read Marx (who was not to become popular again until a few years later). But more of this later.

Disalienation is always partial in that one reproduces alienation in the very process of disalienation. For instance, one may engage in the process of disalienation by acting collectively for the elimination of that guise of alienation represented by exploitation. But in doing so one delegates one's capacity to reason and analyze on the level of collective action to a leadership that, however well founded its pretentions to scientific knowledge, has still appropriated this capacity unto itself and cannot be expected to shrink from wielding it as a weapon to perpetuate its dominion over the "rank and file." Along the same lines, if one rebels collectively against the appropriation of one's sexual capacities by prudish Authority, which has brandished them against one as sin, guilt, fear, taboo, and superstitious ignorance, one, in the process, submits to the verdict of socially determined invidious comparisons as to how "good" one's sexual practice is in terms of "experience," performance, frequency and variety of sexual acts, desirability and quantity of one's partners, and so forth. This might be regarded as tantamount to sanctioning the reappropriation of the same capacities by Authority concealed as a sexual marketplace in whose hands one's sexual capacities once more are manifested as an alien power: this time, by inducing feelings of inferiority; and this new and "higher" alienation is suitably disguised by the traditional bougeois marketplace conundrums of "free will" and "free choice."

We will conclude the discussion of this point by asserting that, generally speaking, only in the context of ongoing social movements, that is, presupposing the forcible assertion of antistructure, does disalienation of human capacities outpace the realienation of the same capacities or the more intensified alienation of other capacities.

Consequences of Disalienation: Mobility and Psychic Healing

The two most conspicuous effects of disalienation, most marked in times of thoroughgoing social transformation, are (1) upward mobility or otherwise-enhanced occupational diversity for a certain minority of dissidents, usually those still fairly young; and (2) psychic healing whose effects may resemble the idealized objectives of psychotherapy.

It should not really be surprising that social movements entailing the collective dissidence of exploited classes should as a rule draw their identifiable leadership from the ranks of the exploiting classes or from occupational and status groups dependent on or associated with the exploiting classes. In rarer cases this leadership may derive from the more privileged strata of the exploited classes; but hardly ever does it derive from the most depressed strata until that point in the development of the movement at which, in accordance with the Law of Emergent Contradiction, society has been stirred to its very depths. Initially, though, it might be anticipated at least statistically that the alienation of capacities to articulate, inspire, lead, organize, plan, negotiate, learn from history (usually but not necessarily implying literacy), establish a favorable image for the movement in the minds of diplomats, journalists, or domestic liberals, command on the battlefield, or generally speaking capacities that may be appropriate to visible leadership in the particular context would be least in the higher strata normally accustomed to command, manage, and be served. Such alienation would be greatest in the lower strata, normally accustomed to groveling servility to their "betters," however much the latter might permit them to brutalize each other (which constitutes additional prima facie evidence of their inferiority). It is in keeping with this that either dissidence commences in the higher strata, which subsequently passes into counterdissidence with the insurgency of the lower; or renegades from the higher strata attempt to instigate dissidence in the lower, sometimes with catastrophic results (as in the instance of the Russian Narodniki of the 1870s, whose initial strategy was to "go to the peasants" but were turned in by those they proposed to liberate); or, alternatively, to present themselves as candidates for leadership at the sign of incipient dissidence stirring in the lower depths (e.g., some of the organizers of the CIO in the 1930s, in particular those who were Communists, derived from strata privileged with respect to the working class—though hardly wealthy—and either volunteered their services as organizers or were trained for the purpose by the Communist party and "went into industry"). The latter, for their part, may initially prefer leaders with "class" or at least a presentable modicum of respectability for much the same reasons; once the enemy's aura of incomprehensible political magic and seeming invulnerability has worn through, the issue of the plebian birth or styles of the leadership may diminish.

With the advance of social transformation, large portions of the former exploiting class and high state officials die, go into exile, or undergo an enforced diminution of status; with the exception of those posts requiring elaborate technical-scientific training, their places are rather more easily taken by the lowborn than outside observers such as foreign journalists and social scientists anticipate. It is thus far easier to recruit a military officer than an engineer insofar as the most crucial part of the training of the former is of the on-the-job variety; the same holds for civil state or party officials wherein their posts do not require lengthy training in the use of sophisticated technical equipment. If relative deprivation and resource mobilization theorists posit that frustrated ambition promotes the impulse to revolutionary social transformation, it might well be posited with at least equal plausibility that the revolution *awakens* ambition in those for whom it would have only a few months ago been inconceivable and would moreover have elicited—had it been manifested anyway—the chiding of peers for presumptuousness. This may be the case in that the revolution promotes disalienation not least among those sufficiently young, adventurous, and insubordinate that they have not yet accommodated themselves to a lifetime in the lowly station of their ancestors. For similar reasons, others who might have succumbed except for the revolution to lives of cretinizing toil become cultural creators under the new order.

The practice of extensive and deliberate downward mobility for the purpose of disalienating capacities in the spheres of manual dexterity, physical strength, grace of movement, and so forth, as transpired among white youth in the 1960s, is far less common and is anyway readily reversible for most who try it following the end of the movement. In the 1970s, the disalienation of such alienated capacities became possible in the alienated form of the physical-fitness industry.

The effects of social movements resembling those touted for so-called psychotherapy have been widely noted by participants at the time and afterward; intrapsychic disalienation may perhaps be credited as the underlying reality making possible the developments we have alluded to as the Law of Emergent Contradiction. It also represents the sort of "color" more likely to be preserved in folk song, oratory, and post-facto musings of the sort collected by Gornick (1977) in her study of American Communists who participated in the labor movement of the 1930s than in the documentary sources consulted by historians or in social statistics compiled by sociologists and political scientists. There is, for example, a Russian folk song called "Dubinushka" (My Oaken Club) in which a worker sings a hymn to this weapon, which, one assumes, he once used in street fighting: "The day came and the people arose,/They straightened out the crooked spines of centuries." More exaltedly, the following aphorism was attributed to the late Mao Zedong by the Chinese People's Army newspaper *Hung Ji* by way of somewhat tortuously establishing scriptural justification for the silencing of critics of the Chinese invasion of Vietnam in February-March 1979: "Revolutionary war is an anti-toxin which not only eliminates the enemy's poison but also purges us of our own filth" (*Economist*, March 13, 1979).

The psychotherapeutic literature, whether psychiatric (Kardiner and Ovesey, 1951; Grier and Cobbs, 1968; Sachs, 1947) or Freudian-sociological (Mannoni, 1964; Dollard, 1957), had either diagnosed "powerlessness" as a mental disease or attributed to powerlessness assorted mental problems such as identification with the agressor, internalized self-hatred, crippled ego, impared identity, and similar diagnoses along those lines. These works, with the exception of Grier and Cobbs, antedate the 1960s; their focus was as a rule upon racially defined victim categories, especially U.S. Blacks, black Africans, or other colonials (e.g., Tunisian Arabs in another work by Mannoni, who, as a native Tunisian Jew, asserted his objectivity as between French and Arabs). With the fragmentary and qualified exception of Wilhelm Reich (cf. the essays in *Sex-Pol*, 1971), who was a far better sociologist than mind healer, influenced as he was by the Frankfurt School perspective on the impact of domination in everyday-life practice upon working-class folk ideology. There was no effort at the therapy of a victim category defined by class and the exploitative relation. In the late 1960s, the analysis of the diseases of "powerlessness" was resurrected by the feminists; explicit analogies between racism and sexism ensued. During the 1960s, a minor intellectual upheaval was precipitated by the dissemination of the works of Frantz Fanon (*Studies in a Dying Colonialism, Black Skin, White Masks, The Wretched of the Earth*). A black man born on Martinique, Fanon became a psychiatrist and was employed in the French colonial administration in Algeria, where he diagnosed diseases attributable to despotic power among the French as well as those attributable to the condition of objects of despotic power among the Arabs. In the last work listed, Fanon—who died in 1961 in the service of the FLN (Front Liberation Nationale) guerrillas—expounded a psycho sociology in the context of revolutionary war: As the Arabs had become mentally disabled by dint of subjection to the despotic violence of the French, they were now engaging in collective mass therapy by employing retaliatory violence to overthrow the colonial regime. The impact of this book included, among other things, the practice of *Fanonization* within the youth movement of the 1960s, which denoted the self-purgation of fears of intimidation by engaging in provocations of members of victimizing social categories.

The difficulty with the Freudian model, as with all variants of the theory of the unconscious derived from it, lay in its positing of a static ahistorical model of the psyche; by contrast, the Marxist model posited a psyche perpetually evolving in history and susceptible to sudden leaps in the complexity and sophistication of consciousness whereby the individual qua participant in a social-conflict collectivity might rapidly be qualitatively transformed.

Heroically futile efforts were made to fuse the Freudian model (and derivatives thereof) with the Marxist. Wilhelm Reich, in the early 1930s, suggested that the "reality principle" was—like the Marxian concept of subsistence—

historically relative; this idea was, however, not developed. There remained the question of the contradiction between an *unconscious* fixed in childhood and *consciousness* existing in dialectical relation to practice. (It is to be conceded that there was a dialectical kernel in Freud never appreciated by the Freudians et al., for whom the unconscious tended to be a species of passive receptacle by day with the capability of going bump in the night.)

The various subjectivist ideologies of the 1960s were more prone to the Freudian than to the Marxian side, that is, if anyone could be induced to read a book without fear of left-McLuhanoid charges of literacy in the postliterate epoch. There was accordingly in each dissident subculture posited an idealized, eternal *true authentic real self*, which the establishment, as variously perceived by Blacks, "freak" radicals, women, and so on, hid, stole, and concealed from "us." To find out who "us" were as opposed to "them" it was necessary to disinter this self and rummage around in it.

By the late 1960s the perfection of the self or the removal of impurities therefrom was the sole objective common to all tendencies within the movement subculture, however much they may have favored cultural radicalism, incipient neo-Leninism, feminism (not quite fully differentiated), overt political conflict without theory, or sheer self-absorption as their top priority. There was no political tract not autobiographical and no argument not ad hominem (or ad feminam); purity of motive had to be established before the merits of one's argument could be taken up. Ideally, the movement participant was "together," this connoting the alleged true self consolidated in a posture of revolt. This posture was sustained by many until 1970–71 when they "mellowed out."

New Humans

The most intense social movements and in particular those that eventuate through social transformations, which by convention are known as Great Revolutions,[1] invariably are associated with the confident assertion that in the light of history the revolution will ultimately be judged on the basis of a wholly new type of human being, collectively created in the context of antistructure, which it is bringing into existence: the Puritan saint, the French citizen of republican virtue, the new socialist man of the Russian Revolution, and more recent Chinese and Cuban claims to promote the creation of a more advanced socialist or communist humanity. In all such instances it has been maintained that the more highly evolved human type advances inextricably and simultaneously the welfare of the collectivity and the individual. This more highly evolved being is the collective idealized expression of disalienation and the "therapylike" intrapsychic effects of social-movement participation. Few are capable of exemplifying it or otherwise living up to it, for they have been molded, crippled, or contaminated by the psychic warpage induced by the old order, now understood from the radical-relativist and environmental-determinist perspective, as a Great Child Crippler. But surely one's children, enrolled in the Young Pioneers or reared on all things natural and organic or sent to Black Consciousness Academy, will attain heights that one cannot oneself contemplate or that perhaps resemble those spelled out by Trotsky: Genius on the order of that of Goethe or Shakespeare would be commonplace, "with further peaks envisioned beyond that." He took it for granted that the Russians would abandon vestiges of tsarist barbarism such as drinking or cursing.

The revolutionary ideal of the new human being, like disalienation and social-movement "therapy," ultimately fades out, for most of the former participants, in that the collective development of the human subject in the context of antistructure transcends the limits of what may be sustained upon the reimposition of "structure." Whether the upheaval has eventuated in social transformation, a change of political regime, mild concessions, or even nothing at all, the reimposition of structure is ultimately dictated by the need to ensure the continuity of the material reproduction of society to first of all guarantee the level of biological reproduction. Otherwise there would be mass privation by hunger, cold, disease, and so forth. This in turn dictates the production and continuity of the levels of political and cultural reproduction, whereby the animals are herded back into their cages—freshly painted ones, perhaps, but cages nevertheless—where they are coerced into "getting things done" while care is taken that these things make a modicum of sense to them while they are getting them done. On the side of the participants there is the sheer impossibility of living for prolonged periods in a state of nervous exhaustion possibly accompanied by extreme material privation and the perpetual threat of death in civil war. There comes a time to take it easy, relax, enjoy the fruits of the revolution or otherwise make one's peace, "cop out," "sell out," or "mellow out." The routine carrying on of everyday life has returned. Also, let us recall that Turner (1966) posited an innate or immanent human need for antistructure by way of complementing the structuralists' positing of a need for structure, that is, that the animal has a need for herd formations of determinate patterns or organization.

When structure is reimposed or reconsolidated, the human subject accordingly shrinks back into the limits dictated by the fact that, given the developments on the level of material reproduction that determine the relative magnitudes of appropriated, redistributed, and collectively consumed surplus, the development of certain human capacities is possible only in the context of exploitation (the cultivated refinement of those who do the civilization as opposed to the labor), cultural alienation (e.g., that art is that which is hung in museums and galleries, which are environments that only the wealthy feel comfortable in, and it is certainly not to be confused with what is painted on the exteriors of subway cars; or that music is what the wealthy pay to listen to and is not to be confused with what members of racial minorities play at deafening volume in the subway on enormous portable radios and in violation of the law), and domination (statecraft, generalship, and the managerial arts). In our lighter moments we have used the expression "the Law of the Destruction of Surplus Consciousness" to denote the post movement consequences upon both individual lives and the cultural ambience of the reconsolidation of structure.

In Gornick (1977), there is an oral history taken from an individual pseudonymized as "Ben Seligman." The latter is now retired from employment by reason of advanced age, though still an enthusiastic Communist. As a youth he had been reluctantly thrust into the trade of a garment cutter. He was a classic Jewish *schlemiel* type, and for his weakness was singled out for extra exploitation by his employer, who denied him normal wage increases. "Seligman" joined the Communist party in 1935 and by his own account was transformed into a veritable tiger of a class-conscious organizer and militant. Even during the less intense labor movement of 1946–48 he was capable of heights of exaltation: "We were thousands! We could have had the whole country!" But at the time of Gornick's interview he is once more the *schlemiel*, shuffling off dejectedly and haplessly to the picket line. Thus, also in the wake of the youth movement of the 1960s, many former participants ultimately found themselves in occupations and careers not unlike those that would have been their lot anyway. ("Some are mathematicians.") We are reminded of one individual who, when we met him in 1970, was an archetypal "freak"-radical of the period. In the early 1970s he studied radical history at the City College of New York while immersing himself in New York left circles. He took an interest in the "oral history" method, which in turn led him to radical anthropology and South America. Five years after that—early August 1979—we met him in Central Park. He was entering his second year of law school, which meant that he was following in his father's footsteps. "Ten years ago, could you have imagined that this would happen?" "No," he answered sheepishly. But there were others whose lives were and remain permanently changed and who have either been sustained by inner conviction and fortitude despite endless psychic pain and soul searching or have been involuntarily fixed in their changed condition by reason of having "dropped out" so far that they can no longer drop back in. ("Some are carpenters' wives.")

Soviet society, having abandoned the ideal of the new socialist man along with the ideal of a noncoercive state operated by the mass participation of the "broad masses" directly in the work of the Soviet organs, has reproduced a state apparatus that in its crude, authoritarian centralism is much in the tradition of tsarism, as well as a stifling cultural atmosphere reminiscent of the Old Regime; this allows, of course, for the modernization of appearances, e.g., in that Soviet policemen do not carry whips. The regime and the surplus-absorbing strata who comprise its principal beneficiaries presuppose for their existence a passive and alcoholic working class whose indulgence in the latter vestige of barbarism would exceed even the worst fears of so harsh a critic of 1930s Soviet society as Trotsky were he alive to see it. The Soviets regard efforts of Cubans to create a new human being emancipated from the need for "material incentives" (this is by now pretty much in abeyance) with a mixture of amusement at such adolescent romanticism and a touch of nostalgia: Richard Barnet, in *The Giants*, recounts the story of a Soviet diplomat who, informed that the Cubans were voluntarily organizing unpaid clean-up brigades, was said to have sadly remarked, "It was the same here years ago." The same sort of doings on the part of the Chinese have if anything aroused fear and loathing in the Soviets.

The withering of the new human ideal in a social movement is always most bitter among those who had been intellectuals once preoccupied with articulating this very ideal. The cultural movement following the Revolution of 1905 among the youth of the intelligentsia known as Saninism (cf. Bertram Wolfe, 1964), whose principal features involved preoccupations—often simultaneous—with eroticism and suicide, for which reason we have characterized it in terms of postmovement adaptation No. 2, "Dissipation," was rather precisely reproduced following the spectacular suicide in 1925 of the poet Sergei Esenin (best known in the United States as the movie lover of Isadora Duncan in

Isadora) whose amorous and alcoholic proclivities were as well-known to the Soviet public as his poetry. There ensued the cultural movement among the younger intelligentsia called the Eseninshchina, which involved a wave of suicides and a preoccupation with the erotic remarkably evocative of Saninism.[2] The culmination of the Eseninshchina was a succession of scandals involving members and even executives of the Communist Youth League (Komsomol), who were found to have been flagrantly involved in spectacular "sexual debauchery," usually drunken orgies. At their 1926 convention, the Komsomol were scolded by one of the luminaries of Soviet literary criticism:

> Polonsky, Editor of *Novy Mir*, to Komsomol Congress, 1926: There is little respect for man because there is little respect for oneself. There is no will-power, no desire to create a good strong type of new man; . . . even the Komsomol does not breed the kind of man who could serve as a model. In our time, when it is said that the quality of shoes, galoshes and other manufactured goods must be improved, *we must first of all improve the quality of socialist man*. [Carr, 1976:179]

Conclusion

As dissidents engage in conflict with their dominators, the experience of the conflict alters their conscious awareness of the nature of the social order and the social meanings within it. This we have referred to as the reinterpretation of social reality. As social reality is reinterpreted, new implications for personal identity are realized as members of dissident collectivities *self-consciously act* in their collective interests. The mere fact that one acts rather than passively accepts one's life situation is bound to have purgative effects on the individual's identity. As identity cannot be separated from social structure (Berger and Luckman, 1966, called it "objectivation") when society evidences the appearance of the forcible assertion of antistructure, the identities of those involved in the struggle are necessarily changed as they are now members of self-acting collectivities. It is in this sense that the limits of human consciousness are the products of history.

Within dissident collectivities, the reinterpretation of social reality and the process of disalienation form a totalization, in that it becomes impossible for one to occur without the presence of the other. They fuse into a dialectical synthesis, with each positing the other as its presupposition. That is, the reinterpretation of social reality cannot occur without having implications for the position an individual occupies within a set of social relations; especially when they are presently under attack by oneself and others, including other dissident collectivities. Moreover, it would be impossible for one to learn new understandings of onself without it having consequences for the understanding of the social relations in which one was engaged—especially if those relations were undergoing transformation.

As we have pointed out, social movement collectivities necessarily undergo processes of collegialization. They also tend to manifest a "cascadation" process, whereby dissidence penetrates downward in the social order. The consequences of these processes are twofold: upward mobility for the more talented of the lower orders and the healing of psychic maladies, such as the lack of self-esteem, which were the consequence of membership in dominated social categories. As social movement members participate in unalienated learning, engage in self-governance, and struggle against their subjugation, they participate in mass therapy, helping each other overcome the crippling effects of their socialization to positions of subordination within the social order. This very process liberates new human potentialities, which, in the following period of social quiescence, are alienated from their possessors and incorporated into new forms of alienation at a higher level of contradiction. Within social movement periods, however, capacities are disalienated faster than they are realienated.

As new human capacities are liberated, images of "new humans" are proffered within dissident collectivities. These images are the idealization of the aspirations of the members of dissident collectivities: more intelligent, egalitarian, humanized, aware, and sensitive than the enemy and even themselves. As the movement fades into the past and the possibility of the achievement of these new capacities in their unalienated form declines, social structure is reasserted. Dissidents are then faced with the prospect of abandoning the idealized image and accepting something less, nothing at all, or punishment for former sins. This necessitates the (often forceful) alienation of those capacities cultivated within the social movement that had been incorporated into the self. Such realienation is a painful process, often requiring authoritarian organizations to impose a harsher and more rigorous control over a former dissident's life than necessary in conventional society. Those for whom the pain is overwhelming, consciousness obliteration becomes an alternative through suicide, use of drugs of consciousness contraction (e.g., heroin, alcohol), or engaging in mindless hedonism.

Notes

1. There is of course an element of racist myopia in the characterization of Great Revolutions: That Oliver Cromwell defeated Charles I is familiar to schoolchildren in Nigeria and India, whereas the feat of his contemporary Li Zecheng in overthrowing the Ming in 1644 is not. The White Lotus rebellion, contemporaneous with the French Revolution, for similar reasons did not "make history" except locally. The Taiping Rebellion, contemporaneous with the U.S. Civil War, was unknown except to specialists in the United States (despite it having been the bloodiest revolutionary struggle of the nineteenth century, if not of all times) until China became a focus of fear and secondarily of admiration in this country.

We should also remind the reader at this point that social movements—even spectacular and cataclysmic upheavals such as the Taiping Rebellion—may leave little trace on the social order without eventuating in social transformation except provisionally prior to their suppression. Contrarily, vast and sweeping social transformations may be carried through, say, by the combined action of the exploiting class and the political regime without the presence of or even in opposition to a social movement, e.g., the eighteenth-century English enclosures and 1930s Soviet industrialization and collectivization.

2. The Soviet Union may be said to have entered a postmovement period following about 1923. The political aspects of this, including the stiffening of authoritarian control and discipline within the party and the Soviets; the economic, including the conciliation of the peasantry and the enforcement of stricter discipline in the factories; and the

diplomatic, including a more conciliatory foreign policy and the enforcement of strict discipline within the foreign Communist parties and their subordination in like manner to the Communist International, which together constituted "Bolshevization," are described at great length in Carr (1971).

Chapter 7

Social Movements Versus Political Violence and Mobilization

Now that the theory of the natural history of social movements has been fully elaborated, we can turn our attention to issues raised previously, but which could only be developed further after gaining familiarity with the perspective presented in the previous three chapters. There are two issues to be taken up in this chapter in relation to social movements: First, what are the relative theoretical benefits of the social-movement perpective to the use of the concept of "political violence"? Second is the problem of "mobilization" in reference to social movements and revolutions. Our efforts will be directed at demonstrating how the social-movement perspective rids the field of confusions that are inherent in such conceptualizations. In addition, as we concern ourselves with the problem of mobilization, we will take up issues related to revolutions and the maintenance of the state.

Before proceeding to the subject matter at hand, we would like to point out that the confusions that have existed in the fields of collective behavior, social movements, and political sociology are related to the overlapping definitions of seemingly similar phenomena. Conceptualization of social-movement phenomena has been most problematic because of the overly inclusive definitions proffered from within the field. Such terminology as "collective action," "political violence," and "resource mobilization" has been erected in its stead as a result.

Political Violence

We must insist most emphatically on the point that "social movements," as defined herein, should not be confused with the currently popular term "political violence" (see, e.g., Gurr, 1970; Laquer, 1977). "Social movements" and "political violence" comprehend overlapping domains. In the first place, though an indispensable defining characteristic of a social movement is social conflict involving the use of force by dissidents, such force is, as noted elsewhere, not necessarily violent, especially in the early stages of social-movement development. A brief consideration of two of the most tremendous popular upheavals of recent years should suffice to drive the point home. The 1968 "Events of May" in France began with occupations of university buildings in Paris in imitation of the U.S. model (the immediate precedent having been the occupation of five buildings at Columbia University, New York City, in April) by "students," i.e., candidate members of the bourgeoisie. The Gaullist regime retaliated by closing the University of Paris (including the Nanterre campus, where the trouble began, and subsequently the Sorbonne, the main campus, whose students had sided with those of Nanterre) and arresting some students. This led to street clashes of a strictly symbolic character—involving barricades, a Parisian tradition since 1588, and weaponry limited to paving stones and truncheons—between students and the Republican Security Companies (CRS, the Gaullist riot police). The political importance of the street clashes in fact derived from their character as media events. Coverage of the rioting, in particular that of May 11–12, had an impact upon affluent and politically connected French "public opinion"—obviously greatest on parents of participants, especially those beaten or arrested—not unlike that of the Chicago "police riot" of August 1968 upon well-heeled liberals in the United States. On May 12, the regime, as a consequence of its own *retaliatory* violence, announced seemingly prudent concessions to student demands, including the release of those arrested. The immediate reaction of the French working class, however, was outrage and *competitive insubordination:* Here were the pampered and spoiled children of capitalists and career bureaucrats getting away with goings-on that, had they been perpetrated by mere workers, would surely have been punished with the sternest repression; this was not to be tolerated. As the sociologist Gilbert Mury (1969) put it, the student movement was "the detonator" and the workers' movement was "the bomb." But the latter was a most peculiar bomb in that it went off without any direct instigation from the detonator or any awareness on the part of the latter that the bomb existed. Specifically, the "bomb" went off on May 13 with the occupation of a state-owned aircraft factory in remote Brittany by workers who had no contact with the action in Paris or any other center of student radicalism. By late May, 10 million workers were on strike and over 3,000 factories were occupied by their employees, surpassing all previous records for general strikes (e.g., Belgium, 1912; England, 1926; France, 1936) in terms of the percentage of factory workers participating, percentage of factories occupied, and extent of economic disruption. In accordance with the Law of Emergent Contradiction, protests and disruptions began to appear among farmers, civil servants, junior executives, entertainers, police (some of whom vowed to refrain from attacking workers, though students were still fair game), and fishermen (who flew the red flag on their boats in Marseilles harbor). Yet in all this social upheaval there was only one death attributable to action by dissidents (a police official in Grenoble accidentally killed by a wagon load of debris rolled down a street by students) and remarkably little destruction of state or private property outside Paris (where cars were overturned to blockade streets and other handy objects cannibalized for barricades; an attempt to burn the Stock Exchange in late May failed).

The other instance, the events leading up to the Iranian Revolution, is even more instructive. Sustained conflict began in November 1977 with demonstrations by the secular opposition in Tehran and by the religious opposition in

Qum. These were of course illegal but in no sense violent. The regime responded with summary massacres of participants; the unofficial figures for the death toll in the Tehran massacre are given in the hundreds and range up to 1,000. (The official figure, twelve, is ludicrously low.) The rhythm of demonstrations was thereby set: Each massacre, by tradition, called for a forty-day mourning period to be observed by processions in the streets in honor of the slain. Whether or not these were sanctioned by the regime, further massacres inevitably occurred. Traditional Shi'ite Islamic days of mourning, which crowd the calendar, also require processions through the streets, and these were forbidden by the regime only at the risk of charges of the gravest impiety. Martyrdom was courted by unarmed demonstrators. During the events leading up to the insurrection of February 9–11, 1979, the correspondent of the *Economist* (February 3, 1979) oberved a youth dip his hands into the blood of a victim shot dead in the street and hurl himself screaming at the troops. The total number of unarmed victims slaughtered in this fashion or in the shah's prisons by SAVAK—the secret service, ranked by former CIA executive John R. Stockwell as, along with the South Korean KCIA, the "deadliest" of its kind in the world; (cf. *In Search of Enemies*)—has been variously estimated from 10,000 to 30,000, with the latter figure officially adopted by the Khomeini-Bazargan regime. Although it is true that a wave of arson, looting, and assassination attended the collapse of the old order from December 1978 to February 1979, this never aproached the level of violence committed by the state apparatus under the orders of the shah and his immediate successor, Bakhtiar. The worst atrocity attributed to dissidents, the Isfahan theater fire of August 1978, in which 477 were killed, was subsequently attributed by the Khomeini-Bazargan regime—according to captured files—to a SAVAK major alleged to have set the fire as a provocation intended to discredit the clergy. (To be fair, we must point out that the alleged perpetrator was shot after a secret trial.) In any case, as the avowed revolutionary organizations had either been domesticated by the shah's regime (e.g., Tudeh, the Iranian Communist party, whose organizational talents were put to use by the shah in the management of the oil industry in a fashion reminiscent of Batista's shrewd dealings with the Cuban Communists) or rendered innocuous by SAVAK (cf. Halliday, 1978). The February 1979 insurrection would scarcely have been possible without the mutiny of part of the armed forces and the passivity of the rest (excepting only the Imperial Guard) in a fashion closely paralleling the events of March 8-13, 1917, in Russia.

In the second place, the usage of the expression "political violence," notably by Gurr, is susceptible to vulgarization to the extent that, according to the latter,

> The concept subsumes revolution, ordinarily defined as fundamental sociopolitical change accomplished through violence. It also includes guerilla wars, coups d'etat, rebellions, and riots. . . . The properties and processes that distinguish a riot from a revolution are substantively and theoretically interesting, and are examined at length in this study, but at a general level of analysis they seem to be differences of degree, not kind. (Gurr, 1970:4–5)

One error in the preceding may be quickly disposed of: Riots, like strikes, may represent episodic dissidence; that is, routine and highly specific forms of social conflict that should they occur in the overall context of a period of social quiescence, are not susceptible to further development as to either the intensity of conflict or the grievances in dispute. George Rude, in *The Crowd in History* (a book cited by Gurr, 1970:6n), pointed out that in eighteenth-century Europe urban riots were quite predictable when the price of grain rose above a certain level regarded locally as traditional; in such eventualities the state would normally take steps to lower the price by decree, subsidy, drawing upon reserves, or importing additional supplies.

There is a species of riot—we might call it the "celebratory riot"—that does not involve a social-conflict intent at all, but rather marks the onset of the New Year, the end of a major war, or the eve or victorious conclusion of football or hockey games in certain cities. (The dangerous condition of the streets of either Austin, Texas, or Norman, Oklahoma, on the night before the annual Sooners-Longhorns game is well known.) These events are commonly replete with drunken brawls and rapes; arson and looting are not unknown but are treated indulgently by the guardians of property. (Nevertheless, the fact that the predictable fisticuffs between partisans of the Greens and the Blues at the chariot races in the Hippodrome at Constantinople did not materialize such that fans of both coalesced into the entirely unpredicted Nika insurrection, A.D. 532, must find its explanation in our "natural history" approach to social movements.) Yet the celebratory riot has in common with episodic dissidence of all kinds its predictability, absence of developmental possibilities, and the comparative lack of significance with which it is treated by both participants and custodians of order. Therefore, though there may be some truth in an assertion to the effect that a social movement that eventuates in revolution differs in degree, not kind, from one that does not, it is yet more truthful to assert that a riot that occurs in the context of a period of social quiescence differs in kind, but not in degree, from one that occurs in a period of ongoing social movement development. A riot that occurs in the context of social quiescence differs in degree, but not in kind, from the routine shootings and stabbings at Mardi Gras time.

Let us proceed to consider coups d'etat. As noted earlier, the professional military in any state-type polity—whether Zulu impi, Roman legions, or the officers and "lifers" of the United States Army—constitute a distinct status group physically and culturally segregated from the civilian population. This status group is itself subdivided into numerous hierarchical gradations of formal status, which themselves mask contradictions of interest and outlook among various groupings such as functional formations (i.e., service arms), the High Command and its privileged staff, ambitious career officers, junior officers, noncoms or "lifers," and conscripts.[1]

Consequently, one may identify a military coup with a social movement only under two circumstances: The first comprises those instances in which the whole military acts qua status group to impose its rule upon society as a whole, especially if in so doing it forces the hand of a reluctant High Command. Coups of this sort presuppose a soldiery ethnically or ideologically distinct from the mass of the population and even from the exploiting class itself; they are, accordingly, typical of states and empires antedating the emergence of the "national army" in modern times (e.g., the Roman Empire, where the legionnaires adopted a distinctive religion, Mithraism, and on several occasions coerced genuinely reluctant commanders to make bids for power; similarly in the Byzantine Empire, Armenian and Isaurian troops twice thrust to power generals who adhered to the iconoclast heresy to the outrage of the ethnically Greek exploiting class; also in the Abbasid and Fatimid caliphates where ethnic Turkish soldiers ruled through shadowy "legitimate" monarchs). The second, previously discussed, comprises instances wherein simmering social conflict in society as a whole is effectively stifled by a despotic regime, yet is reproduced in the guise of sharpened contradictions among interest groupings within the military.

Generally speaking, military coups either have nothing to do with social movements at all or are expressions of counterdissidence carried out by the High Command or ambitious career officers disturbed by the inability of the preceding regime in maintaining "order." Coups of the former type represent the normal type of change of government wherever peripheral capitalism prevails; no more social significance should be attached to coups in such countries than to elections in those of the capitalist core: Orders are given, the troops obey, and Lieutenant General Tweedledum is ousted by Major General Tweedledee who, having promoted himself, institutes policies of minor substantive difference from those of his predecessor; the outs are nevertheless now in, whereas the former ins are now out of the country plotting their return. For example, in 1975, a dispute arose in Ecuador over petroleum policy; the country thereupon held a coup rather than an election.[2]

The paradigmatic case of the military coup is probably Bolivia, which has averaged at least one violent change of government per year during its history as an independent state. Nearly all of these changes were coups of little if any social-conflict significance or were—like the two coups in 1978—of counterdissident intent. The one noteworthy exception was the regime of Victor Paz Estenssoro, president and leader of a radical-populist party, the Popular Revolutionary Movement (MRP), which came to power following uprisings by peasants, tin miners, and part of the army.

Our contention that the coup d'etat is merely the normal form of change of government in the peripheral capitalist countries is fortified by the trend away from absolute monarchies (North Yemen, Birundi, Thailand, Egypt, Iraq, Afganistan, Libya, and probably Morocco) and civilian autocracies installed under other than social-revolutionary conditions (Indonesia, Zaire, Uganda, Benin, Brazzaville Congo, Nigeria, Ghana, Sudan, Central African Republic/Empire, Chad, Syria, Algeria, Comoros, Mauretania, Pakistan, Bangladesh) and toward straightforward military rule.[3] There is a telltale pervasive tendency for military expenditure to rise faster than per capita income throughout the peripheral capitalist world, where few countries can afford to fight any enemy except their own civilian populations without foreign subsidy and even internal security is sustained by lavish military aid in many cases. (The 1978–79 war between Tanzania and Uganda cost the former over $250 million—approximately the box office gross from *Star Wars* or less than a quarter of what is spent in the U.S. on pet food annually—leaving Tanzania broke and Uganda picked clean by troops of both sides. (cf. *Time*, June 25, 1979; cost figure attributed to President Nyerere of Tanzania).

Let us turn now to guerrilla warfare and terrorism. The difference between the two in contemporary usage is frequently dependent on the perspective of the speaker, as in the former Zimbabwe-Rhodesia, where the forces of the Patriotic Front—an uneasy coalition of the Zimbabwe African National Liberation Army, led by Robert Mugabe, a Marxist-Leninist based in Mozambique, a country of similar political coloration; and the Zimbabwe Internal People's Liberation Army, led by Joshua Nkomo, whose politics are less distinct and whose base was in pro-Western Zambia—were called "terrorists" ("terrs" for short) by the Salisbury regime and "guerrillas" by everyone else. The Reagan administration has been accusing the Russians of sponsoring "terrorism" around the globe, especially in El Salvador, where an ill-equipped left-oriented guerrilla force is resisting the junta. The Russian involvement in El Salvador consists primarily of a visit by a leader of one of the guerrilla armies to Moscow on a mission to acquire weapons. The only hard evidence of Russian-sponsored terrorism in El Salvador was a free trip to Vietnam for the weapons procurer.

This confusion of nomenclature is nothing new, and has sound empirical foundation: Guerrilla rebels who are abetted and succored by the mass of the population, from which they also recruit, unquestionably represent ongoing social movements; this has been true for millennia. A "war of national liberation" was led by the Maccabees (or Hashmoneans) against the Seleucid Empire from 166 B.C., when a spontaneous revolt broke out under Matathias, priest of the village of Modin, and his five sons, until 131 B.C. when Simon—the only survivor of the five sons—secured the recognition of his sovereignty (actually as a protectorate of the Roman republic). Guerrilla war, likewise, has been a traditional recourse of exploited masses against homegrown tyrannous regimes for many centuries, especially in the Far East: The first all-China peasant war began about the time of the death of the First Emperor (Shih Huang Ti, who had completed the unification of the country and founded the Chin dynasty in 221 B.C.), 210 B.C. Liu Bang (or Liu Ji), a rich peasant turned petty official, fearing execution because the slave laborers in his charge whom he was conducting to the Great Wall for construction work had escaped, himself fled and raised a rebel army. He then proclaimed himself king of Han; having overthrown the Chin in 207 B.C., he triumphed in a civil war against Xiang Yu, a representative of the old feudal nobility (whose reign the First Emperor had sought to encompass through the establishment of a rigorous bureaucratic administration throughout the country), he founded the Han dynasty (202 B.C.). Other spectacular peasant wars included those that led to the rise of the Ming dynasty (1368) and its fall (1644), as well as the Taiping (Heavenly Kingdom of Great Peace) rebellion (1850–64), suppressed with the aid of Anglo-French intervention. Vietnamese, too, waged peasant wars against Chinese occupiers and indigenous rulers prior to the advent of the Western colonialists. In medieval Europe a problem arises in the identification of guerrilla qua guerrillas, in that the latter are defined in contradistinction to "soldiers" (the word guerrilla derives from the Spanish for "little war")—merceneries or conscripts in the service of a territorial state—and consequently loses a certain applicability in feudal polities where the state is mostly notional; there is a sense in which "feudalism" is merely guerrilla war formalized and legalized. The line was, however, drawn between the petty wars of nobles and knights, which were respectable, and those of peasants and "outlaws," which were not.[4] With the resurgence of territorial states, large-scale peasant wars became a feature of political life—however temporarily—in the fourteenth and fifteenth centuries. Guerrilla wars, in something approaching the modern sense of the term, however, became "traditional" expressions of political strife in modern times (that is, after circa 1550–1600) primarily in Spain, eastern Europe, and Latin America. As in China, regimes threatened by such insurgencies called them bandits and brigands much as their contemporary counterparts call them terrorists.

Eric Hobsbawm, in *Primitive Rebels,* points out the incapacity of the states of southern and eastern Europe even in the nineteenth and early twentieth centuries to suppress brigandage and banditry in remote and inaccessible regions or even in rural areas generally. Banditry, as an obvious recourse for the poverty-stricken and desperate, was hence endemic and there arose in all such places the social type that Hobsbawm calls the "social bandit," who took from the rich and gave to the poor not necessarily from altruism but always from necessity: The rich had what there was to be stolen and the poor could hide, protect, lie to the gendarmerie, and occasionally join up. (This is hardly to say that bandits did not steal from the poor or that the latter did not betray the bandits.)

In places as far apart as China (where guerrilla rebels were depicted living a banditlike existence in the classic novel *Romance of the Three Kingdoms,* set in the third century A.D. but written much later) and Mexico, bandits were drawn into guerrilla armies during major social upheavals; their enemies correspondingly disparaged them as mere "bandits" until quite recent times: In the 1930s the Guomintang army waged four major campaigns against the Communist forces of the Jianxi Soviet under Mao Zedong; these involved hundreds of thousands of regular troops, artillery, field fortifications, and dive-bombers, yet were euphemistically called "bandit-suppression campaigns." The Mexican revolutionary General Francisco ("Pancho") Villa, was beaten in 1914–15 by the U.S.-supported forces of General Obregon. Reverting to guerrilla tactics, he sought to use a Chicano-populated area north of the border in New Mexico as a refuge and staging area, but his forces were pursued into Mexico and destroyed by the U.S. Army under General "Black Jack" (a sobriquet denoting the segregated Black troops under his command) Pershing; the latter is still celebrated in U.S. high school history texts as victor over the "bandit" Villa.

Having established that guerrilla warfare and terrorism (or social banditry) are frequent expressions of social movements, we must now declare that this association is *not necessary and in most cases does not exist.* Guerrillas or terrorists today, for example, have several possible relationships to social movements: (1) those who intend to instigate collective dissidence through exemplary action; (2) those who represent "encapsulated" (see "Postmovement Adaptation Illusions," Chapter 5) vestiges of social movements; (3) those who carry on "armed struggle," which at least a substantial minority of the population actively supports or identifies itself with; (4) those in the pay of foreign states for the purpose of subverting or "destabilizing" the countries in which they operate; (5) those who operate on foreign soil for the purpose of seeking publicity against regimes in their homelands where they may have no support or are even unheard of; and (6) those who operate against genuinely unpopular regimes and claim to act on behalf of the mass of the population although the latter actively favors none of the visible contestants for power. These categories do not have precise boundaries: The IRA, for instance, has endured for decades, i.e., through long periods of social quiescence, and shifting from encapsulation to waging a

VIOLENCE AND MOBILIZATION/115

supported struggle—or even from instigators through encapsulation to armed struggle with support in the populace—during social-movement periods; the latter leave traces on the organization in the form of splits along generational lines as between the "officials" and the "provisionals." The same may be said of the Russian Narodniki (populists, from *narodnaya volya*, meaning "will of the people"). These had genuine popular support during their terrorist campaign of the 1870s among the urban intelligentsia (though none among the peasant masses upon whom they rested their hopes). In 1878, Vera Zazulich shot and wounded the governor-general of Saint Petersburg; when tried she was acquitted by the jury and rescued by a friendly crowd before the police could rearrest her. The organization barely succeeded in assassinating Tsar Alexander II (1881) before the definitive police crackdown. The feeble effort of 1886, in which Alexander Ulyanov (Lenin's elder brother) was hanged, elicited no popular response. The exploits of the Fighting Organization of the Socialist Revolutionary party (SR), doctrinally the heir of the 1870s Narodniki, both preceded and survived the social movement of 1904–1907, which is known to history of the Revolution of 1905.[5]

To conclude: "Political violence" and "social movements" are cross-cutting concepts. Most forms of political violence listed by Gurr can—as we believe we have demonstrated—occur either in the context of social movements or outside them. We have, by the way, refrained hitherto from citing Gurr's definition of political violence, since in this Gurr unwittingly supplies the clincher, as this definition is so vague that one cannot legitimately exclude from its wording even the most routine criticism of a constitutionally elected government by a "loyal opposition":

> In this study political violence refers to all collective attacks within a political community against the political regime, its actors—including competing political groups as well as incumbents—or its policies. The concept represents a set of events, a common property of which is the actual or threatened use of violence, but the explanation is not limited to that property. [1973:3-4]

Does this definition cover, say, situations at election time wherein "liberals" criticize "conservatives" for (1) excessive use of violence against a common enemy; (2) failure to use violence against a common enemy; (3) sanctioning the use of violence by a third group against a fourth group; (4) failure to prevent a third group from using violence against a fourth group; (5) scheming and plotting to use violence without regard for due process of law (e.g., Watergate); (6) pursuing a misguided policy that eventuated in the use of violence unanticipated when the policy was formulated, etc.? One can hardly imagine an election campaign, even in territorial subdivisions (states or provinces, counties, cities), without issues of this sort.

Gurr has called his book *Why Men Rebel*; this does indicate some concern for "social movements" as the object of analysis. Yet the unit of analysis is a sequence of events leading to an act or acts of "political violence," as we have seen, an evidently inapplicable concept. Why? Perhaps because acts of political violence are quantifiable, at least in principle, whereas whole realms of the study of social movements, for example, "the reinterpretation of social reality," are not (e.g., you can't ask people to tell you what they don't know that they know). Quantifiability (at least in principle), even if it explains little or nothing, still affords the authentic look of real simulated science; it is serious. Small wonder Gurr's work on this book was supported by at least three federal agencies and at least three major universities; and that it received the official sanction of organized social science: the Woodrow Wilson Foundation Award for 1970 from the political science profession and a rave review in the *New York Times* by Lewis Coser, president for 1974–75 of the American Sociological Association.

Mobilization

It was not against centralized power that we fought, but in whose hands
it was.
—Member of Parliament, 1653

In social contexts and historical epochs that predispose social movements to formal-organizational cohesion, the military metaphor mobilization fails to distinguish between a mobilization effected by a mass or vanguard dissident (or counterdissident) organization engaged in the contest for power or by a revolutionary dictatorship defending a social order. In the latter case social relations have been newly transformed by revolutionary upheaval against counterdissidence within and interventionist powers without, which are expressions of social movements; and a mobilization effected by a totalitarian apparatus, which is not. That such confusion should exist is hardly surprising in that the objective of the totalitarian apparatus is the simulation of the appearances and ambience of a social movement and the perpetuation of the same indefinitely. The elucidation of this distinction, particularly that between the revolutionary dictatorship and the totalitarian apparatus, requires a digression.

As stated or implied in various places in Chapter 3, "The Reproduction of Social Privilege," the polity (which may be of the state or the feudal type; for purposes of brevity we shall henceforth exclude the latter and simply refer to the "state") in class society guarantees (1) the political reproduction of society by (forcibly) ensuring its own reproduction and that of despotic and patriarchal authority relations in society as a whole. For this purpose the use and possession of the means of violence (but not the effective means of violence) are sanctioned within the household (the *patria potestas* and its variations) and without (by slave overseers, night watchmen, "respectable" citizens permitted to own guns for fear of plunder by the lower orders or as hobbyists, aristocrats as badges of status, and so forth; or on a semiauthorized basis by mafiosi and their Japanese counterparts, the yakuza; the Ku Klux Klan in the United States or the pre-1971 Union of the Russian People, commonly known as "Black Hundreds"; and latterly in capitalist core countries by union goons to enforce discipline upon wildcatters, rank-and-file dissidents, and other troublemakers who threaten mutually advantageous union-management relations). (2) The state also guarantees exploitative relations on the level of material reproduction. It ensures that the normal level of cultural reproduction itself does not threaten the reproduction of the hegemonic ideology whether in a specific doctrinal form (the burning of heretics "relaxed to the secular arm"; or latterly the persecution or "reeducation" of deviationists, Trotskyites, Zinovievist wreckers, Bukhar-inists, Titoists, revisionists, social chauvinists, hegemonists, or "Zionists," also called "rootless cosmopolitans") or as commonsensically understood in society at large. In the latter version, the action of the state—whether effected by prior restraint, suppression, or awareness of the likelihood of these measures, i.e., the "chilling effect"—is commonly called "censorship." The absence of censorship is indicative of the utter innocuousness of overt assaults upon the hegemonic ideology and the absence of subversive implications as stimulants to collective action. The deliberate liquidation by the bourgeoisie of the heg-emonic ideology as found on the level of cultural reproduction for sound business reasons (although its reproduction continues in fragmentary form due to the effects of structure in generating "the normative power of facticity") and the repositing of the censorship function wholly in such extrastate devices as the market mechanism or the academic "tenure" system are also indicative of the inability of subversive implications to stimulate collective action. All systems of censorship break down when they are most "needed," that is, under con-ditions of such intense dissidence that the capacity of the state to deploy the means of ideological supervision has utterly broken down or when efforts at censorship lead to consequences precisely opposite to those intended. A no-torious recent instance of the latter was the assassination in early 1978 of the publisher of the only anti-Somoza newspaper in Nicaragua, Pedro Joauqin Chamorro; this crime set off the chain of events that led to the overthrow of Somoza in July 1979 by rebels far more radical than the bourgeois clique represented by Chamorro. In earlier periods, it is well known that, prior to the English and French revolutions, for example, official censorship was either ludicrously ineffectual or was more trouble than it was worth, for example, when, in 1637, the ears of three heretical Puritan writers were publicly cut off, this instigating far more outrage and opposition to the regime than it instilled fear in the opposition.

It is a commonplace of political sociology, perhaps dating back to Niccolo Machiavelli and certinly to Alexis de Tocqueville—it is certainly restated by Gurr (1970) and Oberschall (1973)—that revolutions, in particular those pro-ceeding to the transformation of social relations, are associated with the over-throw of political regimes understood—rightly or wrongly—as incompetent, socially and politically isolated, lacking the means of violence adequate to the suppression of intense collective dissidence, or irresolute in the means of violence actually at their disposal. Substantially the same effect, as in Iran, may be induced by appeals to the alienated supernatural for succor against a regime ostensibly armed to the teeth, manifestly prepared to slaughter unarmed civilians by the tens of thousands, and self-confident by reasons of the long-standing passive compliance of the mass of the population. Where the trans-formation of social relations eventuates from the overthow of such a regime this presupposes the destruction of the whole state apparatus, which in recent centuries has occurred in only two ways: that of the *classic revolution*, sometimes called "the revolutionary process"; and that of the *protracted war*. The first type includes Bohemia during the Hussite War (1419–33), the English or Puritan Revolution (1640–49), the French Revolution (1789–94), and the Ira-nian Revolution (1979–81). The second type most prominently includes the revolutions in this century in Yugoslavia, Albania, China, Vietnam, Cambodia,

Cuba, Algeria, and Mozambique. Mexico (1910–14) and Nicaragua (1978–79) combined elements of both types idiosyncratically.

In the classic type, the principal political events take place in the capital city, which may be hypertrophied with respect to lesser towns and the countryside (London in 1640) or the nerve center of an administrative apparatus long accustomed to despotic sway over the countryside as well as the locus of cultural and intellectual activity (Paris, Saint Petersburg/Petrograd), or both. The initial overthrow of the regime, or its reduction to political impotence due to popular insurrection or the threat of it, unleashes a wave of collegialization everywhere, usually with the participation or even the numerical dominance of classes or strata previously debarred by law or custom from holding any official post. Events in the countryside may give impetus to this: In 1789, the fall of the Bastille on July 14 set off (or in places was contemporaneous with) a mass panic with admixtures of peasant revolt; the peasants of one village, hearing rumors of "brigands" in the service of the aristocracy, charged off pell-mell so that their approach would be taken in the next village as that of the brigands; in "retribution" the peasants would here and there burn chateaux or otherwise destroy manorial rolls listing feudal dues they owed to their lords (cf. Lefebvre, 1973). This effectively demolished the state administration in the countryside and induced or even compelled the bourgeoisie in each town to supplant the royal officials with improvised administrations and armed forces to teach the peasants respect for private property. In Russia in 1917, a crescendo of rural riots and full-scale peasant uprisings (following the precedent of 1905–1907, as was true of the movement in the cities) likewise reduced to impotence the internal security forces at the disposal of the provisional government.

The initial period of collegialization is often characterized by celebratory euphoria masking potential disunity not yet actualized in keeping with the Law of Emergent Contradiction; and the falsity of the sense of security corresponding to the faith that liberty is at hand, which has not yet been dispelled by the awareness of the absence of organized coercive force capable of defining a revolution whose precise content has not yet been settled. Effective power is in the hands of bodies improvised on the spot: committees of correspondence, patriotic societies, political clubs, county committees (England), communes (France), soviets (councils in Russia), komitehs (Islamic revolutionary committees in Iran). Most important of these are always the bodies that control the streets of the capital itself: Committee of Public Safety (London); Paris Commune; Petrograd Soviet, superseded by the Central Executive Committee of the All-Russian Congress of Society; Islamic Revolutionary Council (Tehran; moved to Holy City of Qum, retaining overall hegemony over komitehs). Provisional revolutionary authorities, such as those of Parliament in England; the Constituent Assembly, Legislative Assembly, and the Girondins in France; and the provisional governments of Russia and Iran, must govern with the consent of these bodies or must take them into account in public declarations of policy while pursuing other policies covertly. (The latter, when exposed, are invariably characterized as "betrayal of the revolution" and "high treason.")

This situation necessarily prevails because collegialization has pervaded the armed forces: In 1639, the army raised by Charles I to fight the rebellious Scots simply broke up. The French army in 1789 was of such dubious loyalty following the attempted coup against the Constituent Assembly that it was patently useless against the rebellious Paris populace; the mere rumor of the approach of foreign mercenaries to the city incited the Parisians on July 12 to plunder military stockpiles, loot gun shops, and—two days later—storm the Bastille. Following these events, soldiers mutinied in various places, refusing to obey the aristocrats—who monopolized the officer corps excepting the artillery arm—and assassinating them. The new National Guard, wherein officers were elected (as they were in new volunteer units sent into battle in 1792), was under the control of the commune in each municipality, most important that of Paris. In Russia the Petrograd Insurrection (March 8–13) succeeded thanks to the fraternization of mutinous troops with the masses in the streets. Mutiny became institutionalized almost immediately when the Petrograd Soviet of Workers' and Soldiers' Deputies issued Order Number 1, which abolished the death penalty in the army and provided for committees of soldiers in each unit to ratify officers' commands, World War I not withstanding. In Iran the crumbling relations between conscripts and officers prior to the flight of the shah (January 19, 1979), which had been punctuated by assassinations, small-scale mutinies, summary executions, and barracks massacres, continued to deteriorate during the following three weeks. On Febraury 9 the Homofars, noncommissioned air force technicians, mutinied and, for their own protection against the fanatically monarchist Javidan Guards, threw open the weapons stockpile at their base to all takers, among whom guerrillas of the Mujaheddin (Warriors of the Holy War) and Khalq-e-Fedayin (People's Suicide Commandos) were especially eager. The rebels repeated the scene at other military bases around Tehran until small arms were distributed in such superfluity that a weapon was unwittingly issued to a supporter of the incumbent Prime Minister Bakhtiar, no questions asked (*Economist*, February, 1979). With the defeat of the Javidan Guards and the completion of the conquest of the capital, the Islamic Revolutionary Council ordered the return of the distributed weapons at the mosques; but compliance was necessarily voluntary and incomplete. Following these events, which were consummated by the execution of most of the High Command, soldiers' committees proliferated throughout the army; this was precisely paralleled by the collegialization of the remainder of the state apparatus, which, even prior to the February insurrection, had contrived to prevent Bakhtiar's ministers from entering the government buildings; now there were scenes of low-level civil servants demanding higher salaries and asserting veto power over the decisions of their superiors.

In the next phase of the "classical" pattern of revolution, collegialization proceeds in conformity with the dictates of emergent contradiction. The state not only cannot guarantee the conditions of exploitation and domination in society at large; it cannot guarantee its own reproduction, which is at the mercy of bodies whose juridical status is very much in flux. Outlying regions inhabited by suppressed ethnic groups may assert claims to autonomy or secede (Ireland and Scotland in the English Revolution; Brittany in the French Revolution; Finland, the Baltic States, Georgia, and—more equivocally—the Ukraine in the Russian Revolution); local bodies behave in a semisovereign fashion, ceasing to collect taxes or to forward the receipts to the center (as in France and Russia, where the currency depreciated; the Russian currency was not even worth the paper it was printed on so that larger denominations were printed on much smaller bills). Social inferiors (English Levellers; French sansculottes;

Russian workers and peasants) assert claims against their "betters," and rivalrous armed forces spring up, choosing sides as their inclinations and the momentary balance of power appears to dictate. The Iranian Revolution illustrated all of these developments to perfection.

By way of background let us explain that Iran under the shah had been a most peculiar parody of capitalism of the periphery, itself further parodied in Nicaragua. The shah in person controlled the economy almost to the extent to which Stalin personally controlled the Soviet economy under the first two five-year plans. This control was exerted through: (1) state ownership of what in the USSR in the 1920s was called the "commanding heights" of the economy, including the oil industry, the basic steel industry, part of the aluminum industry, the (planned) copper industry, industrial-development banking, and agricultural credit; (2) the outright ownership by the royal family of 293 business enterprises in every imaginable sector of the economy; (3) the assets (U.S. $1.1 billion) of the Pahlavi Foundation, including an office building in Rockefeller Center, the ostensible purpose of this foundation having been among other things the provision of eleemosynary aid to hitherto-undiscovered and indigent relations of the Pahlavi dynasty; (4) some fifty-odd private capitalists owning the remainder of large industry, department stores, etc., not in the hands of foreigners and all necessarily on close terms with the shah and his fanatical partisans. (Most of these are in exile. One was shot for Zionism and another for sexual procuring on behalf of high-ranking generals whose proclivities in this area were allegedly exotic.) The shah was a species of multinational corporation dealing with others of his kind; thus it transpired that he purchased—in his guise of the Iranian state—25 percent of Krupp Steel.

The Iranian bourgeoisie was a caricature: Mutilated in its economic or entrepreneurial function, it was consequently reproduced only as politico-military specialists; that is, as state bureaucrats and executives in state-run, state-controlled, or foreign-owned enterprises. Their opportunities for going into business and accumulating capital as private owners or investors depended wholly on a career of service to the state and the shah. The latter was a gigantic tree in whose shadow no capitalist grew. Three groups of would-be capitalists resented this: (1) small industrialists, e.g., Prime Minister Mehdi Bazargan, the owner of a small factory engaged in the manufacture of prefabricated air-conditioning equipment; (2) lawyers, engineers, executives, and others possessing the privilege of Western education who foresaw greater opportunities, whether in business or in electoral politics, upon the shah's removal and constituted the base of the initial "secular" opposition, especially the National Front; and (3) the "traditional" bourgeoisie and petite bourgeoisie—sometimes called "bazaar merchants"—who, without possibilities for expansion under the shah, were destined to liquidation or relegated to the niche of tourist trap and who, consequently, bankrolled the "religious" opposition personified by Ayatollah Khomeini. (This is not intended to imply any generous nature on their part: The working conditions in an Iranian carpet workshop are strictly fourteenth-century, with wages to match.) These groups were sufficiently strong and numerous to demand a semblance of real capitalism, but far too weak to sustain it. Consequently, the question of capitalism or socialism was never very serious. The expropriation of the royal family (January and February 1979), other large industrial capitalists (completed by early July except for foreign business), "private" banking (mostly foreign-owned subsidiaries, including an agency of the Soviet state and a state-owned French bank) on June 8, and insurance companies on June 10 saw to that. *Cultural* issues, including the autonomy of national minorities, the status and rights of women, the power of the clergy, the prohibition of hashish in the land of the hashishin,[6] the execution or whipping of prostitutes and homosexuals, the banning of any and all music from (entirely state-owned) radio and television, etc., aroused the most passion. Meanwhile, the following—as reported in a periodical distributed by the Iranian Students Association in Southern California—has been transpiring:

> Workers and other employees of the "Lavan" Oil Company,[7] have asked for the nationalization of the company which is owned partially by the four American corporations; Sun Oil, Union Oil, Murphey [sic] Oil, and Atlantic Richfield. . . .
>
> On March 28, 20,000 people marched in the Northern city of Bandar Turkoman in support of the just and democratic demands of the Turkoman people. Marchers condemned the killings of Turkoman people in the previous days. One of the slogans was: "Yesterday in Kidistan, [sic] Today in Turkoman Sahra, where will it happen next?"[8] They demanded the immediate release of all those who had been arrested in Turkoman Sahra, and also the freedom of political acitivities for the Turkoman people.
>
> Workers of "Jean Mode" factory in Amoul[9] established their syndicate after they went back to work to get their postponed salaries. The representative of the employer at the beginning was not willing to confirm the workers' organization, but finally with the strike of the workers recognized the syndicate and agreed to pay the postponed salaries of the employees. But he didn't honor his promise on the specified date. The elected council of the workers compulsorily decided to sell the factory's products, and collected $10,000 which was distributed among the workers.
>
> Peasants of many villages around Iran, have sent letters to the government and expressed their support for the revolution. They have also categorized their demands into three articles which are the following: 1) Cancellation of all the peasants' financial debts to the Agricultural Bank. 2) Providing loans to the peasants with no interest. 3) Providing agricultural machines for peasants' use. [*Iran News & Review*, vol. 1, no. 1, June 1979.][10]

The same source also lists the eight-point "Demands of The Kurdish People," undated, attributed to "representatives of the revolutionary councils from the cities of Kurdistan Province of Iran, in a gathering in the city Mashabad" and submitted to the Bazargan government. These include:

> 2. The Kurdish people, like other peoples of Iran, demand the elimination of "national oppression" and ask for the right of self-determination in a "federation" from within the country of Iran, and deny the charge of being seperatist. [sic] . . .
>
> 5. All the garrisons in Kurdistan must be operated under the supervision of revolutionary councils. Therefore, a joint military committee, from patriotic officers and representatives of revolutionary councils, must be formed.

6. The criminal officers who ordered shooting and martyred thousands of people must be sent to the revolutionary courts. In order to transform Shah's reactionary army into a people's army, all its anti-revolutionary elements must be filtered. . . .

That is, in other words, that the Iranian state and army may undertake nothing or appoint nobody in Kurdistan without the prior agreement and subsequent supervision and control of a Kurdish political entity whose powers are to be defined by the Kurds.[11]

In keeping with the conservatism customary in revolutionary nomenclature, former Prime Minister Shahpur Bakhtiar, overthrown in February, was called the "Iranian Kerensky" by his enemies. At the time we said, "Nonsense. Bazargan is Kerensky. Bakhtiar is Rodzianko (the leader of the state duma, the tsarist parliament, who arranged the abdication of Nicholas II and forthwith disappeared from the political scene along with the duma) or Prince Lvov (first prime minister of the provisional government formed in mid-March; overthrown the next month in the "April Days"). This was borne out: Like Kerensky, who was constantly embroiled with the Soviet for the purpose of acquiring more than titular power, Bazargan and his ministers—originally appointed for their reassuring bourgeois respectability, strove to become more than mere marionettes. Imam Khomeini—the title "imam" must be bestowed by popular acclaim, as it is blasphemous heresy to claim it for oneslf; there had previously been only twelve canonical imams, of whom the last, the "invisible imam," is said to have disappeared into thin air in the tenth century—and the Islamic Revolutionary Council played cat-and-mouse with the government, the latter cast as the mouse: When, for example, Bazargan offered to resign unless the summary executions by ad hoc Islamic courts were halted, the resignation was refused by the imam, who also agreed to Bazargan's demand; but executions resumed the following day (March 1979). Subsequently, conflict developed over the government's desire to subordinate the Islamic militia or Pasdarans, an undisciplined rabble constituting the armed support of the komitehs, to the regular army in the interests of public order. This was suspect in that the officer corps—however innocent of murder or torture under the shah—were *eo ipso* vestiges of the monarchy. In the politics of revolutionary social transformation it is not what one did but who one is or was that constitutes the crime. On July 2, Bazargan caved in and offered an apology: " 'This country needs the Pasdarans more than any other time. When the Imam gave me the mission of leading the Government, I did not appreciate this need. I thought the old regime was gone and the new regime had replaced it. But later we saw that this was not the case.' "(*New York Times*, July 3, 1979).

Spectacular indiscipline ensued within the regular armed forces: The Homofars, their heroic role in the February insurrection notwithstanding, were suspect to the dominant religious faction by reason of their secular-technical bent, and not least because this was imparted to them by U.S. instructors. Stripped of their political importance, e.g., as Bazargan's bodyguards, and otherwise harassed, they staged a sit-in at their base; several dozen were arrested by order of General Rahimi, commander of the military police (*New York Times*, July 11, 1979). This raised the broader issue of the need for technically trained personnel, which seemed to the Bazargan government to dictate not only the release of the Homofars and acceptance of their demands but additionally the recall of some of the U.S. instructors; without these measures the air force was so much very expensive junk.

The Marxist-Leninist Left—the Khalq-e-Fedayin and its supporters, inclusive of the Iranian Students Association of Southern California—called for the outright dissolution of the regular army and its presumable replacement by a force of its own persuasion. In an editorial entitled "Why shah's Army Must Be Dissolved" the Iranian students declared:

> The establishement [sic] of a new revolutionary army along with the dissolugion [sic] of the Shah's anti-people army, are among the issues which are most vital. The resolution of these two issues is necessary to safeguard the victories of the revolutin, [sic] and to facilitate the struggle of the people against imperialism and reaction.
>
> We believe that the revolution can't reach its final goal, unless it destroys the nerve center of the enemy which is the anti-people army, and replaces it with a new revolutionary army made-up [sic] of the people themselves and the revolutionary personnel of the old army who have shown their loyalty by joining the people. We believe that the Shah's army, in all aspects, had been formed and extended to serve the interests and desires of imperialism.

This divided the secular Left not only from the Islamic Revolutionary Council, inevitably hostile to Marxist atheism, but also from the Bazargan government, which, faced with secessionist revolts and possible war with Iraq (which finally materialized in 1980), secretly hankered for a modified form of the alliance with the United States to revive the firepower of the military. Otherwise, given the curious politics of the situation, Bazargan regarded the Marxist-Leninists as de facto allies against the IRC in that the Fedayin were at least secular. Consequently, it was not until Bazargan delivered his self-abasing speech of July 2 (*New York Times*, July 3, 1979) that he was finally compelled to denounce the Marxist peril.

Like Kerensky, too, Bazargan was steadily compelled to replace the aging pillars of bourgeois respectability in his government with figures reflecting the power in the streets: Dr. Karim Sanjabi, leader of the National Front, resigned as foreign minister in April; in May the post was filled by Dr. Ibrahim Yazdi, thirty years younger, rhetorically more militant, and a close associate of the imam. Justice Minister Assadollah Mobasheri resigned in June; his duties had become patently impossible given the predominance of extrastate courts enforcing the Higher Law. In late July, Bazargan finally offered to appoint to his government a number of high-ranking clergy from the Islamic Revolutionary Council; but the precise identity of these personages was not known to the public nor was there any evidence that they wished it to become known.

All this was only the beginning: The seething unrest among the masses of workers and peasants was not reflected in the Islamic Revolutionary Council nor were the autonomist demands of Kurds, Arabs, Turks, etc. One recalls that much the same was true of the Soviet until shortly before Kerensky's overthrow; the convening of a new Congress of Soviets with a Bolshevik majority in fact dictated the timing of the coup of November 7. Similarly, the Girondin regime in France did not reflect the growing disaffection of the sansculottes before the Jacobins came to power in the insurrection of May 31–June 2, 1793.

The latter two events marked the installation of revolutionary dictatorships in power in the respective countries. The coercive power bestowed by control of the means of violence at the disposal of these regimes was initially negligible; but in the face of counterdissident insurrection to the point of civil war supplemented by the intervention of reactionary foreign regimes, they were charged with the defense of the revolutionary order by whatever means, as delegated by the resolute or even fanatical support of strategically located minorities of the population. With this support they organized recentralized despotic states; created huge well-disciplined armies that defeated their enemies; and massacred counterdissidents whether overt or merely suspected. (This was the "reign of terror" in France, 1793–94, and the "red terror" during the Russian civil war, 1918–21; in fairness it must be recalled that in each instance there was a "white terror" on the other side at least as bloody.) Throughout 1981, partisans of Khomeini engaged in bloody street fighting with the People's Fedayin. The head of the Islamic Revolutionary Party was lopped off by assassins who apparently infiltrated the Islamic Guards, their security force, and were able to plant bombs in meeting places of the party leadership. In response to the threat, the regime summarily executed over 1,600 suspected members of the leftist opposition. The violence was maintained at a high level, but did not compare to that which led to the overthrow of the Shah's regime. The French revolutionary dictatorship was overthrown with the passing of the military emergency in mid-1794. The Bolshevik regime, on the other hand, managed to hang on, though not without difficulty; the difference can be attributed to the circumstance that the sansculottes were a status group riven by mutually contradictory economic interests whereas the Russian proletariat constituted a class; and to the development of formal-organizational technique for political purposes throughout the intervening period. The Bolshevik regime was thus enabled to make the transition whereby it became the first totalitarian state. Even so, the end of the Russian Revolution as a social movement may be dated rather confidently in 1923 and the full panoply of totalitarianism established by 1926 (cf. Carr, 1971).

Where social transformation is the outcome of protracted war, the transition to totalitarian mobilization is far more difficult to detect. The Cuban, Yugoslav, and Albanian wars were relatively brief and, in the Cuban case at least, it is clear that the guerrillas triumphed over Batista long before the social movement had reached its peak intensity. Hence the Cuban regime quite visibly went through the phase of revolutionary dictatorship during 1960–62 (the arming of the population; the formation of committees for the defense of the revolution analogous to the revolutionary committees under the Jacobins; etc.) prior to the transition to the totalitarian state.

On the other hand, the Mozambican Revolution (1961–75), the Chinese Revolution (1925–49), and the Vietnamese Revolution (1940 or 1945–1975) involved wars of such length that it is out of the question to consider that the same social movement persisted throughout. It is more reasonable to infer that totalitarian mobilization was effected by counterstates within zones wholly or partially or even intermittently under their military control, whereby the mass of the population was affiliated to numerous and cross-cutting mass organizations (e.g., the party, military and paramilitary units, village cells, peasant organizations, women's organizations, workers' organizations, youth organizations, schools, medical services, financial apparatus, the other officialdom of the counterstate, etc.), the complexity of all this being unimaginable to U.S. observers at their first sight of squalid peasant villages (cf. Douglas Pike, 1966, for organizational charts, auxiliary bodies, and assorted entities loosely affiliated with or under the clandestine control of the party and in opposition to the regime). Protracted war, like the classic model, gives rise to what Trotsky called *dvoyevlastiye*, or "dual sovereignty," whereby two would-be states, representing irreconcilable social interests and disposing of rival means of violence contest control of the same territory by means partly political and partly—and ultimately—military. The protracted war model, though, does not necessitate the persistence of the social movement until the final destruction of the state by the counterstate, as the latter may through totalitarian mobilization achieve a social transformation immanent within the social movement whose prior existence is the precondition of the initial emergence of the counterstate as a revolutionary dictatorship.

Summary

Our pupose in this chapter has been to demonstrate the shortcomings of the conceptions of "political violence" and "mobilization," while offering the social-movement perspective as an alternative that adds clarity to the field. "Political violence" and "social movements" comprehend overlapping terrain. However, the problem with the terms "political violence" and "mobilization" is that they are defined so broadly as to include everything from routine political behavior to social revolutions. Second, they make no distinctions between qualitatively different phenomena. For example, "celebratory" riots that are not dissident actions are grouped with social-conflict riots. In the case of "mobilization," no distinction is made between mobilization effected by dissident vanguards or by a revolutionary dictatorship defending a social order. Terrorism, social banditry and guerrilla warfare may be defined, not by the nature of the activity, but in terms of perspective. That is, what the Left considers guerrilla warfare is likely to be called terrorism by the Right. No distinction is made between episodic dissidence and that which is susceptible to further intensification. Third, "political violence" makes no distinction between violence and force that is non-violent. The social-movement perspective treats collective action occurring within a social movement context as qualitatively different from that which does not. In so doing, political actions can be analyzed in terms of their social meanings—whether they are dissident, counterdissident, or routine (as in the case of coups d'etat in the capitalist periphery). By virtue of the fact that we seek to understand the meaning of political action, we can gain a more comprehensive—and historical—analysis of the phenomena.

"Mobilization," with its overtones of militaristic maneuvering, presupposes formal-organizational cohesion and downplays the process of collegialization within social-movement collectivities, which, as we have pointed out above, in the cases of classical revolutions, can even pervade the military. Such was certainly the case in both the Russian and Iranian revolutions. By overlooking the collegialization process, resource mobilization theory distorts the reality of social movement phenomena, especially the process whereby the dissidence of one collectivity triggers the dissidence of other collectivities in conformity to the Law of Emergent Contradiction. Even in the case where revolution is the consequence of protracted war, the revolution itself may cover several social-movement periods, thus making it difficult to detect the transition from social movement to a formalized revolutionary dictatorship.

Notes

1. The contradiction between the latter two groupings was perhaps nowhere sharper than in the eighteenth-century African kingdom of Dahomey: The standing army cadre, that is, the "lifers," consisted wholly of women, the famous "Amazons," about 5,000 in number. These were all volunteers. Men were by contrast conscripted for the annual campaigns; their distaste for service may be deduced from the fact that a village chief's life was forfeited when the number of recruits specified in his local draft quota was not met at muster (cf. Polanyi, 1968).

2. The analogy may be pushed further: Coups of the so-called "Nasserite" type (a term in vogue among political analysts in the early 1970s), whereby avowedly radical-nationalist officers seize power, might be fancied as the parallel in the peripheral-capitalist world of the election of social-democratic governments in capitalist core countries. In either case the extent of the transformation of social relations is not comparable to the rhetorical militancy of the regime's (or government's) declared objectives (or electoral manifesto). "Nasserite" regimes in most cases have come to power in the absence of intense dissidence among the civilian masses, and have usually dealt harshly with those groups, civilian leaders, and organizations actually intent on revolutionary social transformation. Pursuing our analogy, this might seem comparable to the repression of socialist revolutionaries by German Social Democratic party governments from 1918 to the present. (The 1958 Iraqi coup by General Abdul Karim Kassem presents an exception. This touched off a massive outbreak of revolutionary mob violence in Baghdad in the course of which King Faisal was torn to pieces in his palace and Prime Minister Nuri as-Sa'id was hanged from a lamppost. General Kassem legalized the Communist party and gave it a subsidiary role in his regime; but this apparently constituted grounds for his overthrow in the 1962 coup.) Moreover, "Nasserite" regimes have in most instances been replaced (Egypt, the prototype) or overthrown (Peru) by more conservative ones, or else have survived by moving to the right (Sudan). Colonel Qaddafi of Libya relies on magical authority at least as much as on his army; but the same personality that animates the regime is also stifled by the circumstance of being confined to a country—however oil-rich—whose population is about 4 million; consequently, the regime may have begun to autodestruct thanks to Qaddafi's foreign adventures, in which he has made numerous enemies and incurred disasters (most dramatically during the Libyan intervention on behalf of ex-Field Marshal Amin in the Tanzanian-Ugandan war, March–April 1979, when the entire Libyan force was killed or captured); presumably he will be overthrown by more "level-headed" if not "moderate" (U.S. media code for "conservative" or "pro-Western") officers.

3. The issue of whether President Sadat of Egypt was a military or a civilian autocrat should be confined to the plane of image manipulation. He liked to pose in a business suit abroad and in uniform at home.

Syria and Iraq underwent successive military coups after 1956 and 1958, respectively. They are presently governed by rival wings of the Ba'ath (Arab Renaissance) party which affects a civilian appearance in each country. Although both states are allies against Israel and clients of the USSR, not to mention their espousal of the same official ideology, they have until recently been bitter rivals. (In June 1979, they announced the formation of a joint military command. [*New York Times*, June 20, 1979] This may have had more to do with the anticipation of war with Iran than with military planning against Israel: During the preceding months Iraq demanded that Iran evacuate three islands in the Perian Gulf; detained a religious leader—who had been a close friend of Ayatollah Khomeini while the latter was in exile in Baghdad—on charges of fomenting religious subversion; and warmly encouraged Arab secessionists in Iran's oil-rich Khuzistan Province.) There are two possible explanations for this enmity. The *religious* interpretation points to the circumstance that the Iraqi Ba'athists are a Sunni minority governing a country with a Shi'ite majority, whereas their Syrian counterparts constitute an Alawite (Shi'ite) minority governing a Sunni majority. The military explanation points to the enormous military establishments maintained by both countries, which dominate the state apparatus in each (e.g., the Syrian minister of the interior is a brigadier-general), and to their geopolitical rivalries (specifically, the right of the Syrians to use the headwaters of the Euphrates for irrigation, and Syrian charges for the passage of Iraqi oil through a pipeline to the Mediterranean). These analyses should not be taken as mutually exclusive, in that the officer corps in each country is recruited from the dominant religious minority. The "Islamic revival," personified in 1979 by Ayatollah Khomeini, predictably aggravated Shi'ite dissatisfactions in Iraq; but simultaneously—and to the U.S. observer somewhat paradoxically—encouraged Sunni dissidence and terrorism in Syria: Sunnis have been blamed, for example, for the assassination of the country's attorney general on April 11, 1979 and for a massacre of military cadets—thirty-two dead, fifty-four wounded—on June 16, 1979 (*New York Times*, June 23, 1979). This may explain part of the Syrian motive in the decision to huddle closer to the Iraqis, presumably under the common denominator of "Arab socialism."

4. The legendary exploits of "Robin Hood" are a composite of the deeds of several individuals, often déclassé knights, who operated circa 1200. One of these gave King John so much trouble that he had to be bought off with an official post (cf. Painter, 1949).

5. Type (1)—instigators—is mainly to be found in the countries of the capitalist periphery, where its contemporary practitioners are commonly Marxist-Leninist in political thought. In Latin America, guerrilla war has been a traditional participatory sport of the *jeunesse doré*, going back at least to the time of Simon Bolivar (who finally succeeded in his third try, 1818); it is even older as the recourse of African slaves (Republic of Palmares, Brazil, seventeenth century) and downtrodden Indian serfs (rising of Tupac Amaru, Peru, eighteenth century, whence "Tupamaros"), though these latter groups were always squashed by a united front of all factions of white "civilization." Even Fidel Castro did not break with the tradition whereby privileged urban contenders for power took to the hills: Contrary to subsequent myth, he did not mobilize the peasants, but awaited reinforcements and arms from young radicals in the cities—whose friends, especially the Revolutionary Directorate in Havana, played a key role in eroding the morale of Batista's army (cf. Hugh Thomas, 1971)—and disarmed public opinion in the United States by holding press conferences for successive yanqui media representatives. The mass of the Cuban population may properly be said to have become participants in the movement only with the outbreak of strikes in 1958. Thus Castro, who was clearly in type (1) at the time of the Moncada attack (July 26, 1953), had become type (2) before his conquest of power and still more strongly so after his victory when he appealed to the mass of the population against the pro-U.S. strata.

Epigones of Castro in Latin America have almost uniformly fallen into type (1). The strategy of creating guerrilla forces in the rural areas failed, possibly because of the tedium encountered by young educated rebels in rousing skeptical peasants (much like the experience of the Russian Narodniki in the 1870s), and possibly because of the greater lure of more publicity-laden activities such as urban terrorism and press conferences (cf. Laquer, 1977:178ff.,217ff.).

Type (2)—encapsulated—is today most commonly found in the capitalist core countries as a vestige of 1960s student or youth radicalism: Weather Underground (U.S., defunct); Red Brigades (Italy); Red Army Faction (West Germany); Japanese Red Army; Quebec Liberation Front (Canada, defunct); Black Liberation Army (U.S., perhaps defunct; and possibly also the Symbionese Liberation Army (California, defunct). The strategy of such groups has as its common denominator the unmasking of the parliamentary regime in each country as a mere facade of police despotism (this having to some extent "succeeded" in West Germany, but only to the enhancement of the prestige and power of the police). Their substantive importance lies elsewhere, specifically in their incomprehensibility to liberals and the legal-parliamentary Left; in this respect perhaps the SLA was most "successful" because of its manifest "senselessness" to the rest of society as a whole.

Type (3)—those paid by foreign states—included such historical specimens as the Serbian "Black Hand," an outfit funded by some officials of the Serbian secret service prior to World War I; their objective was the creation of a Greater Serbia at the expense of the Hapsburg Empire, and their most notable success was the assassination of Archduke Franz Ferdinand at Sarajevo in 1914. In the same class was the Internal Macedonian Revolutionary Organization (IMRO), which between world wars was on the payroll of the Bulgarian state for the purpose of detaching the Macedonian region of Yugoslavia for its annexation by Bulgaria. More recently, the CIA funded the war of the Khmer Serei ("Free Khmers," i.e., rightists) against Prince Sihanouk of Cambodia (deposed March 1970); that of the FNLA (National Front for the Liberation of Angola) and UNITA (Popular Movement for the Liberation of Angola); that of the Kurdish Democratic party in Iraq, only to leave it to the slaughter when the latter country struck a deal with Iran, which subsequently unraveled during the Iraq-Iran War); and the terrorism of the Chilean Right from 1970–73.

Type (4)—operating on foreign soil—comprises the South Moluccan terrorists of the Netherlands, few of whom having ever seen their "homeland"; and the tiny and mutually-hostile bands of Serbs and Croats whose activities in the United States (one airplane hijacked by Serbs, one by Croats; one New York City policeman killed by a Croat bomb; threatening letters, etc.) and Europe mystify the public and sometimes amuse it. (Sources cited by the *New York Times*, June 22, 1979, give the figure of Serb "activists" in the U.S. as six, though Croats are said to be "more numerous.") Though we are not certain of this, the FALN terrorists who set bombs and rob banks in the cause of the independence of Puerto Rico may well have more popular support on the mainland (where the terrorist acts take place, where the terrorists are not easy to capture, and where—like Willie Morales—they readily escape) than on the island.

It is possible these days to start a "guerrilla movement" with only a set of initials and a dime for a phone call: With the latter one takes credit for a fire or explosion set by someone else or wholly accidental. This possibility is not merely theoretical: When in April 1979, a bomb wrecked part of the Rome headquarters of the Italian Communist party (CPI), both leftist and rightist terrorists called to claim credit. The claims of either group to represent any sort of social movement must be taken advisedly, especially those of the ultra Right, since these in their guise of a legal political party call themselves the Italian Social Movement (MSI).

6. These were the original Assassins, founded as a Shi'ite mystical brotherhood circa 1070 by Hasan-i-Sabah at the fortress of Alamut in Tabaristan (south of the Caspian Sea) for the purpose of eliminating heretical and infidel rulers. Hashishination continues in Iran, among the most deadly have been:

a. *Forghan.* The name is a Persian word for either the *Koran* or "that which discriminates between good and evil." It designates a terrorist organization inspired by Dr. Ali Shaariatei, murdered by SAVAK in 1975, who was, it is hardly necessary to add, a sociologist. He advocated extreme social egalitarianism legitimated by a literal reading of the *Koran*. This egalitarianism—a species of communism with God—extended to advocacy of the suppression of the Schi'ite clerical hierarchs and the end of their moral hegemony over the faithful. Since the February insurrection *Forghan* shot several close associates of the Ayatollah Khomeini, including a general and two or three important clerical figures in the Islamic Revolutionary Council.

b. *Black Wednesday*. These are terrorists supplied by Iraq, which covets the Iranian province of Khuzistan; the latter is the site of the Iranian oilfields in their entirety and its Arabic-speaking population is rife with autonomism and separatism. Black Wednesday would rather blow up pipelines than people, but does not shrink from killing persons in the vicinity of flammable substances.

c. *Khomeini Crusaders*. Elite gunslingers who fanatically support the Ayatollah/Imam Khomeini and the rule of the Islamic Revolutionary Council. These are deployed to protect the members and high-ranking adherents of the council, especially against *Forghan*.

7. Lavan is a small island in the Persian Gulf.

8. This refers to the killings of people in those provinces.

9. Amoul is a city on the coast of the Caspian Sea.

10. As an indication that this is no mere propagandist eyewash, here is the story from the capitalist side: "Some of the big farms were occupied by peasants during the revolution. In many, the owners have vanished. Those who remain wonder whether the regime's attempts to buy off discontent will push it into nationalisation of land. . . ." (*Economist*, July 28, 1979). Having described the heroic efforts of a textile manufacturer to break even, the same source notes:

> In other plants, operations are hamstrung by committees led by enthusiasts for workers' control; by the discontented (e.g., locally trained engineers at last able to lord it over their foreign-trained rivals); or by workers furious at their betrayal by employers now safely abroad with the company's funds.
> One Iranian banker, newly appointed by the revolutionary government, said it was difficult to lend because he could not find anyone capable of taking responsibility in many firms. Managers have nominal legal responsibility for the actions of the company, but find their actions thwarted by committees who mistrust them, or are determined not to pay out to firms and foreigners they dislike.

11. "We've got independence, but we are willing to compromise and settle for autonomy within post-revolutionary Iran," said Amir Qazi, one of the leaders of the Kurdistan Democratic Party.

The armed Pesh Mergo guerrillas are the only authority in many towns and villages throughout Iranian Kurdistan. Qazi's claim of "independence" apparently leads the government to doubt the Kurds are willing to settle for autonomy instead of secession. . . .

Kurds have a historic reputation as tough mountain warriors, and Qazi estimated that as many as 500,000 are armed. Four million members of the ethnic minority are believed to live in the region.

"They love guns and are ready to fight for their rights," Qazi said. [*New York Daily News*, July 30, 1979]

But these are not the same Kurds whose demands are published by the Iranian Student Association of Southern California. Those Kurds, in their Demand Number 8, denounce these Kurds as CIA agents and warn the Bazargan government to have no dealings with them. So contradiction begets contradiction. . .

Chapter 8

Thematic Recapitulation

The Definition of a Social Movement

We argue for a definition of social movements wherein the *decisive* criterion is the resort by members of dissident social categories to *nonroutinized* countercoercive *physical force*. The latter criterion demarcates social movements from cultural, artistic, and religious movements; from "reform" movements abiding strictly within the confines of routine politics; from the nutritiously edible "social conflict" of the Simmel/Coser (1962) variety or routinized dissidence, e.g., strikes at the expiration of contracts, which "function" to reinvigorate the bureaucracies on either side; and from recourses to force situated from beginning to end within established elites. Our criteria are noninstrumental and nonteleological. We reject the position that they occur as rationally calculated efforts to attain goals envisioned at the outset. As we have seen, "goals" are provisional artifacts of the level of intensity of conflict behavior.

An admitted drawback of our definition, at first sight, at least, is the fact that social movements can, and in "real" history, *have* emerged from the phenomena listed above, from which we have distinguished them. We must, therefore, apply a modicum of hindsight in delineating the course of a social movement (subsuming the issue of whether it existed at all). We offer no comfort to those who, with premeditated rational calculation, would snuff out or divert a social movement before it occurs (the hidden agenda of a Chalmers Johnson or a Ted Gurr) and we offer none to those avowed subversives who would, with premeditated rational calculation attempt to "build a movement" and thus mix their metaphors before they hatch. Woe betide subversives who are simultaneously sociologists, for in the former capacity they must give a prospective social movement the benefit of the ontological doubt on the basis of scattered early returns, whereas in the latter capacity they must refuse to concede until the returns are nearly complete and perhaps they must even demand a recount.

Our definition offered in Chapter 1, "The Guises of Social Movements," is the most restrictive in the field—and for good reason. At the writing of this

130

work, sociologists still do not have a clear understanding as to the distinction between "protests" and social movements. A glance at the conceptual confusions deriving from the 1960s gives evidence as to the nature of the problem: Was there an "antiwar" movement? A student movement? A civil rights movement? A hippie movement? From our perspective, none of the above were, of themselves, social movements, but, rather, aspects or phases of other social movements. Antiwar protests, student disruptions, hippie and civil rights protests were all parts of a middle-class youth movement. Civil rights protests, however, were more centrally located in the Black movement, which, in 1963, intensified into Black nationalism and moved north. Though the antiwar protests recruited from a larger constituency than the youth movement, certain manifestations began on college campuses, and only later did antiwar protests spread to other sectors of the population. According to our definition, there were at least four and perhaps as many as six social movements between 1960 and 1973 appearing in strict conformity with the Law of Emergent Contradiction: the Black movement, reciprocally influencing and coterminous with the middle-class youth movement, the women's movement, and the gay rights movement, the latter two of much shorter duration than the former, which lasted the whole decade from 1960–70. In addition, these movements, especially the Black, spurred collective dissidence by Hispanics and Native Americans. We speculate that the women's movement began in 1967 and had been effectively coopted by 1972. The Gay Rights Movement was even shorter, beginning in 1969 and ending in 1973. Dating them is difficult because of the the small amount of overt physical conflict manifested in each.

Social categories are accepted a priori at the outset of social movements. Social-movement participants, comprising minorities within them, act in their name ("we the students," "we the workers"). ("What is the Third Estate? It is nothing, yet it is everything."—Mirabeau)

A social category is *not* a behavioral entity. It designates the specific location within the system of social classification from which social-movement participants are drawn. It may even be a *residual* category, i.e., defined negatively by reference to those categories accorded special privileges and prerogatives, e.g., "Third Estate."

In the course of intensification of social conflict and the unfolding of emergent contradiction, social categories are renamed and redefined. For example, during the French Revolution, "Third Estate" became "the people," which then legislated a distinction between active and passive citizens. Subsequently, this distinction was erased (e.g., 1792) and replaced by the category of "patriots" within which the sansculottes, a newly delineated category, furnished the political muscle for a faction of bourgeois politicians to organize a revolutionary dictatorship. Note that, throughout, the lines demarcating categories remained subjective and tangential to "class consciousness." The sansculottes were more aware of their common interest as consumers than of their "relation to the means of production"; they were hence easily aroused against "hoarders," "speculators," and "middlemen," but had no sense of "class interest" antagonistic to that of the bourgeoisie. Duby (1981) makes the point that a system of social classification, once established in subjective awareness is extremely conservative despite its having been nonempirical from its inception and progressively more counterempirical with the passage of time. The case of the "three orders" dates from 1025–1030 and persisted until 1789, becoming progressively irrelevant to empirically observable social behavior from about the year 1100 onward. The Indian caste system, a hierarchy of ritual purity, has had at all times only the most notional relation to the distribution of wealth and power in India.

In defining social movements as confined to *major* social categories, whose collective action *interferes* with the cultural and/or political reproduction of society, we have given sociologists conceptual tools by which they can judge whether or not collective action is part of an ongoing social movement. That is, when a social category forces its way into the system of historical action (to borrow from Touraine, 1977) to the point of disrupting the normal functioning of cultural or political institutions, one can conclude that a social movement has begun. However, a definition is not sufficient. As we have indicated elsewhere, institutions can be disrupted episodically. The difference between a social movement and episodic dissidence is that it builds upon itself in a process of intensification, wherein the hegemonic ideology is rendered problematical by dissidents. This "reinterpretation of reality" provides the subjective basis for further—and more drastic—action. As social reality is reinterpreted in the struggle, movement participants attempt to reclaim those aspects of human subjectivity that have been alienated from themselves as part of their socialization to positions of social subordination. So long as these three aspects of a social movement are a mutually reinforcing totality—intensification of conflict, reinterpretation of social reality, and redefinition of the self and its capacities—a social movement is ongoing. Their fragmentation signals the point of incipient decline of the movement. When movement participants retreat from confrontation or when they begin to believe that revolutionaries can (or must) be made prior to or independent of the revolution, the point of incipient decline has been reached. Such phenomena must be viewed as a whole, since there are often temporary defeats and retreats within the process of intensification of a social movement, as well as phases of overt conflict alternating with cultural (or subjective) intensification.

Our definition of social movements differentiates them from periods of quiescence and, therefore, establishes boundaries around social movement periods. The advantages of conceptualizing social movements as recurrent (as opposed to continuous) phenomena are manifold: It prevents lapses into idealism and reification (i.e., the study of trends and ideas), allows for the examination of social movements without necessitating the use of conceptions abstracted from periods of social peace, and it helps to understand the distinction between movement and postmovement phenomena. The latter is important, since the concept is relatively new in social-movement theory. Bureaucratic organizations and other flotsam and jetsam from social-movement periods call themselves "movements" beyond the social-movement period and have rather easily deluded sociologists into believing that they in fact are social-movements. Take for example, the fall-out from the youth movement of the 1960s: religious organizations (Hari Krisnas, Jesus freaks, Nichiren Shoshu, Divine Light Mission, etc.), organizations that practiced dissidence only at the cultural level (e.g., the new American movement, the human potential movement), and Marxist sectarians all claimed themselves to be "movements" or "building movements," especially since their recruiting grounds were among former social-movement participants, many of whom joined thinking they were carrying on the revolution by alternative means. However, none of these organizations engaged in overt conflict, unless with each other, often over minute distinctions in doctrine, and they had quite different functions than groups within the movement. The sociology of "new religions" has been fairly unanimous in its characterizations of "new" religious organizations as conduits back to conventional life from social-movement participation (see, for example, the review by Robbins, Anthony, and Richardson, 1978).

The one exception to the above characterization has been the isolated underground terrorist organizations. In the wake of the 1960s, a number of such organizations existed, including the best known: the Weather Underground, the Black Liberation Army, and the Symbionese Liberation Army. All engaged in violent acts of terrorism. However, none had a mass following. None of their acts precipitated increased action on the part of the masses in whose name they were acting. In the case of the latter, its acts were as incomprehensible to the then-existing Left as it was to the rest of the population. To conclude, in our conceptualization, society moves from periods of quiescence to movement, with a transitional phase following the movement, whereby former movement participants are forced to accommodate themselves to the recrudescence of dominant structures. Dissidence during the postmovement period is fragmented, ritualized, and isolated.

Reproduction

Social movements are extremely complex phenomena, and, if the literature is any key, are more difficult to apprehend and understand than ongoing social structure. Asking what "causes" social movements is a bit like asking the causes of social structure. That is, causality is overly narrow in conceptualizing the origins of complex social phenomena. Instead of looking for "causality," which presupposes variable analysis, we must look to the reproduction of social relations in order to understand the recurrent outbreaks of social movements. Such an effort requires historical rather than teleological explanations.

More specifically, since social movements are attacks upon the prevailing set of social relationships extant at the time of the movement, we focus on the reproduction of social privilege. This provides correctives to such theories as relative deprivation, which attempt to assess the psychological "mood" of the masses in order to predict "political violence," or the alienated "dialectic" between trends and movements as advanced by Roberts and Kloss (1974). For us, the important phenomena that underlie the cyclic recurrences of social movements are contained in the processes of the reproduction of social relations in class-based society. Exploiting classes are able to exploit because they have effective control over the means of violence and the means of ideological reproduction (the latter of which has become increasingly important during the twentieth century). The former may be characterized as "power," and the latter can be described as "legitimacy." Thus, the social relations of privilege become the bases of our explanation of the recurrence of social movements, instead of the tried and not so true, industrialization, urbanization, relative deprivation, and anomie.

As noted in Chapter 1, "The Guises of Social Movements," social movements are engaged in by all sorts of social categories, spanning practically every possible social distinction. It is because of this that economistic and psychologistic theories are inadequate. A more "totalistic" analysis of social relations is necessitated at the material, political, and cultural levels, since social categories are primarily differentiated by their mental life; they are differentially affected by alterations at the material and political levels; and society is continually manifesting new divisions. Since social collectivities (having been social categories in periods of social peace) are the main actors in social movements, it only makes sense that we analyze social reproduction as a foundation for understanding their historical development materially, politically, and culturally.

We have now arrived at the question "When is a class of itself for itself?" Although this question tends to make scholars' eyes glaze, suffice it to say that the identity of groups engaged in social-movement behavior begins with the *appearances* of the social order. That is, social categories assume political and cultural identities prior to identification at the material level of social reproduction. "Consciousness of kind" appears as a consequence of both the reproductive process and the forcible assertion of antistructure. Within the reproduction process during periods of quiescence, a common mental life evolves out of similar material and political relations. The forcible assertion of antistructure allows for the rapid development of the subjective: (1) The social category becomes a social collectivity in that members begin acting in behalf of the collectivity; (2) the members of the social category experience new relations within their collectivity and between themselves and other collectivities; (3) their social action alters their understanding of the nature of the social order; and (4) they collectively experience altered states of consciousness.

Though a social category may share a common mental life, it is reproduced in alienated form such that members are being socialized along parallel lines without a clear understanding that other members are subject to the same social forces and experience alienation in similar ways (cf. Kenniston, 1959). In bourgeois society, this is reproduced in the form of the isolated individual. Thus, consciousness of kind is repressed or obliterated until events occur that raise common experiences within a significant sector of the social category to the level of consciousness (e.g., the consciousness-raising groups of the women's movement). Therefore, in order to understand the recurrence of social movements, one must be able to grasp the mechanisms and forms of development within a given historical period, major social categories and their shifting relationships, contradictions and fractionations, and internal laws of motion operating within a given social formation. Without analysis of the relations of exploitation, domination, and hegemony, this is impossible.

The Natural History Approach to Social Movements

James Rule and Charles Tilly (1972) have strongly criticized the conceptualization of natural histories of revolutions and cite evidence from the overthrow of the Bourbon monarchy in France and the elevation of Louis Philippe of Orleans to the throne, known to history as the Revolution of 1830. Rule and Tilly's main targets are Crane Brinton (1965) and his revisionists. Brinton develops what he calls a "fever-chart" theory of revolution that posits several distinct stages: escalating discontent, the fall of the old regime, the honeymoon period, the rule of the moderates, the accession of the radicals, the reign of terror, and the period of reaction; that is, the phases of the "classical" revolution. (The term "fever chart" has become a pejorative among contemporary theorists.) In addition, sociologists have set forth a variety of "natural histories" of social movements, such as Blumer's (1948) phases of collective behavior and institutionalization, Touraine's (1977) utopia, confrontation, and institutionalization, and so forth. The evidence that Rule and Tilly advance is in the form of tabular data indicating that the incidence of violent uprisings was highest in 1830, when the king was deposed and again in 1832, when the regime used violence to consolidate itself against the populace. (The Revolution of 1848 had a similar progression in France, with collective violence at its height in 1848 and 1850, the former resulting in the exile of Louis Philippe of Orleans and the latter the consequence of the Bonapartist coup d'etat.) Rule and Tilly use this evidence to demonstrate that natural histories are not of much use, since in the case of 1830 and others like it, the emergence of violence was neither gradual, nor escalating, but rather cyclic.

Rule and Tilly demonstrate only that the intensity of social conflict is no guide to political outcomes: In 1830, the political issue, i.e., distribution of the political pie between titled and untitled rich was settled rather quickly by the removal of Charles X (1824–1830) despite and largely because of the imperative, faced by all sectors of the propertied classes, to stifle the claims of the propertyless class for whom July 1830 was merely the opening round.

The problem with such natural histories is that if they are specific in their designation of phases, they are doomed to have more exceptions than cases that adhere to the rule. Contrarily, if they are too generalized, they become useless and subject to gross distortion as in the case of Blumer. The problem has been that theories of social movements and revolutions that have employed the natural history approach have used *descriptive* categories. Each social movement has its own natural history depending on the historical conjuncture. For example, the middle-class youth movement of the 1960s increased steadily in intensity throughout the decade, alternating between phases of overt politics and cultural intensification until its most radical phase in 1968–69. The women's movement, which was spawned full blown from the youth movement in 1967, had its most radical phases at the beginning, until it was coopted and deradicalized in the early 1970s. Likewise, in the Iranian Revolution, there was no honeymoon period to speak of since the civilian populace was able to rapidly arm itself following the overthrow of the shah. The natural history of social movements must be determined on the basis of *analytical* categories. That is, the internal laws of the development of social movements must be determined and the natural history must be constructed in light of the interaction of those laws.

We have posited that social-movement natural histories are the consequence of two major factors: historical conjuncture and the internal laws of motion of the movement. Historical conjuncture includes the forms and means of domination and exploitation, the level of development of social relations, the reproduction of social categories, the development of apparatuses by which social order is maintained, the nature and level of contradictions within the social formation, the historical development of relations between social categories and the level of development of the historical subject. By internal laws of motion we mean that all social movements develop in conformity to the laws detailed in Chapter 4 ("The Intensification of Conflict"): the Law of Mounting Stakes, the Law of Emergent Contradiction, and the Law of Shifting Terrain. These laws are not merely asserted a priori, but are the consequence of detailed analysis of social movements through recorded history. They are the logical consequences of the forcible assertion of antistructure by dissident collectivities that occur whether or not the regime under or overreacts to collective dissidence. Dissidence, by definition, is not a social movement unless it builds upon itself and collective action becomes a spur to further collective action. It is an empirical fact that dissidence by one collectivity will stimulate action by other collectivities, both within a particular state and between states. (One only needs to look as far as Eastern and Central Europe during the Polish labor crisis of 1980–81, as industrial worker strikes in the shipyards of the north spread to miners, farmers, and students nationwide in a process of rapid collegialization. Regimes in Hungary, Czechoslovakia, and Rumania passed legislation in attempts to head off similar confrontations in their own countries.) A necessary condition for a social movement to build upon itself is the collective reinterpretation of reality, which means that boundaries between "issues" as defined and isolated within the hegemonic ideology are breached and become increasingly understood as manifestations of conflict between two major social categories. (Again, the Polish worker movement of 1980–81 is instructive. Within the movement emerged the notion that the Communist party was responsible for the operation of the "state," whereas Solidarity was responsible for "society," a term consciously rendered problematic, since "society" subsumes "state." As protectors of society, Solidarity took on issues of state; that is, all relations of political domination.)

It is generally regarded as pretentious to refer to any social (or historical) phenomenon as a "law," although a few have been pointed out from time to time, such as Michel's "iron law of oligarchy," or Parsons's law of social differentiation. In science, a phenomenon is termed a law by virtue of the fact that it has been observed to operate without exception on repeated occasions. Once the phenomenon has been characterized as "lawful," such lawfulness becomes a defining characteristic of the phenomenon (e.g., "differentiation" becomes a defining characteristic of modernization). Subsequent discoveries may present a variety of exceptions to the law, which then can be used to proscribe the conditions under which the law works. If we return to the internal laws of motion of a social movement, we find (1) they become visible as a consequence of the development of a definition that separates phenomena that conform to these laws from that which does not; (2) through the process of reification, they are raised from observations of consistently recurring phenomena under a given set of circumstances to laws of historical development. By raising them from universally repeated observable phenomena within the process of the forceful assertion of antistructure to laws of historical development, we have elevated them to defining characteristics of social movements.

Laws are tools of science that allow the researcher to make distinctions between phenomena. The application of laws allows the scientist to make order out of the universe of phenomena he or she is studying. Although, as Kuhn (1970) has shown, laws can interfere with the understanding of disjunctive phenomena, i.e., that which violates the laws or assumptions of the observer is systematically screened out; they paradoxically also allow for the possibility of their own supersession in that they establish an order that, when violated, leads to the undermining of the paradigm of which they are part. Though some may believe that the theory of social movements is too primitive to assert the existence of laws, we would point out that there are 2,500 years of historical record from which to draw. In addition, the question we should, as social scientists, ask ourselves is whether or not they provide clarity over earlier conceptions. Obviously, we think they do.

Sociocharacterological Revolutions

We have indicated that within social movements the locus of motivation among movement participants changes; that such alterations in the human subject lead to movement conceptions of "new humans" who are perceived to be an advancement over earlier *sapiens*, including the most recent forms out of which the movement participants have evolved. Following social movements, including revolutions, the human subject must be forced back into boundaries necessitated by the reimposition of social structure, which is, in itself necessary for the material reproduction of society. For the most part, then, the psychic consequences of a social movement become denatured in the forms of psychic healing and upward mobility of former members of dissident collectivities. We have referred jokingly to this process as the law of destruction of surplus consciousness, in which movement sensibilities are effaced by the necessity to return to the production of the material necessities of existence.

Under certain conditions, such as when social movements combine with a rapid increase in the material surplus, movement sensibilities are incorporated into the social structure and are institutionalized as a characteristic of an emergent social category. We have alluded to just such a phenomenon in the English Revolution of 1640–49, in which a rational-calculating, profit-maximizing merchant class emerged victorious over a status-conscious, military-maximizing aristocracy. Additionally, those sectors of the gentry and upwardly mobile yeomanry that sided with bourgeois elements against the crown were forced by historical necessity to engage in rack renting, intensive cultivation, refraining from conspicuous consumption, and watching the ledger, all characteristics of rational calculation and profit maximization. Thus, out of the English Revolution, we see the rise of a new social type as dominant in English society—the rational calculator. From this time forward, England has portrayed itself as a nation of shopkeepers. Out of the revolution, then, emerged a qualitative change in English character that was institutionalized in the occupational structure. This we have referred to as a sociocharacterological revolution.

Of course, the emergence of the rational calculator was not limited to England, but was manifested throughout the north of Europe as capitalism evolved out of feudal social relations and mercantile capitalists gave way to industrialists. While Max Weber (1950) may have attributed this to Protestantism, such characterological changes affected capitalists who did not become Protestants, such as the Fuggers and Amsterdam bankers. Nevertheless, the rise of Protestantism in the areas of capitalist development in the sixteenth through the nineteenth centuries indicates the extent of the characterological change necessitated by bourgeois society. As E. P. Thompson (1966) has demonstrated, the industrial laboring classes of England used Methodism as an instrument of self-discipline for the purpose of altering rural-based peasant orientations into a working-class consciousness necessary for functioning in subordinate positions in industrial society.

Thus, we see the dialectics of character. First, the altered characterology emerges as a necessary element of newly rising accumulators in the seventeenth and eighteenth centuries. By the latter part of the eighteenth century, such characterology was being imposed on an industrial working class as part of their being forged into a reliable labor force. The working class resisted such imposition when they were insurgent. When worker movements were supressed and structure was reimposed, they flocked to such Protestant religions as Methodism to help increase their value as individual workers in the labor market.

Within the social movements of the 1960s, all of which developed a "subjectivist" reinterpretation of reality and were organized around dissident subcultures, each dissident collectivity intensified its subjective awareness of the imposition of the forms of domination that pervaded bourgeois society: ageism, racism, sexism, and homophobia. More important, each social movement at its most radical phase rendered the whole of bourgeois social relations questionable, including the sacrifice of the human subject to the discipline of the reality principle. That is, the necessity of performing labor under the conditions of the capital/labor nexus was called into question to the point where opinion surveys routinely assessed the perception of the public as to whether or not business had a right to make a profit.

Within dissident collectivities, there was a perceptive characterological change that resulted in a relative deemphasis of the reality principle vis-à-vis the pleasure principle. There were strong indications that the characterology of the rational calculator had been eroding throughout the twentieth century as the fundamental problems of capitalism altered from inadequate forces of production to inadequate modes of consumption. Capital attempted to solve this problem by creating consumption formations and "producing" culture in the form of consumer hedonism (see, e.g., Mills, 1951; Riesman, et al., 1956; Ewen, 1976; Bell, 1976); however, it was not until the 1960s that the characterology of the rational calculator came under attack by a self-confident minority. The social history of the 1970s attested to the alteration in the American character structure. Scarcity-based bourgeois institutions, such as education, the nuclear family, patriarchy, and work were on the defensive. The forms of bourgeois discipline have all suffered a decline in legitimation since the 1960s. The state, business, organized religion, and the media all lost "trust" among the populace throughout the 1970s. The "work ethic" has been a major issue in presidential campaigns since 1968; three recessions have been induced since then to assure labor-force discipline. Their consequences have been to both conservatize and alienate workers, who, if current assessments are correct, seem to be compelled to conform out of sheer necessity. "Management" has been able to increase its power over "labor" since the mid-1970s and demand such "give backs" as a declining standard of living; increased control over the labor process, hiring and firing procedures, and strikes; and fewer benefits. This has increased the facticity of bourgeois social relations.

The new characterology is reproduced primarily within capitalist consumption formations; that is, the surplus-absorbing strata. However, it is not limited to those strata. It has also infiltrated sectors of lower strata, especially the younger elements of the industrial laboring class. One is reminded of such examples of age stratification in the working class as younger members of unions have been at odds with and more radical than union officialdom. This cleavage was demonstrated most dramatically in the Lordstown wildcat strike of 1972 and the unruliness of young workers in the union-sponsored "March for Jobs" against the Ford administration.

The new characterology emphasizes the following: (1) increased sensitization to the imposition of authority, (2) desire to experience states of consciousness outside the boundaries of bourgeois rationality, (3) the questioning of the necessity of having life controlled by the market mechanism, (4) liberation of the sexual impulse from bourgeois prudery, and (5) the increased importance of "love" as a necessary component of life. Each sensibility can be expressed in an oppositional or alienated form. For example, number 1 can be manifested in open conflict or as mass apathy. Number 2 can be experienced as an artifact of opposition (see, e.g., the next section, "The Greatest 'High' There Is") or as altered states of consciousness induced by drug use, sexual contact, psychotherapy, religious rites, violence, or in combination, with conflictual elements vetted. The third element can be demonstrated by making attempts to extricate oneself from the market as did landed hippies in the late 1960s and early 1970s under the guise of self-sufficiency and ecology, or in its alienated form of profligate spending, gambling, and dissolusion as engaged in by Elvis Presley before his death. Sexual liberation in the 1960s took the form of an attack on bourgeois sexual taboos and body alienation. However, in the 1970s, sexuality was reincorporated into the social structure in the forms of an intensified and extended sexual-competitive struggle. As for "love," in the 1960s, it became a code word for a new form of social order that included erotic love with the love of humanity and admonitions to love neighbors and even enemies. Within dissident collectivities, members were called "brothers" and "sisters." Following the 1960s, there was a visible increase in romantic love, with a concomitant increase in fear, hatred, and yearning for times when interpersonal competition was not so intense and people could feel as members of a cohesive collectivity. This has been the underlying motivation for the nostalgia that has been characteristic of the post-1960s period.

At the writing of this work, the five aspects of the altered locus of motivation are experienced in their alienated forms. However, they remain as important traits in the American character, especially the middle-class surplus-absorbing strata. They did not recede as ephemera of the 1960s and therefore must be viewed as manifestations of a sociocharacterological revolution.

The Greatest "High" There Is

In Chapter 3, "The Reproduction of Social Privilege," we contended that the continuity of culture, that is, its *reproduction*, presupposes the periodic interference with its reproduction. The adaptive and innovative character of the human subject dictates the interference with cultural reproduction for intrinsic reasons even without the extrinsic provocations that precipitate those responses Anthony F. C. Wallace (1966) calls "revitalization movements": Few archeologists, for example, would assert these days that a change of pottery style here or burial customs there—as one digs into the accumulated garbage of millennia—necessarily implies demographic change, conquest, or even "cultural diffusion." The empirical observation of interference with cultural reproduction undertaken by Victor Turner (1969) among the Ndembu was, however, inevitably limited to ephemeral events, themselves periodically reproduced: the *isoma* and *wu'bwang'u* fertility rituals. These in turn assert *within* the "liminal" state[1] the resolution of the contradiction between matrilinearity and virilocality on the spiritual plane. This, as noted above, has the effect of limiting Turner's attention, in his extension of his concepts of "antistructure," "liminality," and "communitas" in class societies, to such festivals as Holi and Mardi Gras, which despite the blatant "status reversals" are equally ephemeral as well as socially conservative in their effects (in that, e.g., the untouchables of India and the Blacks of New Orleans are permitted "safety valves"); to religious movements without conflict dimensions, specifically those of Saint Francis of Assisi (Italy, early thirteenth century; subsequently throughout western Europe) and Sri Chaitanya (Bengal, late fifteenth century; revered by U.S. Hare Krishnas as their founder while rejecting the sexual practices instituted by him); and subcultures such as the Hells Angels, who despite their perpetration of acts deemed revolting by the "citizens"—the conventional people of California—are not in revolt (though they did dabble with both dissidence and counterdissidence during the 1960s).

"The battle of the sexes" described by Turner as the culmination and conclusion of *wu'bwang'u* gives a clue to a slightly different perspective: The central contradiction of Ndembu society is at bottom that of gender, that is, patriarchy. This central contradiction is common to all preclass societies. It may be mitigated or aggravated by changes in social structure like those discussed by Levi-Strauss as found among the "faddish" Australian aboriginals; but it is invariably reproduced. This contradiction, obviously, is located on the level of *biological* reproduction; we posit that explanation as follows: It is evident that in some ultimate sense and with the benefit of epochs of hindsight that, as Erving Goffman puts it in *Gender Advertisements*, "gender is not really all that important." But, though "anatomy" is certainly not "destiny," it is likely that—especially under conditions of low levels of material technique—possession of female bodies as opposed to male ones is conducive to *slight* differences in the construction of "reality." That is all that is required, since two "realities" cannot coexist *permanently* in the same culture (as opposed to "alternative realities" deriving from "nonordinary states of consciousness," such as those peculiar to mystical transcendence, sex, and violence, which may be situationally encapsulated or delegated to specialists). "Reality," to be convincing as such—and that, in a sense, is its "job"—must consequently be *either* male or female: In the beginning the former was decided upon.

Class society posits patriarchy as its presupposition. However, the material basis for the transcendence of class society has been built in a number of countries. Class society is of course defined by the production of products by some people in part for consumption and possession by entirely different people who do not produce but instead provide "service," including repression, military command, administration, organized religion, indoctrination, marketing, and surveillance of the population, all of which entail the *consumption* of products. (Note: To repeat, only the production of products is production and only that labor power objectified in products is productive. This is not to imply a moral condemnation of those not directly engaged in production but rather of structural conditions that *require* some do the work while others do the civilization, especially wherein this is no longer necessary.) The rising levels of technique, especially in so-called "industrial society," proliferate standardized products—"commodities"—whose relation to cultural reproduction is taken for granted, as they are produced collectively and increasingly consumed collectively (freeways, office buildings, data processing equipment); they constitute the "ground"[2] against which products more patently associated with the reproduction of mental life represent the "figure." While specific human capacities are developed pari passu with the introduction of new products, a point is reached where the emergence of the human subject in history comes, generally speaking, into contradiction with the acquisition and accumulation of products-in-general, especially the standardized kind; the human being simply has more important things to do. Yet the environmental envelope comprised of products constitutes a *de facto* ideology promoting the acquisition and accumulation of products-in-general and implicit in "reality" itself, with the corresponding legitimation of the exploiting class in capitalism—"the system delivers the goods," though increasingly to itself as collectivized consumption—and derivitively in socialism. This human predicament is perceived, however dimly and confusedly, by reason of the "sociocharacterological revolution" (defined earlier) of the present epoch.

Capitalism (and by extension socialism, where it is rich enough) compensates for the consequences of the sociocharacterological revolution by "scarcity-simulation"; that is, the restraint upon the level of household consumption and the relative shift to collectivized consumption, in particular that of the state as consumer of last resort (which unlike the household may go indefinitely into debt and unlike the "private sector" need not fear Japanese price competition). At this point, too, the maintenance of the industrial working class at an artificially large magnitude for the purpose of enforcing social discipline ("functioning") upon the surplus-absorbing strata above it stands revealed. But the new society has been gestated in the womb of the old, since the objective for which the human subject unfolding itself in history is striving posits as its *precondition* the carrying on of collective production for collective *use*, this to objectify as little human labor as possible and to be deemed appropriately insignificant. (Elsewhere we suggested that industrial production be relegated to "those with a romantic urge to return to the primitive.") Human beings would then get on with whatever it is they have to do. It is here and now that the central contradiction shifts—though patriarchy and exploitation persist—to *the level of cultural reproduction:* that is, the struggle for the control of *"reality" itself.*

The location of the central contradiction on the level of *material* reproduction precludes the easygoing suspension of the "status hierarchy" as with the Ndembu; and in fact the holding of "status reversal" festivals in class societies presupposes their geographical isolation (e.g., Mardi Gras in New Orleans, the Carnival in Rio, Holi in encapsulated Indian villages), a docile and disarmed population (as is true wherever Mardi Gras is held and even more so in India, ruled for centuries by Muslim princes and English Protestant administrators), or the watchfulness of a lurking constabulary (the lack of which during the 1979 New Orleans police strike caused the cancellation of Mardi Gras). It will be obvious that, whatever underlying antagonism between the genders may be comically ventilated by the Ndembu during *wu'bwang'u*, male and female must still combine to reproduce society biologically; the same is not true of classes, especially prior to the advent of capitalist industrialization; a mass of dependent peasants could observe empirically that they produced the wealth of the exploiter whose exactions may have palpably interfered with the biological reproduction of the peasant community in the form of malnutrition, war, overpopulation promoted by enserfment, and consequent vulnerability to disease. Until quite recent times, specifically until the point when the decomposition of the bourgeois hegemonic ideology in the capitalist core countries turned out to be very good business (see Chapter 3, "The Reproduction of Social Privilege"), the tendency of exploiting classes and political regimes has consistently been toward the interference with society's own spontaneous tendency to interfere with its own cultural reproduction. They tended to restrict "communitas" to pallid imitations: the mysteries, rites, and public celebrations of organized religion; and local village festivities of the exploited mass. The latter were often observed bemusedly by the local representatives of the exploiting class or even conducted by them as officiants, as for example at the slave wedding on an antebellum southern plantation: These occasions would reinforce their sense of superiority and paternalistic noblesse oblige vis-à-vis their charges, who were obviously simple pious children or savage drunken brutes or both.

The *real* "communitas" is, as the argot of fifteen years ago would have it, "really something else," and emerges most clearly in the context of major social upheavals when the dissidents have forced at least a local interference with the political as well as the cultural reproduction of society. Readers with long memories will recall the refrain of white youth at "be-ins," music festivals, or the first heady flush of campus building occupations: "Why can't it always be like this?" They will recall, too, the street festivities in flaming, riot-sacked cities like Newark and Detroit prior to the arrival of the troops; or perhaps a pop song hit, "Dancing in the Streets," best known among whites in the version released in 1966 by the Mamas and the Papas, but originally Black soul music: Whites understood the title literally, but to Blacks it had the additional connotation of Watts-like riots and insurrections. "Communitas" might be posited as a "nonordinary state of consciousness," that is, more colloquially, a "high," perhaps comparable to states of mystical or sexual transcendence with which it is frequently reported in combination: the former in religious movements and in social movements exhibiting religious solidarity (e.g., the Taoist-derived revolutionary sects of China, from the Red Eyebrows and Yellow Turbans down to the Boxers, or Loyal Order of the Harmonious Fist); the latter especially in the 1960s, whence the French student slogan of May 1968, "The more I make revolution the more I make love. The more I make love the more I make revolution." Unlike the other states, though, "communitas" is accessible to the individual *only* as part of a social collectivity.

Social movements are, in terms of the collectivity that emerges during the social-movement period, in a sense comparable to so-called peak experiences in the life of the individual. For movement participants the imprint of "communitas" upon their lives may be even stronger than that of major wars upon the soldiers who fought them, since dissidents are not conscripted (except perhaps by dint of peer-conformist pressures in the most intense phases of movements). This is the "it-changed-my-life" syndrome, after a common feminist refrain in the 1970s (and used as a book title by feminist Betty Friedan). But by contrast to the "peak experiences" of individuals, the "communitas" felt by members of a dissident collectivity during a social-movement period survives as idiosyncratic memories of the constituent individuals once each has undergone a "postmovement adaptation" to the return of social quiescence and may be subsequently able to communicate with each other about what the movement had been "all about" no better than an individual of merely average linguistic skills may be capable of informing a stranger as to the precise nature of a "peak experience" such as mystical transcendence. Social movements exhibiting formal-organizational solidarity and secular-rationalist doctrinal ideology may mask this development, or perhaps even defer it; but movements exhibiting subcultural solidarity and subjectivist ideology displayed the process quite dramatically.

"Communitas" and the "peak experience" each provide a standpoint for the critique of everyday life, but quite differently: The latter posits "individuality," takes it for granted, and points the way only to the individual enhancement of it *qua* individual. The former progressively dissolves "individuality" into the *human subject evolving in history*, whose level of development is an artifact of the density and complexity of human interdependence; that is, of social relations (cf. Marx, Introduction to *Grundrisse*, 1973). Human interdependence itself develops pari passu with human capacity to transform "nature," that is, the material and in this capacity *the level of development of the human subject is paramount, the most important objective "material" condition*, capable of further developing itself once it has become *conscious* of its existing level of development. The relation between the "human subject" and "individuality" is thus dialectical: The heightened, more developed powers of the human subject is the presupposition of greater individuation, whereas the latter implies—among other things—an enhanced capacity to discover its own preconditions and thereby contributes to the former.

Let us in conclusion restate the three processes found in social movements yet again: (1) the intensification of social conflict, that is, the forcible assertion of antistructure; (2) the reinterpretation of social reality that is, the collective development of the thought forms of antistructure; and (3) the redefinition of the "self," "human nature," and human capacities, that is, disalienation and the collective refashioning of the human individual in the context of antistructure (this process having been colloquially connoted by the expression "getting it together").

The second and third of these processes must fuse into a totalization (given, of course, sufficient intensity and duration of the movement as a whole) expressive of the historical condition of the emergence of the human subject *and* the form of ideological critique—e.g., religious, secular-rationalist, subjectivist—characteristic of the particular epoch.

Notes

1. Latin *limen*, threshhold; whence Turner's "liminality" (noun) and "liminal" (adjective) denoting a state of the social collectivity wherein the routine behavior and status hierarchy prevailing in everyday life are suspended and "communitas" is experienced.

2. Until they are suddenly unavailable:

> But growing anger and frustration all too often erupted in name calling, fistfights, occasional stabbings and shootings. While a gas-station owner in Freemansburg, Pa., rushed to help his bleeding wife, who had been accidentally struck by a car waiting in line, other motorists filled up their tanks and drove off without paying. In Levittown, Pa., in an outbreak originally caused by truckers demonstrating against high diesel fuel prices, some 2,000 motorists and thrill-seekers clashed with the police in three days of rioting. Police arrested nearly 200. Local officials declared a state of emergency and enforced a curfew that prohibited more than five people's getting together on the streets after 9 P.M. Pennsylvania Governor Richard Thornburgh helped restore order by bringing another 500,000 gal. of gas into the area and imposing a statewide odd-even purchase system. Said Bristol Township Police Chief Richard Templeton: "We're sitting on a powder keg." [*Time*, July 9, 1979]

At the bottom of the same page is a photograph captioned, "Angry rioters burn automobiles as violence erupts over continuing gas shortage in Levittown, Pa." In the picture, a shirtless young man whose hair falls below his shoulders is shown in what appears to be the act of consummating the fiery destruction of the twisted wreck of a car listing to starboard against what might be a gasoline station-entrance signboard painted over with a grafitto in fifteen-inch letters, which reads "!MORE GAS NOW!"

This is a localized instance of people refusing to "function" and interfering with the functioning of others.

Chapter 9

Conclusion

In attempting to interpret the 1970s, we quite understandably saw the period in terms of a "recuperation," or a recoil from the political dissidence of the 1960s whereby some of the cultural dissidence was incorporated, shorn of oppositional content, into a drive to expand the domestic market, in particular by replacement of the market-limiting "nuclear family" by a more frivolously consuming household or family type.

The substantive issue of the 1970s was how to stimulate personal consumption in a period of declining—absolutely or psychologically—purchasing power or, from a somewhat different angle, how do you get people to enjoy themselves harder and harder on less and less money? The solution adopted by both the state and big business was the generalization of "repressive desublimation" in the direction of a societal norm. "Repressive desublimation," epitomized by "the *Playboy* philosophy," had initally manifested in the 1950s as socially and subculturally encapsulated among young men who, it was understood, were within a few years to cofound their own isolated nuclear families and commence the "serious" business of life. The notion of the isolated nuclear family pursuing an idealized consumption career, the "family home," the "family car," and so forth, formerly known as "the American Dream" had been dinned into the heads of the population for years; the American Dream would have constituted a formidable obstacle to the generalization of repressive desublimation had cultural history proceeded unbroken after the 1950s since it posited as a presupposition the isolated nuclear family. It in turn posited as its own presupposition, as did the rest of bourgeois cultural and institutional forms, the rationally accumulating individual to whom the endless accumulation of exchange values for its own sake appears to "make sense" even if said individual is for reasons of class relations or personality deviation precluded from engaging in it. In bourgeois culture it is by definition impossible to develop a "sense of worth" if one lacks a "net worth" since one is unmistakably a "worthless good-for-nothing bum."

Given the availability by the 1970s of millions of under-35 well-educated, hip, quasi-hip, radicalized, consciousness-raised, personally growing, or merely vulgarly hedonistic surplus absorbers, it was clearly going to prove impossible to fit them neatly back into the framework of the American Dream and the isolated nuclear family. On the other hand, it was definitely possible to convince them, given a hint of recession, a whiff of tear gas, and the inevitable tendency of social movements to expire after a few months or years of intensifying social conflict, of the advisability of continuing or resuming "functioning," however reluctantly in the interests of what has come to be called "survival." In 1970s argot, this meant either "maintaining a level of social privilege commensurate with one's educational qualifications" (e.g., "What do you mean, why get tenure? The name of the game is survival," said an ex-colleague who did not get it) or "obtaining additional educational qualifications commensurate with one's expectations of future social privilege" (e.g., "Why am I in law school? Survival, that's why," a law student told us).

Thus, throughout the 1970s, in addition to the generalization of repressive desublimation, the scarcity-simulation function of the state has become increasingly important as an apparatus of social discipline. These two mechanisms are in many ways antithetical and mutually contradictory: (1) Repressive desublimation is based on the assumption that the system "delivers the goods," whereas the scarcity-simulation function posits that there is not enough to go around. This particular contradiction contains explosive possibilities. As long as such "scarcity" is structured into social relations in the form of intensification of competition in the sexual, hipness, and self-development spheres, it will continue to be experienced as individualized malaise. It is, however, entirely possible that large sectors of the population may come to the collective conclusion that the struggle is not worth it, given the ever-intensifying competition and the decreasing rewards for participation. (2) Repressive desublimation presupposes a payoff for political submission, whereas the scarcity simulation function exacerbates the fiscal crisis of the state making it less able to make the payments. (3) Repressive desublimation operates by harnessing the pleasure principle to commodity consumption, whereas the scarcity-simulation function operates through the reality principle, enforcing the necessity of "functioning" in the "real world." The former presupposes the repression of political freedom, and the latter presupposes the repression of emotional freedom. Thus, functioning in the 1970s and 1980s requires a dual repression that demands even greater self-vigilance than was demanded in high-Victorian bourgeois society of the late nineteenth century. One aspect of the cultural revolution of the 1960s was an attack on the "performance principle." In the period following, we have found that the performance principle has rebounded back in a more pervasive and vigorous form than it existed prior to the 1960s.

As the cultural revolution of the 1960s, now divested of its dimension of social conflict, was chopped up into its constituent parts—sex, hipness, human potential, feminism, mysticism, nature and the organic produce thereof, drugs, music—and turned into competitive struggles or packaged as new-product fads or both, the younger and more fashionably inclined surplus absorbers were confronted with more and more dimensions of human life in which they could be identified as *publicly* inferior, e.g., if you did not trade in your obviously unsatisfying mate, you were a failure in the human potential competitive struggle because of your indifference to "personal growth." Meanwhile, the traditional occupational-competitive struggle raged more fiercely than ever because the objective necessity—"survival"—had increased while expectation did not diminish. Meanwhile, the objective rationality of "functioning" had not been enhanced, but the subjective necessity for it had, so a tremendous psychic toll was exacted: Though college students were not rioting, in the 1970s they were committing suicide in record numbers; in addition, within youth culture, the punk subculture developed in the mid-1970s, which glorified suicide, violence, failure, and drugs of consciousness obliteration (e.g., heroin, PCP or "angel dust," and Quaaludes), and disco, in which the consciousness was obliterated through mindless dancing to a never-ending beat. By 1977, 8 million Americans were said to suffer from a mysterious disease called "depression" of whom 1.5 million were so incapacitated that they could not function. In 1975, 100 million prescriptions were written for tranquilizers, of which 56 million were for Valium, consumed by an estimated 18 million addicts. When it was determined the following year that some of the addicts had become so strung out that they could no longer "function," the drug was classified as a controlled substance, forcing the addicts to see doctors more often for renewals, generating a new industry of "stress clinics" which are thinly disguised covers for downer dealers with MD's who charge $75, on the average, per prescription. There is a thriving business in self-help books, and instant therapies are consumed by millions desperate to "function more effectively" or feel less inferior about something; if their message could be boiled down to a least common denominator, it would be: There is no such thing as right or wrong, virtue and guilt; only winning and losing. Everything that happens is your fault. You have no obligation to any other person unless you are paid hard cash; your sole obligation is to be whatever it is necessary to be in order to win. Likewise, don't count on anybody else's help, because if you need them that means they've outgrown you and don't need you; but if you concentrate on outgrowing them then you'll get to the point where you don't need them and can get rid of them at your leisure.

With the growth of predatory anarchy in the personal sphere, faith in love and happiness reaches the point of mania. Sexuality had always assumed the form of market relations in bourgeois society, with romantic love serving as the fig leaf covering the dirty secret of rational calculation. But the market had, up though the 1950s, been twofold, with each positing the other's existence as its own presupposition: There was, first of all, an extramarital sex market, which posited marriage, in which women were scarce; if women were not "cheap" then they were expensive. There was simultaneously a marriage market, in which men were deemed scarce, which posited extramarital sex; the height of Victorian prudery was the veritable golden age of prostitution. In the post-1960s period the two are combined into one, which you are debarred from leaving by the possibility of getting traded in, which in turn requires you to periodically ascertain your market value. But in that case, the bourgeois iso-lated-nuclear-family form has been qualitatively liquidated, i.e., the *modular* family, vulgarly known as the "relationship."

The nuclear-family form posits the permanence of the couple in principle. There may be adulteries and separations, of course; but as late as the 1950s, divorce, desertion, and "living in sin" definitely constituted deviance, and conferred upon the women involved "bad reputations" even if—as was usually the case—the men took the initiative. Even the men, if they belonged to the surplus-absorbing strata, could be looked at askance by their employers and deemed unsound, immature, or unstable. So it is implausible to us that any social institution that has undergone such a high level of "structural deviance" (divorce, desertion, and cohabitation), not to mention "role deviance" (which, after all, is what feminism is about), can still be said to exist. The vulgar language is appropriate: The "relationship," whether or not legally formalized, is not anything in particular.

In construing the 1960s as a rebellion against "functioning," i.e., the mechanism whereby social discipline is implanted and reproduced in "everyday life" routine, we posited a *sociological law of motion* according to which a limit of capitalism had been reached whereby a ceiling on household consumption was necessitated by the erosion of the fundamental bourgeois ideological construct of "scarcity"; the state would henceforth act as a "scarcity simulator," rendering the construct plausible by highlighting the privileges of a minority against a backdrop of a stagnating or deteriorating material standard of living for the majority (a trend that appears to have been sustained), low productivity growth (as to which we are less sure), and high *apparent* unemployment (which, even apparently, may not be true).

To recapitulate and clarify: A historic watershed had been reached or approached such that employment, first and foremost that entailing the performance of unproductive labor, was no longer necessitated for primarily economic reasons, i.e., as the "incidental costs," *faux frais*, of capitalist production, but as a device whereby the employed were inured to having someone else prescribe where and when their bodies were going to be placed under bureaucratic supervision. This is the essence of "functioning": It entails departure from the domicile at a (preferably) inconveniently early hour of the morning; and the partition of the day into "getting ready for work," "working hours," and "after work." It represents the minimum criterion for both moral virtue and mental health; and those who do not do it, and lacking valid "student deferments" from the "labor force," are partitioned into relatively small privileged groups (academics, practitioners of the creative and performing arts, the hereditary rich, and the virtuously retired who have served their time for forty-five years), and large stigmatized social categories (the insane, criminals, "bums," women who must admit to being "just a housewife").[1] In pecuniary terms alone, the normative prescription of universal labor force participation was irrational. According to Lester Thurow (1984:45): "Analysis demonstrated that it was often cheaper to give many low-skill individuals a lifetime income than it was to raise their earnings capacities by the same amount." We would add that it's even cheaper to do the same for a high-skill individual the necessity for whose job is of a subjective character and whose activities entail the consumption of lavish office space, sophisticated equipment, and a supporting staff.

In 1980, we believed that the observed low productivity growth in U.S. industry, i.e., retaining larger numbers of productive laborers than was warranted by existing productive technique and preserving their jobs by means of subsidies, import quotas, "trigger pricing," state purchases, and so forth, against more efficient foreign, especially Japanese, firms was dictated by the soberly disciplining effect their very presence had upon the nonproductive workers, whose sense of privileged exemption from the worst degradation of the "capitalist labor process" was thereby enhanced. The totality of these charges upon society, we thought at the time, represented the underlying, essentially noneconomic, cause of the seemingly indefensible inflation of the 1970s.

In 1980, André Gorz (1980) in France and Rudolf Bahro (1977) in East Germany were putting "free time" at the head of the agenda of the liberation struggle against capitalism and "actually existing socialism," respectively.

If something wicked this way came, it would be the condensation of relations of cultural alienation in guise of forms previously developed to subserve the administration of the extraction of surplus value such that opposition would be liquidated without resistance, without the realization on the part of anyone that it was occurring; without it being conceivable what an opposition that opposed would be against.

In 1980 we lacked the words to describe it, no portable high-level language code, just an isolated cross-section here and there, no two of which we could link into an executable module; that is, the future is here, debugged, and it works!

We call it the Garbage State.

The Garbage State flourishes by secreting a poisonous miasma of pure information into the sphere of cultural reproduction. Its purity inheres in the fact that it is not about anything in particular; just endless lists of things that can be printed out, displayed, formatted, stored on-line or on tape, just any old (or new or projected) thing that someone else finds necessary or desirable or advisable or a good thing just in case (you never can tell) to have accessible.

The life energy of most people misleadingly called "productive" is consumed in keeping track of things and keeping track of the things that have been kept track of or keeping track of the people coding literals in the *working-storage section* of the *data division* so that more things can be kept track of. The Garbage State is made possible by, and spawns the proliferation of, what is glorified as high-technology industry.

Hi-tech works like this: In August 1981, the *New York Times* included in a Sunday edition an advertising supplement paid for by the office-equipment industry. It featured an essay by the best-selling writer Alvin Toffler. This was quite informative, though perhaps not for reasons intended by Toffler and his paymasters. Fifty-two percent of employed citizens were at that time "working," or whatever it was they did, in offices. Every day (it was not clear from the context whether weekends and holidays were included) these functioning appendages of collectivized consumption output 600 million pages of computer print-out, 245 million pages of photocopies, and 76 million pages of business letters (that is, real letters, exclusive of junk mail, form letters, computerized mailings, "mailgrams," what have you); all of which represented an average of forty-five pages of documents generated per employee daily. The authors would like to take this opportunity to declare, in the words of the slogan of the National Recovery Administration (1933–1934), "We do our part!"

As we have noted above, given the impossibility of adequately quantifying the "productivity" of those paid to consume, plus the steady cheapening of the costs of consuming information-processing machines relative to the cost of the labor of those paid to implement the consumption of the machines, it was inevitable that managers would be inundated by an exponentially growing deluge of information. Toffler's essay actually cited executives' complaints of deepening obfuscation the better "informed" they were. The office equipment industry's remedy, in the proffering whereof they were perfectly sincere apart from the element of "relative use value creation" to be found in any advertisement, was redolent of iatrogenic disease: Faster, more sophisticated machines capable of generating yet vaster masses of information at the hands of still more ignorant and untrained employees at even lower unit cost.

As so often happens in social life, what was substantively rational on the "micro" level, much like the lone farmer increasing acreage under the plow in hopes of selling more crop for incremented income, had begun to turn into substantive irrationality on the "macro" or aggregate level: The more information that was output faster, the more complex, difficult, and expensive it was becoming to keep track of its flow, evaluate its importance relative to the mass of other information with which it competed for attention, ensure that it was stored in orderly fashion ("database management") and up to date, and troubleshoot the bugs, flaws, bottlenecks, and malfunctions, any of which could precipitate chaos without backup equipment, backup files, and backup personnel. Less than two years earlier, the North American Air Defense Command had been sent on a World War III alert due to a programming error. It was entirely reasonable for any given office to deal with the inundation of information by acquiring newer, faster, more sophisticated equipment that could process vastly more information coming in and send information out in the same proportion. The latter then became someone else's problem.

That was in 1981, a long time ago. The apparently successful intensification of social discipline in the "Let's catch up with Japan!" ambience of the early 1980s has at last permitted a drastic shrinkage of the "classical"—or, in the more contemptuous usage, "smokestack-industry"—working class, whose continued high visibility is dispensable: In these pitiless times it has become possible to enforce aversion to a "bad attitude" upon the "information processors," not by the mere threat of manual labor, but by the outright terror of a shelter for the homeless—if lucky: sleeping in doorways otherwise.

The Reagan administration, elected in 1980 principally because the pitiful policyless political drifter, Carter, deserved to lose, generated an amazing amount of out and out blind faith in the empty slogan "supply-side economics." We are not professional economists, but naively bewildered readers of the political press who cannot make any sensible distinction between encouraging an increase in supply and the stimulation of aggregate demand by an increase in purchasing power somewhere: the so-called Keynesians would have done it by means of deficit spending accompanied by a redistribution of income to encourage household consumption. Part of the subsidizing of the latter would have taken the form of "social programs," too small in the aggregate to subserve anything but a legitimation function, aimed at raising the consumption levels of households in dire need of basic necessities.

The Keynesian school is now in disrepute and has been the explicit target of the "supply siders." But the fiscal policies of the latter have certainly entailed deficit spending, and that unprecedentedly. The purchasing power "pumped" into the economy was, however, now sloshed onto the upper- and upper-middle income strata, i.e., those who already had acquired plenty of practical experience in squandering money and the only people in a position to save part of their incomes in that they could not possibly spend it all.

The monetary policies of the early 1980s complemented and supplemented fiscal policies: High interest rates subsidized such savings as the domestic rich chose to make, while draining capital out of Europe: $83 billion in 1983 alone. As, partly by consequence of this, Europe languished in the depression from which the United States was emerging just in time for the 1984 elections (sheer coincidence), the hi-tech sector of U.S. industry was crushing its feeble counterparts: In late July 1984, the ITT subsidiary in England was scheming to acquire that country's largest computer manufacturer, while IBM did a deal with British Telecom that "revives fears among its rivals that an IBM standard may come to dominate data communications as effectively as it already does mainframe computers" (*Economist*, August 4-10, 1984). In New York, as if in rebuttal, *Time* (August 13, 1984) ran a feature story blaming the Europeans' troubles on obsolete national rivalries while, a couple of pages later, announcing U.S. plans to abolish the withholding tax on interest payments to foreigners.

Part of the proceeds of the Reagan tax cuts was indeed squandered on luxury goods and frivolous speculation. Some was saved, thus potentially available for investment as the Reagan administration hoped. Other tax subsidies were handed over directly to corporations. Some "investment" did take place, but in terms of the categories of bourgeois economics it is most difficult to differentiate "productive" investment, i.e., on facilities and machinery for increasing the output of goods, from expenditure on office buildings, office equipment, computers, interoffice and intraoffice communications equipment, and other tinker toys wherewith management keeps better track of things while cosmetizing itself with a more advanced, hi-tech appearance. All of the latter is unproductive.

We got our most recent figures from a glance at a *Newsweek* column by Robert J. Samuelson:

> The 1981 business tax cuts . . . bloated corporate treasuries and made new investment highly profitable. In 1983 corporations collectively covered their investment needs from internal cash flow—that is, retained profits and depreciation allowances. . . . The Federal Reserve estimates that the effective corporate tax rate dropped from 56 percent to 32 percent from 1980 to 1983. [August 13, 1984]

Where is the demand coming from, though? Barring centralized control of investment decisions, as practiced by the Japanese Ministry of International Trade and Industry, wherein it is guided by the opportunities for creation and penetration of markets perceived by the mammoth export trading companies, it is quite fantastic to expect corporations to invest, rather than raise dividends, bloat salaries, squander money on advertising to marginally increase market shares, export capital, indulge in international currency speculation, or, most spectacularly, consummate gigantic mergers.

The answer was given in the following paragraph: the office.

> The boom is concentrated in computers and electronics gear as prices drop while computing power increases. Last year the proportion of business' equipment spending on computers and office equipment (14.2 per cent) was nearly double the 1978 level. Communications and electrical generating equipment, instruments and office copiers also rose; together these items now constitute about two-fifths of all equipment investment.

(Equipment accounts for about two-thirds of business investment; the rest is buildings.)

So, between 26 and 27 percent of all business investment is on nonproductive office—read "information processing and information generating"—equipment, which as we hinted above, has a way of ensuring the expansion of its own market by the very nature of its output. To this must certainly be added a portion of the 33 percent spent on buildings, as it is obviously necessary to put the equipment somewhere. Of the remainder, the portion of investment actually spent on machinery and factories for manufacture of products, a not inconsiderable fraction may be presumed to be destined for the expansion of, and research and development for, the "hardware" output of the information processing industries themselves. This is not to mention "software," of course: That is a can of worms on the level of theory, which we approach with the greatest trepidation.

An applications program written, usually in COBOL, by 500 denizens of cubicles for keeping track of inventory or personnel efficiency ratings is common clerical work. Entertainment software, e.g., home electronic games, is part of the sphere of cultural reproduction with potential for soon becoming one of the fine arts. An operating system and related system software—loaders, linkers, assemblers, compilers, file-management services, peripherals interface programs—is at least as important to the machine as any of its parts, of which by the way, none move except the peripherals (tape and disk drives, printer card reader if any).[2] Deciding whether writing system software constitutes "productive labor" may well be comparable to a rabbinical decision as to whether opening a refrigerator door on the sabbath constitutes building a fire, hence performing labor as prohibited in the Torah, if the light goes on.

To the collectivized consumption in the office must be added the collectivized consumption in the military. The predominant industry in which the energies of Americans who are paid to get through the day are expended is, materially, using stuff up; on the political level, keeping themselves under surveillance and fostering the readiness and refinement of the means of violence, and on the cultural level, generating the fog of information pollution whereby their monitored behavior is qualitatively transformed where it is not actually thereby constituted.

Considered exclusively in terms of the level of material social reproduction, the office is parasitic. It consumes products and human labor while producing nothing within its confines. The office-in-particular keeps track of things and people, as it has always done. The office-in-particular, as the facilitator and radiator of domination and exhibitor of the magical metalanguage associated with domination remains as it was since the beginning of recorded history, which was of course first written down in an office. But it was a computer scientist, not a sociologist, who pointed out that, in order to maintain the reproduction of domination at the *same level* of intensity in the period following World War II, the development of the digital computer was dictated (Wisenbaum, 1969). Otherwise, the bureaucracies of the major capitalist states would have "collapsed" under the weight of information to be processed.

We find the aggregate impact of the *office-in-general* even more interesting for purposes of abstract speculation: Over half of those recorded by the payroll-program-output-in-general as being paid money to do something are keeping track of things. That is, they are monitoring behavior.

The office-in-general is, via its ever-growing capacity to monitor an ever-expanding range of behavior, engaged willy-nilly in the reproduction of stupidity and inferiority on an extended scale: All behavior monitored, from the extent of your debt to your scores on assorted "instruments," is susceptible to the construction of being reflective of your degree of inferiority in terms of ever-proliferating invidious distinctions, i.e., who is inferior to whom on something or other and, this being bourgeois society, by *exactly* how much. A determinate relation is posited between inferiority and stupidity (nothing new here excepting only quantitative precision; recall Mencius, "Some labor with their minds and rule others..."), though it is that exception, in its mass, the very magnitude of the quantity of quantities, which imparts the quality of "reality" to the results): The inferior must be stupid; some kind of "cognitive deficit" can always be yanked from the files, printed out, or displayed on the screen.

Curiously, these inferiorities, as measured, may have little of a causative nature to do with aggregate inequalities. Economists take the word of psychologists and sociologists that "skills," "work ethic," "intelligence," and suchlike are important, but according to Lester Thurow, "standard economic variables (skills, IQ, hours of work, etc.) could explain only 20 to 30 percent of the variance in individual earnings" (1984:44). Earlier, Bowles and Gintis (1976), had found that, in explaining variance in intergenerational mobility, operationalized as the probability of movement from parents' income decile to children's income decile, found that IQ contributed nothing at all.

It is curious that the social sciences have never seriously explored the alternative interpretation, by which inferiorities and stupidities, rather than representing intrinsic personal attributes determining human fate, should rather be construed as mediators of the hereditary transmission of social rank, hence concomitants of purely stylistic aspects of behavior. This corresponds to the picture that emerges when one groups the scores of children or adolescents on any standardized test: The larger the parents'-income interval used, the closer do the observed correlations with children's test scores approach unity.

Beyond the measurement of relative inferiorities, which has come to be the entire practice of the academic social sciences and their applied versions, i.e., the "management sciences," there is a realm of not-yet-quantifiable behavior susceptible to monitoring; slip-ups therein, usually of a stylistic character, can have consequences most painfully quantitative, especially in the upper-middle strata; and equally so for the professional-academic and the corporate-managerial sectors: a deficiency in your "way of relating" here or a violation of intricate "dress for success" rules there; and in either case any violation of the demanding ritual norms of bodily purity, as legitimated and medicalized in terms of "health." The advertising industry, whose business it is to propagate insecurities, reminds you of the terrible consequences: "I've had poor scotch and I've had rich scotch. Believe me, *rich is better!*"

The detection and communication of advantageous behavioral styles, deemed simultaneously fashionable and intrinsically good, for and to the relevant specialized audiences, and standardized therein, is accomplished with amazing rapidity by journalists, scholars, artists, writers, and other wielders of formidable capacities for shorthand depiction and conceptualization of the doings of fast-rising young upper middles. Some of these, in select circles, may even pass for radical social critics. We mention no names.

There transpires a generalized "speed-up" of life: Sex roles persist, but have become more difficult and complicated on either side. Men are required to become passably adept at the domestic and emotional skills formerly relegated to women, and increasingly essential for the maintenance of appropriate appearances during foreseeable episodes of singleness in the epoch of the modular family; and they must "achieve" at least as ferociously as before to outcompete and outrank the women they intend to be good enough for. Women are held to standards of pulchritude and fashionable display at least as exacting as before, to which have been added criteria of physical fitness previously enjoined—and less stringently—on men, while psychosexual passivity is taboo among the better sort as clinical norms of good sex are propagated in explicit detail by experts and their popularizers; and meanwhile women must be at least passably good as "achievers" to maintain an upper-middle standard of living both before and, again foreseeably, *after* marriage (especially with custody of children) to be good enough for men who somewhat outrank them.[3]

In the mid-1970s, it occurred to us that monitored behavior—whether kept track of by bureaucratic superiors and minions of agencies with which one has dealings; phone company and credit card computers whose presumed purpose is compiling your monthly charges only moderately inaccurately, media operatives, survey takers, market researchers; pollsters, and last and least social and behavioral scientists—is somehow qualitatively different from "naive behavior."

Monitored behavior, or potentially monitorable behavior, occurs as if it might be documented by someone else, or even oneself as surrogate, for other, and necessarily higher, purposes, precisely because of its realistic-seeming ostensibility as ordinary quotidian activity. Monitorable behavior finds its reflection in the impulse to self-document—whose remote origins are found in diary keeping and writing letters at least in part for their ultimate collection and editing by future scholars for publication and eventual textual analysis by specialist scholars yet unborn—whether by audio or video cassette devices, home movie cameras, 35mm cameras for slides, or, today, by personal computer: A behavioral scientist of the authors' knowledge keeps an Apple IIe at each of his business locations—and of course at home—whereon he maintains a log of what he does, accurate to the half hour or less, while somehow he manages to do it all ("5:00–5:30, update references including references to instrumentation; 5:30–6:00, Eat"). If Daniel Boorstin could term a news conference or a press release a "pseudoevent," the totality of monitored or monitorable or self-documentable behavior is "information pollution." This is not pseudo anything—as the imitation fur coat commerical would have it. It's real whatever-it-is.

Whether or not one agrees with Barbara Ehrenreich's reconstruction of the cultural history of the 1950's "Silent Generation" in her *In the Hearts of Men*, it is reasonable to believe that there was a single "middle-class" behavioral style stigmatized by the epithet "conformity," and, further, that this was itself a legitimate heir of nineteenth-century high bourgeois culture whose passing was so eloquently—if vapidly—mourned by Daniel Bell in *The Cultural Contradictions of Capitalism*. It was, by contemporary standards, both less demanding to conform to, the sixties having not yet occurred or been imagined, drugs having not yet been invented, "good sex" having been hitherto a mere rumor; and sufficiently coherent as to have been rejectable (as well as, of course, acceptable), at least conceptually—all sorts of behavioral compromises short of the beat generation having been tried—as a totality. Even at the most abstract theoretical levels (cf. Foss, *Freak Culture*), its seamless unity was posited if not hallucinated: Parsons's *The Social System* presenting the benign version; Marcuse's *One-Dimensional Man* the malign.

In the 1980s, there are several contending jigsawed fragments of culture, all in part confusedly interpenetrated and unto each there corresponds its variant of "appropriate behavior," each difficult to perfect, expensive to sustain, demanding of time and energy, and rigorous in its standards. Behavioral lapses, often, as noted, stylistic and superficial, may precipitate the disasters that once accrued to ideological lapses in the Joe McCarthy era: Academics do not get tenured, law-firm associates do not make partner, executives are "dishired" with exquisite delicacy.

What is appropriate behavior?

About "appropriate behavior" very little is known, scientifically speaking. A great deal was learned about interactional rituals in everyday life in the 1960s and 1970s by sociologists. This body of knowledge may or may not have some bearing on a definition of appropriate behavior: Mention of sociology is inappropriate behavior in the presence of behavioral scientists.

Of inappropriate behavior a great deal is known, as it is measured on rating scales and symptom checklists. Usages such as "role-inappropriate behavior" and departures from "age-appropriate behavioral norms" suggest that, first, inappropriate behavior must be highly contextual, second, appropriate behavior is definable merely by not being noticed; and third, inappropriate behavior invariably gets the perpetrator into trouble.

Already, by 1960, secular-rationalist doctrinal or theoretical interpretations and reinterpretations of social reality had become "deconstituted," even for purposes of lame political reformism, to such a degree that a leading candidate for the ruling political idea of the time was called "the End of Ideology," after the title of a book of essays by Daniel Bell. To the extent that "ideology" was generically identified with intellectually coherent formulations in the realm of political economy, the point was well taken. The ensuing social-movement period, witnessing as it did an innovative exuberance of subjectivist ideologies followed by the dawning awareness that the latter are no less vulnerable to standardization, trivialization, and recuperation than the ideological forms they replaced, did not at its close yield to a recrudescence of "isms" of the traditional sort, with the minor exception of a flurry of neo-Leninism among former movement participants and a more influential school called "Neoconservativism." In a period generally characterized by every form of conservatism from the knee-jerk reactionary to the mock evangelical to the steely-eyed murderous, the "neo" may have alluded to prominent practitioners applying argumentative styles acquired in the Jewish socialist intellectual subculture of New York City to the irrititation of their former friends by opposing that which, in the given situation, it had been uniquely conventional to favor and vice versa. Note the telling implications of Norman Podhoretz's book title: *Breaking Ranks*.

Withal, it is acknowledged that the post-1960s period must surely rank as one of the great eras in the intellctual history of the United States and its culturally kindred satellite states, though we insist that this impinged not at all upon the image huckstering and sophisticatedly contrived "political process." Perhaps this had something to do with the sheer mass of the cultural practitioners or the volume of their output, ever increasing under the lash of the familiar quest for wealth and fame and the increasingly more typical need for tenure. In our highly mannered civilization we have developed what heretofore might have been a contradiction in terms: a vigorous, vital, dynamic decadence, subsumed within which, in a small corner to be sure, are hitherto unimaginable cultural contradictions of socialism.

We have focused here upon the "upper-middle" strata in a desperate and rather tortuous effort to account for an obvious political fact: There is today no political opposition; and not only is this of no great concern outside an exiguous subculture of career politicos; it is hardly noticed.

In the political sphere all sectors of the upper-middle strata are collectively known as "public opinion." This is the upper 5 to 10 percent of the population that comprises the popular support of the regime as a whole. Within it, the nominal opposition chose as its candidate an entity who could not even be characterized as a gray blur, rather, he seemed a mere patch of smog: His major career advancement had been due to his capacity for making Jimmy ("Who?") Carter appear exciting by comparison. A nothing who stood for nothing, he was thought mismatched against a president who was naught but a fabrication seeking to become a facade.

Before Mondale's nomination, curiously, he faced what could only have been a serious challenge to one as insubstantial as himself. This was from a certain Senator Hart(pence), exuding mock glamor, who won a string of primaries by announcing "new ideas." This was too good to be true, and indeed it was fraudulent. There was nobody capable of generating any "ideas" whatsoever; the habit and practice of political thought had been lost.

Daniel Bell (1960) had already announced that political "ideas" were obsolete. The Germanic depths of this notion were plumbed by Marcuse (1964). The recrudescence of social-movement political dissidence in the 1960s did, in fact, bypass what had been *conventionally* understood as "ideas," "ideologies," "policies," "issues," and "positions" altogether. For this reason the 1960s movements passed the socialist tradition, which was uncomprehending utterly as liberal and reactionary adherents of the conventional interpretation of social reality, in that all of these continued to posit the primacy of the material level of social reproduction in social development.

In the 1980s, we have attained a new level of distortion in social reality. The conventional interpretation continues to posit the primacy of the level of material reproduction, ever harping as it does so on "productivity," technique, employment, and "the bottom line." The liberal variant, in the elections held in 1984, typically emphasized *material* social justice as opposed to the *material* rewards of predation, and was rejected by the voters as mustily obsolete, albeit neither winners nor losers even attempted to analyze wherein this was so.

The predominance of the level of cultural reproduction combined with new technique—so-called high-tech—yields a new social formation wherein the most privileged large stratum of the population, and occupationally the most prestigious, comprises those paid to concoct plausible excuses for other members of their own stratum, not to mention vastly more numerous subordinate strata, to waste their time generating, printing out, copying, text editing and formatting, publishing, inputting, outputting, mailing out, or throwing out strings of characters and digits. This is the *informationalizing of mental life*. An elaborate prestige hierarchy, from "knowledge" at the top to mere "data" at the bottom, corresponds to the range from professionals to minimum wage-earning data entry clerks.

At the core of Marx's (1973) analysis of capitalism is the notion of *using-up*—or consumption—of the *time* of human life. In the 1850s and 1860s, this was *productive consumption*. A solid majority of those "gainfully employed" in the most advanced version of bourgeois society are enduring the consumption of their time in the reproduction of symbols (or their symbolic representation as eight-bit characters in EBCDIC or ASCII) of which only a diminishing portion ever attains material existence.

Never before has so much of human lifetime been so unproductively consumed by capitalism, literally for nothing, with this nothing embodied in a commodity—information—which ever cheapens itself while air and water become more expensive! As earlier noted, the delusion as to this commodity's importance reproduces social discipline whose underlying logic thus becomes social discipline for its own sake. This is compounded, in turn, by the facticity of the dataness—the aggregate of all data bases—whose content, with quantitatively speaking, minor exceptions, is the monitoring of human behavior at greater or lesser degrees of abstraction.

As hinted, social theory—our own not excepted—must be subsumed within the process of the informationalizing of mental life. To ask social theorists to transcend this new stage even to the point of acknowledging its advent is to ask them to become unserious, unprofessional, unconcerned with external grant support, unaware that "previous studies have found that . . . " whereas "the present study . . . " suggests "the need for further study." This is not merely the problem of "abstracted empiricism" first noted by Mills (1959), but the ultimate dilemma of sociology: the point at which the investigator construes that he, she, or perhaps it, has stepped outside the object of investigation is a matter of subjective judgment that posits as its presupposition the prior existence of the critical faculty for making such a judgment. The constraints upon this critical faculty reflect the impossibility of construing that those with whom one wishes to communicate are in the aggregate wrong and that one is oneself wrong to the extent that dialogue is maintained. That is, all the individuals the investigator *knows* are "doing good work," and one does and should ask for reprints, but the *whole* is hallucinated. All individuals *qua* individual can generate high quality knowledge-product, but the product *in the aggregate* has the effect of legitimating the structure of information production and the monitoring of behavior.

What has been presented here is not a theory in the scientific sense. We can neither predict qualitative changes in the bases of social-movement cohesion, nor in the emergence of wholly new ideological formulations. Social movements have shifted bases in relation to the industrial era. Preindustrial social movements were formed on religious-ethnic bases using religious interpretations of reality; social movements during the industrial era (1820–1950) used secular-rational interpretations of reality and formal organizations constituted their bases of cohesion. In postindustrial societies, social movements have taken the form of dissident subcultures and the interpretations of reality have been subjectivistic-experiential. Yet it is problematic to posit that the next social movement—we promise there will be a next one—will cohere around dissident subcultures, since as we have already noted, dissident subcultures posited as their presupposition a unitary bourgeois culture.

What we have done is present a reconceptualization of an accepted body of fact. This reconceptualization has, we hope, provided a framework to clarify the nature and processes of a social movement and to delimit them as episodic and recurring processes in social development. Although this reconceptualization does not have predictive power, it does provide a point outside conventional social theory from which currently popular theories can be shown to be egregiously inadequate for the understanding and interpretation of social movements and social revolutions.

There is an inevitability to the recurrence of social movements in class society. Eruptions that have occurred would have occurred anyway, because issues raised within social movements are artifacts of the historical conjuncture in which they emerge. Issues do not create social movements, but vice-versa.

Since the founding of the United States, social movements have roughly followed a cycle of recurrence every thirty to thirty-five years. Peak years were: 1828, in which laborers in major cities struck and fought for union representation and the first stirrings of feminism were heard; 1860, in which one of the bloodiest social movements ever occurred in the West, combining abolitionism, labor insurgency, and regional conflict; 1894, with labor troubles and the Populist revolt; 1912, again labor was rebellions and feminists were on the move; 1921–22, working-class and racial insurgency; 1937, working-class revolt, with Blacks as a category subsumed within it; and 1968–69, insurgency of middle-class youth, Blacks, women, homosexuals, Amerindians and Hispanics, this time with the working class being counter-insurgent.

In 1959, we had no notion that there would ever be another Left, little idea that we ourselves would be in it, and certainly no inkling of what sort of Left it would turn out to be. The 1960s were capable of giving rise to those who knew somehow that they were a "New Left," though not why this was so nor why there had, of necessity, to be an "Old Left." In the future, we cannot count on participants in whatever social movement may emerge of having any sense of what a "Left" is or was, or that they are it. Of the next Left, we are sure only that it will laugh at us and that we will be too old to know it for what it will *post facto* be known to have been.

The social movement to come will somehow confront, and itself invariably bear the mark of, the recuperations of the 1970s, the emergent Garbage State, and the informationalization of mental life. We wish we could identify the rebels of tomorrow and tell you how they will do it. We do not have the slightest idea.

Notes

1. A loose formula translates exemption from functioning into privileged high income within the same occupation: We informed the graduate program director in clinical

psychology at a large State University of New York campus of the base salary rate of a clinical psychologist with the title of Research Scientist V, but required to show up at the office at 8:30 A.M., who might be employed at a research institute, an arm of the Office of Mental Hygiene, housed on the same campus; the figure excluded seniority "step" increases and raises for favorable efficiency ratings. The professor exclaimed, "Why, that's twice what they're paying me!"

2. "As measured by the number of moving parts, the System/370 operating system is undoubtedly mankind's most complex creation. The computer hardware is less complex, but complex nonetheless" (Gary DeWard Brown, *System/370 Job Control Language*. New York: Wiley, 1977. pp. 1-2). "Moving parts" is to be read figuratively.

3. There is no sign that the hypergamy-hypogyny rule (cf. Jessie Bernard, *The Future of Marriage*, pp. 25-26, for a pithy formulation thereof and certain logical corollaries therefrom) is in desuetude; witness the chronic complaint of career women that "there are so few good men around," i.e., that they have priced themselves out of the market; notwithstanding, of course, the conspicuous flouting of the rule by a few celebrities. It is arguable that the rule is sexist, but we didn't make it. The rule is to such an extent embedded in social relations as to represent a sufficient explanation for the so-called Cinderella Complex in that the logical consequence of "success" is a drastic restriction of mate selection. The structure of bourgeois social relations that constitutes the "career" as both mental structure and configuration of behavioral dictates is equally accountable for other psychic disasters discerned by mental health professionals; notably, the "identity crisis," i.e., the trepidation at "career" inception; and the "midlife crisis," i.e., that point at which definitive consignment to one side or the other of the "success-failure" dichotomy is made by conventional definition. Fortunately, the vast majority of the population is spared all this anguish in that, by conventional construction, they never had "futures" ahead of them to begin with, being left with the comparatively manageable problem of living with being inferior by reason of some combination of "lack of ability," moral depravity assessed post facto ("not motivated," etc.), and deliberate intentions of which they were never aware yet "really wanted to."

References

Amin, Samir. *Accumulation on a World Scale*. New York: Monthly Review, 1974.

Aronowitz, Stanley. *False Promises*. New York: McGraw-Hill, 1971.

Bahro, Rudolph. *The Alternative in Eastern Europe*. London: New Left Books, 1978.

Baran, Paul and Paul Sweezy. *Monopoly Capital*. New York: Monthly Review, 1966.

Barnard, Jessie. *The Future of Marriage*. New York: World, 1972.

Barnet, Richard. *The Giants*. New York: Simon and Schuster, 1977.

Baskir, Lawrence and William Straus. *Chance and Circumstance: The Draft, the War, and the Vietnam Generation*. New York: Knopf, 1978.

Bell, Daniel. *The End of Ideology: On the Exhaustion of Political Ideas in the Fifties*. New York: The Free Press, 1960.

————. *The Coming of Post-Industrial Society*. New York: Basic, 1973.

————. *The Cultural Contradictions of Capitalism*. New York: Basic, 1976.

Berger, Peter and Thomas Luckmann. *The Social Construction of Reality*. New York: Doubleday, 1967.

Bettelheim, Charles. *Class Struggles in the USSR: 1917–1923*. New York: Monthly Review, 1978.

Billington, Ray. *The Protestant Crusade: 1800–1860*. New York: Quadrangle, 1964.

Block, Fred. "Contradictions of Capitalism as a World System." *Insurgent Sociologist* 5 (1975).

Blum, Jerome. *Lord and Peasant in Russia*. Princeton, NJ: Princeton University Press, 1961.

Blumer, Herbert. "Social Movements." In A. M. Lee, ed., *New Outline of Principles of Sociology*. New York: Barnes & Noble, 1948.

Bowles, Samuel and Herbert Gintis. *Schooling in Capitalist America*. New York: Basic, 1976.

Braudel, Ferdinand. *Capitalism and Material Life: 1400–1800*. New York: Harper, 1973.

Braverman, Harry. *Labor and Monopoly Capital*. New York: Monthly Review, 1974.

Brinton, Crane. *Anatomy of a Revolution*. New York: Vintage, 1965.

Carr, E. H. *Foundations of a Planned Economy*. Harmondsworth, England: Penguin, 1971.

———. *Socialism in One Country*. 3 vols. Harmondsworth, England: Penguin, 1976.

Cheyney, Edward. *The Dawn of a New Era 1250–1453*. New York: Harper, 1936.

Cohen, Norman. *The Pursuit of the Millennium*. New York: Oxford, 1961.

Coser, Lewis. *The Functions of Social Conflict*. New York: The Free Press, 1956.

Davies, James. "Toward a Theory of Revolution." *American Sociological Review* 27 (1962): 5-19.

Dill, William. "Environment as an Influence on Managerial Autonomy." *Administrative Science Quarterly* 2 (1958): 409-443.

Dobson, W.A.C.H. *Mencius*. Toronto: University of Toronto, 1963.

Dollard, John. *Caste and Class in a Southern Town*. Garden City, NY: Doubleday, 1957.

Douglas, Mary. *Purity and Danger*. London: Routledge and Kegan Paul, 1966.

Duby, Georges. *The Three Orders: Feudal Society Imagined*. Trans. by Arthur Goldhammer. Chicago: University of Chicago, 1978.

Ehrenreich, Barbara. *The Hearts of Men*. New York: Doubleday, 1983.

Ewen, Stewart. *The Captains of Consciousness*. New York: Harper, 1976.

Fanon, Frantz. *Black Skins, White Masks*. New York: Grove, 1967.

———. *Studies in a Dying Colonialism*. New York: Grove, 1967.

———. *The Wretched of the Earth*. New York: Grove, 1968.

Farber, Jerry. *The Student as Nigger*. New York: Pocket, 1969.

Foss, Daniel. *Freak Culture*. New York: Dutton, 1972.

Foss, Daniel and Ralph Larkin. "From 'The Gates of Eden' to 'Day of the Locust': An Analysis of the Middle Class Youth Movement of the 1960s and its Heirs in the 1970s—the Postmovement Groups." *Theory and Society* 3 (1976): 45-64.

———. "Roar of the Lemming: Youth, Post-movement Groups and the Life Construction Crisis." In H. Johnson, ed., *Religious Change and Continuity*, San Francisco: Jossey-Bass, a special issue of *Sociological Inquiry* 49 (1979): 264-85.

———. "Lexicon of Folk-Etymology of the 1960s." In S. Sayres, et al. (eds.). *The 60s Without Apology*. Minneapolis, MN: University of Minnesota, a special double volume of *Social Text* 3 (3) and 4 (1), 1984.

Gamson, William. *The Strategy of Social Protest*. Homewood, IL: Dorsey, 1975.

Goffman, Erving. *Asylums*. Chicago: Aldine, 1961.

———. *Gender Advertisements*. New York: Harper, 1976.

Goodwyn, Lawrence. *The Populist Moment*. New York: Oxford, 1978.

Gornick, Vivian. *The Romance of American Communism*. New York: Basic, 1977.

Gorz, Andre. *Farewell to the Working Class*. Boston: South End, 1980.

Gramsci, Antonio. *Letters from Prison*. New York: Harper, 1973.
———. *Selected Writings*. New York: International, 1977.
Grier, William and Price Cobbs. *Black Rage*. New York: Basic, 1968.
Gurr, Ted. *Why Men Rebel*. Princeton: Princeton University, 1970.
Habermas, Jurgen. *Legitimation Crisis*. Boston: Beacon, 1975.
Halliday, Fred. *Iran: Dictatorship and Development*. Harmondsworth, England: Penguin, 1978.
Higham, John. *Strangers in the Land*. New Brunswick, NJ: Rutgers, 1955.
Hill, Christopher. *Puritainism and Revolution*. London: Secker & Warburg, 1958.
———. *The Century of Revolution: 1603–1714*. New York: Norton, 1961.
———. *The World Turned Upside Down*. Harmondsworth, England: Penguin, 1973.
Hobsbawm, Eric. *Primitive Rebels*. New York: Praeger, 1963.
Hofstadter, Richard. *The Age of Reform*. New York: Harper, 1955.
Huizinga, Johan. *The Waning of the Middle Ages*. London: E. Arnold, 1924.
Josephus, Flavius. *History of the Jewish War*. Harmondsworth, England: Penguin, 1970.
Kardiner, Abram and Lionel Ovesey. *The Mark of Oppression*. Cleveland: World, 1951.
Kenniston, Kenneth. *The Uncommitted*. New York: Dell, 1959.
Kolko, Gabriel. *The Triumph of Conservatism*. New York: The Free Press, 1963.
Kuhn, Thomas. *The Structure of Scientific Revolution*. Chicago: The University of Chicago Press, 1970.
Laquer, Walter. *Terrorism: A Study of National and International Political Violence*. Boston: Little, Brown, 1977.
LeBon, Gustav. *The Crowd*. New York: Viking, 1966.
Lefebvre, Georges. *The Great Fear*. London: New Left Books, 1973.
Levi-Strauss, Claude. *The Savage Mind*. Chicago: University of Chicago, 1966.
Livy, Titus. *A History of Rome*. Trans. by Moses Haddad and Joe Poe. New York: Modern Library, 1962.
Lyon, H. R. *The Norman Conquest*. New York: Harper, 1967.
McCarthy, John and Meyer Zald. "Resource Mobilization and Social Movements: A Partial Theory," *American Journal of Sociology* 82 (1977): 1212-41.
McNeil, William. *Plagues and Peoples*. New York: Doubleday, 1976.
McPhail, Clark. "Civil Disorder Participation: A Critical Examination of Recent Research," *American Sociological Review* 36 (1971): 1058-72.
Mannoni, O. *Prospero and Caliban*. New York: Praeger, 1964.
Marcuse, Herbert. *One Dimensional Man*. Boston: Beacon, 1964.
Marx, Karl. "Economic and Philosophical Manuscripts of 1844." In T. Bottomore, ed. *Karl Marx: Early Writings*. New York: McGraw-Hill, 1963.
———. *Capital*, 3 vols. New York: International, 1967.
———. *Grundrisse*. New York: Vintage, 1973.
Milliband, Ralph. *The State in Capitalist Society*. New York: Basic, 1969.
Mills, C. W. *White Collar*. New York: Oxford, 1951.
———. *The Sociological Imagination*. New York: Oxford, 1959.
Mury, Gilbert. *La Societe de Repression*. Paris: Editions universitaires, 1969.

Oakley, Ann. *Housewife*. Harmondsworth, England: Penguin, 1976.

Oberschall, Anthony. *Social Conflict and Social Movements*. Englewood Cliffs, NJ: Prentice-Hall, 1973.

O'Connor, James. *The Fiscal Crisis of the State*. New York: St. Martins, 1973.

———. *The Corporations and the State*. New York: Harper, 1974.

Olson, Mancur Jr. *The Logic of Collective Action*. Cambridge, MA: Harvard, 1971.

Painter, Sidney. *The Reign of King John*. Baltimore: Johns-Hopkins, 1949.

Parsons, Talcott. *The Social System*. New York: The Free Press, 1951.

Pike, Douglas. *Viet-Cong*. Cambridge, MA: MIT, 1966.

Polanyi, Karl. *The Great Transformation*. Boston: Beacon, 1961.

———. *Primitive, Ancient, and Modern Economies*. Garden City, NY: Doubleday, 1968.

Poulantzes, Nicos. *Classes in Contemporary Capitalism*. London: New Left Books, 1975.

Reich, Wilhelm. *Sex-Pol*. New York: Vintage, 1971.

Riesman, David, Nathan Glazer and Ruel Denny. *The Lonely Crowd*. New York: Doubleday, 1956.

Roberts, Ron and Robert Kloss. *From the Balcony to the Barricade*. St. Louis: Mosby, 1974.

Rowbotham, Sheila. *Women, Resistance, and Revolution*. New York: Vintage, 1972.

———. *Woman's Consciousness, Man's World*. Harmondsworth, England: Penguin, 1973.

Rude, George. *The Crowd in History: A Study of Popular Disturbances in France and England, 1730–1848*. New York: Wiley, 1964.

Rule, James and Charles Tilly. "1830 and the Unnatural History of Revolution." *Journal of Social Issues* 28 (1972): 49-76.

Sachs, Wulf. *Black Anger*. New York: Greenwood, 1947.

Satin, Mark. *New Age Politics: The Alternative to Marxism and Liberalism*. Vancouver, BC: Whitecap, 1978.

Sinclair, Andrew. *Era of Excess: A Social History of Prohibitionism*. New York: Harper, 1964.

Smelser, Neil. *Theory of Collective Behavior*. New York: The Free Press, 1963.

Snow, C.P. *Two Cultures*. New York: Cambridge, 1959.

Stockwell, John. *In Search of Enemies: A CIA Story*. New York: Norton, 1978.

Stone, Laurence. *The Crisis of the Aristocracy*. New York: Oxford, 1965.

———. *The Causes of the English Revolution: 1529–1642*. New York: Harper, 1972.

Tawney, R. N. *The Agrarian Problem in the Sixteenth Century*. Santa Fe, NM: Gannon, 1970.

Thomas, Hugh. *Cuba; or the Pursuit of Freedom*. London: Eyre, 1971.

TenHouten, Warren. *Cognitive Styles and the Social Order*. Springfield, VA: National Technical Information Service, 1971.

Thompson, E. P. *The Making of the English Working Class*. New York: Viking, 1966.

Thurow, Lester. *Dangerous Currents*. New York: Vintage, 1984.

Tilly, Charles. *The Vendee*. Cambridge, MA: Harvard, 1964.

———. *From Mobilization to Revolution*. Reading, MA: Addison-Wesley, 1978.

Tilly, Charles and Edward Shorter. *Strikes in France: 1830–1968*. New York: Cambridge, 1974.

Tilly, Charles, Louise Tilly and Richard Tilly. *The Rebellious Century: 1830–1930*. Cambridge, MA: Harvard, 1975.

Touraine, Alain. *The Self-production of Society*. Chicago: University of Chicago, 1977.

Trevelyan, G. M. *England Under the Stuarts*. New York: Barnes and Noble, 1965.

Trotsky, Leon. *History of the Russian Revolution*. New York: Sphere, 1957.

Turner, Victor. *The Ritual Process*. Chicago: Aldine, 1969.

Useem, Michael. *Protest Movements in America*. Indianapolis, IN: Bobbs-Merrill, 1975.

Veblen, Thorsten. *The Theory of the Leisure Class*. New York: Macmillan, 1899.

Wallace, Anthony F.C. *Religion: An Anthropological View*. New York: Random House, 1966.

Weber, Max. *The Protestant Ethic and the Spirit of Capitalism*. New York: Scribners, 1950.

Wedgewood, C.V. *The Kings Peace: 1637–1641*. London: Collins, 1955.

Weinstein, James. *The Corporate Ideal in the Liberal State*. Boston: Beacon, 1968.

Weizenbaum, Joseph. *Computers and Human Reason: From Judgment to Calculation*. San Francisco, CA: W. H. Freeman, 1976.

Wiel, Andrew. *The Natural Mind*. Boston: Houghton-Mifflin, 1973.

Willis, Paul. *Learning to Labour*. London: Saxon House, 1977.

Wolfe, Bertram. *Three Who Made a Revolution*. New York: Dial, 1964.

Wright, Eric Olin. *Class, Crisis and the State*. New York: Schocken, 1978.

Yglesias, Jose. *In the Fist of the Revolution*. Harmonsdsworth, England: Penguin, 1970.

Zagorin, Perez. *The Court and the Country*. London: Routledge & Kegan Paul, 1969.

Index

Accumulation: conditions of, 33–34; capitalist, 37, 46; function of the state, 52

AFL, 66

Ageism, 138

Albegensianism, 16

Alexander II, 115

Ali, Caliph, 63

Alienation, 14, 90, 134; and disalienation, 98–99; and hegemony, 41–43; as domination, 50; cultural, 103, 149; defined 39, 50–51; as exploitation, 50; as false consciousness, 50; of authority, 50–54; of human sensibility, 139; of individual capacity, 94–99, 106; of the dialectic, 133; worker, 138

Amin, Field Marshall Idi, 126n

Anabaptists, 92

Anarchists, 79–80

Anarchy, 51, 92

Anomie, 23, 133

Anti-Communists, 84

Antistructure, 1, 8, 58, 71, 140; and human subject, 103; forcible assertion of, 21, 25, 54, 99, 105, 134, 136; need for, 97; thought forms of, 86–92

Appropriate behavior, 155

Aristocracy, 137

as-Sa'id, Nuri, 126n

Authority, legitimate, 48

Bahro, Rudolf, 149

Baktiar, Shahpur, 110, 119, 122

Bernard, Jesse, 159n

Barnet, Richard, 104

Baskir, Lawrence, 81–82

Batista, Fugilencio, 127n

Bazargan, Mehdi, 110, 120–123, 128n

Belief, religious, 42

Bell, Daniel, 154–156

Bettelheim, Charles, 6

Billington, Ray Allen, 85

Black Hand, 128n

Black Liberation Army, 128n, 133

Black Panther party, 16, 55, 67

Black power, 67

Black Wednesday, 129

Blacks, 8, 19, 61, 66–67, 88, 90, 96, 101–102, 142, 158; movement of, 131; working class, 82

Blumer, Herbert, 135

Bohemianism. See Counterbourgeoisie, cultural

Bolivar, Simon, 127n

Bolsheviks, 6, 73, 75, 79, 123–125. See also Russian Revolution

Sociocharacterological revolution, 90, 137–139, 141
Soldiers, 30
Solidarity. *See* Polish workers movement
Somoza, 117
Sparticist revolt, 24
Stalin, Joseph, 9n, 120
State, 3, 37, 97, 111, 113, 138; and accumulation, 34; and counter-states, 124–125; and society, 136; and the English Revolution, 66; as alienated authority, 50–54; as guarantor of the exploitive relation, 116; -building, 24; Italian corporate, 66; maintenance of, 108; reproduction of, 119
Status groups, 2; exploiting class as, 72; gentry as, 4; in bourgeois society, 45; yeomen as, 65; within the working class, 66
Status: hierarchy, 141; inconsistency, 59; reversal, 141
Stockwell, John R., 110
Stone, Lawrence, 4, 9n, 59
Strafford, execution of, 64
Straus, William, 81–82
Strikes, 21, 60–61, 110, 130, 138; sit-down, 66
Students. *See* Youth
Subcultures, dissident, 17, 89, 102
Subjective, 25; elements in movement behavior, 26
Subjectivism, 7, 143, 155
Subsistence, 30
Surplus: 103, absorption of, 30–31; aggregate, 56n; appropriated, 30–31, 33, 36; consumption of, 41, 43; redistributed, 30, 35, 36, 44; unappropriated, 30, 36
Surplus absorbing strata, 35, 50, 56n, 104, 139, 141, 146; lower, 80
Symbionese Liberation Army, 128n, 133

Taboos, 38–39
Taiping Rebellion, 106n, 113

Task environment, 20
TenHouten, Warren, 96
Terror, 124
Terrorism, 84, 112–115, 125, 127n, 133
Terrorists, South Moluccan, 128n
Thompson, E.P., 9n, 89, 91–92
Thurow, Lester C., 148, 153
Tilly, Charles, 20–26, 134
Tocqueville, Alexis de, 10, 117
Toffler, Alvin, 149–150
Totalitarianism, 124
Touraine, Alain, 20, 132, 135
Trade unions, 5, 52
Transcendence, 142
Trotsky, Leon D., 75, 79, 102, 104, 125
Trotskyism, 88
Turner, Victor, 38, 58, 97, 103, 140, 143n

Ulianov, Alexander, 115
Underground, 84
Urbanization, 133
Useem, Michael, 13–14
Utilitarian economics, 20

Vanguard: 26; dissident, 116; revolutionary, 75; party, 1, 16
Value: exchange, 33; surplus, 30, 34, 44, 149; relative use, 150
Villa, General Francisco, 114
Violence: 43, 139; and social movements, 108–109; collective, 11, 25–26; means of, 31, 33, 48, 51, 53, 61, 116–117, 124–125, 133; political, 11, 13, 26, 49, 108–116, 125, 133; relations of, 31; retaliatory, 109; terrorist, 133

Wallace, Anthony F. C., 140
War: 110; Albanian, 12; Cuban, 124; German Peasant War, 56n; Hundred Years, 54, 56n; Hussite, 54, 117; Korean, 82; Napoleanic, 91; peasant wars, 113; protracted, 117, 124–125; Vietnam, 68, 70, 81–82; World